I Believe in the Creator

I Believe in the Creator

by

JAMES M. HOUSTON

WILLIAM B. EERDMANS PUBLISHING COMPANY
GRAND RAPIDS, MICHIGAN

231.7
H843

Copyright © 1980 by James M. Houston.
Printed in the United States of America. First published 1979 by Hodder and Stoughton, London. First American edition published 1980 through special arrangement with Hodder and Stoughton by Wm. B. Eerdmans Publishing Co., Grand Rapids, Michigan 49503.

Library of Congress Cataloging in Publication Data

Houston, James Mackintosh
  I believe in the Creator.

  Bibliography: pp. 258-259.
  Includes index.
  1. Creation. 1. Title.
BT695.H67 1980 231'.7 79-13452
ISBN 0-8028-1749-1

To my children, Christopher and Jean,
Lydèle, Claire and Penelope, with the
hope their generation may learn to
trust the Creator richly.

Acknowledgments

The author and publisher gratefully acknowledge permission to include extracts from the following works:

pp. 17-18   from the poem by Frederick Peers cited in *Belief and the Counter Culture*, by Robert A. Evans. Copyright © MCMLXXI, The Westminster Press. Used by permission.

p. 22   from poems by Hart Crane, published by The University of Alabama. Used by permission.

p. 23   from "The Lesson for Today" from *The Poetry of Robert Frost*, edit. Edward Connery Latham. Copyright 1942 by Robert Frost. Copyright © 1969 by Holt, Rinehart and Winston. Copyright 1970 by Lesley Frost Ballantine. Reprinted by permission of Holt, Rinehart and Winston, Publishers.

pp. 45-46   from *The Secret Trees*, by Luci Shaw, © 1976 by Luci Shaw. Used by permission of Harold Shaw Publishers, Box 567, Wheaton, IL 60187.

pp. 125-126   from *Collected Poems*, by John Betjeman, published by John Murray (Publishers) Ltd. Used by permission of John Murray and Houghton Mifflin Co.

pp. 123 & 175   from two poems in *The Collected Poems of W. B. Yeats*, published by Macmillan. Used by permission of Mr. M. B. Yeats and Macmillan Publishing Co., Inc.

p. 192   from *The Collected Poems of A. E. Housman*. Copyright 1922 by Holt, Rinehart and Winston. Copyright 1950 by Barclays Bank Ltd. Reprinted by permission of Holt, Rinehart and Winston, Publishers.

p. 207   from *Caring for Animals* by Jon Silkin. Copyright © 1954 by Jon Silkin. Reprinted from *Poems New and Selected* by permission of Wesleyan University Press.

p. 207   from *The Days* by Edwin Muir, published by Faber and Faber. Used by permission.

pp. 179-180, 242-243, 244, 256   from *Collected Poems 1909-1962* by T. S. Eliot. Reprinted by permission of Harcourt Brace Jovanovich, Inc.; copyright 1943 by T. S. Eliot; copyright 1971 by Esme Valerie Eliot.

Editor's Preface

Abraham believed in the Creator, and in obedience to Him he went out of Ur of the Chaldees. Dr. James Houston is in many respects a modern Abraham. He left the security and comfort of a Fellowship at Hertford College, Oxford, teaching geography in the University, and accepted the call to go to Vancouver in order to try to found a Christian interdisciplinary college. He had no staff, no students, no home, car or assured salary when he went out. He simply trusted the Creator.

The story of how Regent College, Vancouver, was born and grew, of how it overcame all opposition and was incorporated into the University of British Columbia, of how buildings were provided and a superb faculty assembled, of how God has laid His hand on this place and made it a centre of Christian teaching in Western Canada—all this is a minor epic of our times. But if you were to ask James Houston, he would humbly and cheerfully give all the credit to the Creator.

The point I am emphasising is this. There are plenty of books that argue the theistic hypothesis of cosmic origins against other views. There are plenty of academic treatises on the existence of a Supreme Being. Jim Houston has not written a book of that nature. His book is like a powerful, fast-moving river, composed of three streams. The first is a strong biblical foundation which has been with him since his youth. The second is a fearless academic scrutiny of alternatives to the Christian belief in a good and loving Creator, a scrutiny made all the more impressive by his professional expertise in environmental studies and his careful research into all sides of the question. The third is his passionate personal affiance in this faithful Creator God; quite literally he has staked his family, his career and his whole life on the existence and faithfulness of God. It is not surprising, therefore, that this book is a little out of the ordinary. Jim Houston has wrestled with the subject for four years. He has lectured on it in many parts of the globe. He has written and rewritten various drafts of the book, while seeking advice, clarification and correction from colleagues, students and opponents. He has taken pains to include an astonishing mixture of illustrative material and has undertaken a no less astonishing breadth of reading. Here is a man who knows the God he writes about. I cannot imagine anyone coming away from this book unrewarded.

Ours is a generation which for the most part has deemed the God hypothesis unnecessary. It is a generation on the edge of shipwreck. The confrontation course being pursued by rich and poor nations of our planet, the food scarcity, the shortage of non-renewable resources, the population explosion, the social and marital breakdown, the nuclear threat, the silicone chip, the emptiness of belief and purpose—all these factors bid us sit down while there is still time and consider whether we have not been mistaken. Could it be that the supreme purpose and fulfilment of man is to know God and to enjoy him for ever? Is such an old-fashioned view reconcilable with the present state of scientific and sociological knowledge? Jim Houston's book will help us to find an answer to that question. It is unquestionably one of the most important issues in our day. And Dr. Houston's book is one of the most important contributions to the *I Believe* series.

Michael Green
St. Aldate's,
Oxford

Foreword

I write as a layman, who has long struggled with the challenge of how to integrate one's professional training and outlook with one's Christian faith. At bottom the issue rests on one's views of God as Creator of all things, so I was grateful to the editor of this series, Canon Michael Green, when he first asked me to write on this vital subject. I am indebted to him for his trust, encouragement and patience with me. When first asked to write on 'I Believe in Creation', it seemed to be putting the cart before the horse, for we can only speak of the creation as we trust the Creator. This further comforted me, since I could write only with a deep sense of inadequacy, neither as a theologian, nor as a philosopher, nor indeed as a hard scientist, each of whom would approach the issues more rigidly than I have done. Indeed, I have resisted doing so, because to me the mystery of the creation is too great to fit neatly into any logically developed system of explanation. I have been content with indicating some signposts that I hope will help the ordinary Christian to walk in his pilgrimage towards a deeper understanding of God as Maker of Heaven and Earth. I have in mind to publish later another biblical study on the Promised Land, which has been deliberately omitted from this outline.

I am grateful to several classes of students who helped and encouraged me by their responses to lectures on the subject of Creation. My former colleague, Dr. Clark Pinnock, helped me in my first course to gain a little theological confidence when I had none. A number of friends, especially while engaged in teaching Summer School courses at Regent College, read various parts of the book. I am particularly indebted to

Professor F. F. Bruce, Professor Donald MacKay, Professor Bruce Waltke, Dr. Carl Henry, Professor R. Hooykaas, Professor Richard Longenecker, Miss Ruth Etchells, Mrs. Luci Shaw and Professor Donald J. Wiseman, who read one or more chapters or earlier drafts. I am also indebted to my relative, Mr. Raymond Forrest-Hall, for helpful criticism. Nevertheless, whatever blemishes and errors the book may have are entirely my own responsibility.

My research assistants, Beat Steiner, Dori Perrucci and George Davis, helped me respectively in the initial preparation of a bibliography, in the improvement of style, and in the compilation of the index.

I wish to thank the Board of Trustees of Regent College, who generously granted me a six months' sabbatical leave to complete this book. I am grateful also to Dr. Richard Halverson and the elders of Fourth Presbyterian Church, Washington, D.C., who invited me as Visiting Scholar to speak on the issues of this book, in a congenial atmosphere of fellowship and encouragement. Mr. and Mrs. Ken Smith kindly gave me permission to use their summer cottage when I began writing the book, and the bulk of it was completed in the friendly atmosphere of Fellowship House, Washington, D.C. Finally, I wish to thank my daughter Lydèle, Mrs. Kathy Robins and my two most loyal secretaries, Mrs. Marion Bromley and Mrs. Ilse Fleischmann, for their uncomplaining typing and re-typing of this manuscript.

Vancouver
Aug. 31st, 1978   JAMES M. HOUSTON

Contents

CHAPTER ONE

The World We Live In

The world we see is the mirror image of our hearts. We perceive reality as we conceive it to be. If we have given up hope of finding meaning in our lives, then we see the world as a desert, a threatening wilderness. If, however, we have hope in God the Creator of all things, then we can, and shall, see it very differently. We are always experiencing two landscapes at the same time: the landscape before our eyes—the phenomenal world—and the landscape in our minds, what the poet Gerard Manley Hopkins has called 'inscape'. The one is constantly interacting with the other. If, therefore, we conceive the world to be a desert, we also make it such.

That is why symbols and other forms of imagery have such powerful effects upon man and his world. Images such as the garden, the wilderness, the sea, mountains, and the city frame so much of our imagination. But back of them all, either we are possessed by our images, or we are possessed by our Creator, of whom no graven image can be made.

Creation is the landscape of the Bible. It sees God as the 'Maker of heaven and earth', the Creator of all things. There is activity, 'creation', where things happen. The energy of God's will, not just the energy of the sun, sustains the biosphere where grass grows and animals feed, and man depends upon them for his own food. God's creative power also produces diversity. All things are different from God, for He created all things, and He is holy, other than all else. From this basic distinction, all other distinctions arise. So creation is rich in variations. Things differ in degree, in kind, in distribution, in style. Trees differ from rocks or animals, one species of mam-

15

mal from another, one individual flower from all the other flowers of the same species in a meadow, one particular branch or petal from another on a single plant. Each thing that exists is unique. Likewise each change is an event that is unique. All things change without ceasing. Yet there is form, content, structure, rule, in all the changes. Thus creatureliness, individuality, variety, distinctiveness and alteration are by definition good. They are consistent with that from which they are derived.[1]

In the story of creation there is no hint whatever that there are inferior or superior forms of existence. Neither matter, nor plants, nor animals are less good, less removed from their Creator. He created them all good, not in spite of their materiality, but with their own significance and purpose in mind. Each thing has its proper capacity and fitness in relation to the rest of creation. Having blessed their reproductive capacities, their variations and complementarities, God blessed them. That is to say, He gave them the power of continued existence, of fulfilment of their purpose, so that in their creative energy they would display ever greater diversity and multiformity. This is a unique story, for no other religion or philosophy has ever been able to ascribe such significance and power to matter as Christianity has.

The biblical view of creation sets man uniquely in the world, created in God's image. Given the capacity for relationship with his Creator, he has mind, will, emotion, soul—all the functions of spirit by which man is under God yet set over the world. Man has the mandate to change the landscape of the world according to the landscape of his mind. That is why we now face the environmental crisis. All is not well in the world; man is out of joint with the rest of the household (oikos) of life. That is why we call it an ecological issue; man is a poor housekeeper of this planet. The environmental crisis may not be an emergency situation—yet—but it is rapidly approaching such a stage. It reflects, like the writing on the wall in Belshazzar's palace, the warning that, in the midst of affluence and revelry, we 'are weighed in the balances and found wanting' (Dan. 5:27). For, says the prophet, man has lifted himself up against the Lord of heaven.

All creation, says the biblical story, is one system of inter-dependence. Grass depends upon the soil, animals upon the grass. Fish inhabit the sea, as birds live in the air. While each generates its own kind, all life consists of interaction and interdependence. Charles Williams has called this play of inter-action among the separate identities of creation 'Coinherence'.[2] Its basic principle of activity is exchange, and its fruits are joy and love. We all live *from* each other, in order to live *for* each other. Our identity depends upon God, our surrender to each other depends upon the goodness of God. Thus self-sufficiency is the outrage of creation. The loss of community wounds creation. Creation 'groans' in the absence of coinherence.

The landscapes of the mind and spirit of man without God the Creator are few in number. There is the view that nature is its own creator, which ends up with the belief that man is his own creator and lord. The attempt to live sub-merged, identified with the whole, is called 'monism' or pantheism. The admission of two realms, of matter and spirit, of the world and man, is called 'dualism'. The reverence of nature is some form of 'naturalism'. The fantasy that man is his own creator, the source of his values and meaning, is 'sec-ularism'. Beyond these, there is 'nothing new' for those who live 'under the sun' (Eccl. 1:3) rather than under God who made the sun.

Nevertheless, our society does not believe this. For one of the most significant aspects of our conception of what it means to be 'modern' is the idea that we can consciously change our own character and that of our society, and be 'new'. We can, and do, deliberately change. We plan. We make the future. Whereas formerly man lived historically, that is to say, rooted in the past, now he anticipates his future, whether in family planning, in lifestyles, or in the roles he wishes to perform. The 'new' appears to be the only thing many now live for. With this loss of a beginning, there is also the loss of coinherence. One of the gurus of the counterculture, Frederick Peers, ex-presses the mood of the new generation when he says:

I do my thing, and you do your thing.
I am not in the world to live up to your expectations
And you are not in the world to live up to mine.

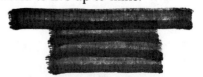

You are you and I am I
And if by chance we find each other—
It's beautiful.[3]

No society, of course, can survive with such an ethic. Perhaps that is why our age is mesmerised by the motif of 'the waste land', not only in the poem of T. S. Eliot, but in a whole sequence of plays and novels about its character.[4] Many of our writers are helping us to see this landscape of wilderness where the Creator is absent from His world.

A GODLESS WORLD

1. A Speechless World

The play *Waiting for Godot,* by Samuel Beckett,[5] has shown by its immense popularity in the last two decades that it touches the nerve of our generation. The play is a plotless description, in two scenes, of two tramps, Vladimir and Estragon, who wait on a lonely road in a barren wilderness. There is no sign of life other than a lone willow tree. They are waiting for Godot, who, when he comes—the next day, the day after—will save them and fulfil their lives. But he does not come, although in each scene a child messenger assures them he will come.

Vladimir: Well! What do we do?
Estragon: Don't let's do anything. It's safer.
Vladimir: Let's wait and see what he says.
Estragon: Who?
Vladimir: Godot.

There is something mandatory about the promise of his presence to them.

Meanwhile they are bored, have nightmares, lack sleep, contemplate suicide. Action is substituted for contemplation. While they wait they decide: 'We could do our exercises—our movements—our elevations—our relaxations—our elongations—our relaxations—to warm us up—to calm us down.' Their survey of space and time is hazy.

Estragon: And all that was yesterday, you say?
Vladimir: Yes, of course it was yesterday.
Estragon: And here where we are now?
Vladimir: What else do you think! Do you not recognise the place?
Estragon: (suddenly furious) Recognise! What is there to recognise? All my lousy life I've crawled about in the mud! And you talk to me about scenery! (Looking wildly about him.) Look at this muck-heap! I've never stirred from it!

The two tramps have never heard the story of creation, or if they have, they have forgotten it. They are enveloped instead by silence, the silence of dead voices that murmur and rustle meaninglessly.

Vladimir: What do they say?
Estragon: They talk about their lives.
Vladimir: To have lived is not enough for them.
Estragon: They have to talk about it.
Vladimir: To be dead is not enough for them.
Estragon: It is not sufficient.
          Silence

Then Estragon suggests: 'We should turn restlessly towards Nature.' Vladimir replies: 'We've tried that.' Nature has the silence of a mirror, which reflects the images cast upon it, but it cannot speak.

Yet as Estragon remarks, 'They have to talk about it.' The whole play is composed of the endless chatter of the two tramps and of two passers-by, Pozzo and his slave Lucky. But their conversation breaks up into formlessness, with loss of words, loss of meaning, loss of coherence. Language is used only to show its own uselessness. For it is an absurd world, and words do not reach reality, nor can they convey truth. The slave Lucky, in the first scene, makes a long speech on scholarship, which is *caca* (the French for excrement). Compulsively the two tramps talk, but they do not speak to each other. They are unwilling to listen to each other's nightmares, so that their incapacity to communicate means their incapacity to be friends—real friends. There is no real speech, for there are no real people, and no real community. Instead, all the sounds of the earth have merged into an indistinguishable buzzing and murmuring gibberish. There is no transcendence, only the closed system of the lifeless lives of unreal people, in a wilderness. Pozzo, the arrogant and cruel master of Lucky, is a void of mock seriousness. Both master and slave are dehumanised in their reciprocal roles, intensified in the second scene when Pozzo is blind and Lucky is dumb.

If man is distinguished from all other creatures by being a user of language—he speaks—then language becomes a crucial reality for man. The sheer futility and insanity of man in *Waiting for Godot* is that the chatter that fills the air means nothing. What then is man? Nothing! This then is the antithesis of the biblical story of creation; it is a story—the story—about reality. If man is made in the image of God, then God has made Himself known to man through His Word (John 1), so that man's nature is constituted by his being a language user. We may say that as man listens to God's Word, man is really man. Authentic man sees the biblical landscape of creation as he listens to the Word of God, who spoke all things into being and who 'sustains all things by His Word of power'. Likewise, it is through his words that a man ultimately reveals whether his heart is good or evil: 'For by your words,' said Jesus, 'you will be justified, and by your words you will be condemned' (Matt. 12:37). Vladimir and Estragon condemn themselves as dead by the absence of communication.

To live in a closed world—either of nature or the secular—is to be dead. At one point Vladimir wants to embrace his companion, but Estragon reacts violently: 'Don't touch me! Don't question me! Don't speak to me! Stay with me!' The two men desperately seek community—coinherence—but they want it on impossible terms: without intimacy, without challenge, without communication. God's challenge—'Adam, where art thou?' —is unheard. Near the end of the play, the two tramps have one more opportunity to be real people by showing compassion and helping blind Pozzo to his feet. But because they live in an unreal world, with no specificity of time or place, they do not grasp the opportunity. It slips by like a flowing river. Their loss is the lack of commitment to anything. They summarise their efforts to be human in shadowy words.

Estragon: We always find something, eh Didi, to give us
          the impression we exist.
Vladimir: Yes, yes, we're magicians.

That is the summary of modern man. If God the Creator does
not exist, Godot never turns up, and man does not exist. Technicians, magicians, may swarm and thrive, but man is dead.
But if God is, then every blade of grass He has created is real
and every dewdrop weighs a ton of glory, for creation is the
speech of God.

2. Man, the Cosmic Orphan

When man lives without faith in the Creator, then, in
another dominating metaphor of our age, man is 'the cosmic
orphan'. For he alone, of all the creatures known to him in the
universe, can probe the night sky with his telescope, or examine all the teeming forms of life with his microscope. Man's
alienation intensifies his expectation of signs of 'other intelli-
gences' elsewhere in the universe. The biologist Loren Eisely
argues that the flux man senses all round him, without eventfulness, without rootedness, makes man an orphan indeed. He
does not fit into the coinherence of nature, for unlike creation
nature has no fittingness:

> Life is indefinite departure. That is why we are all or-
> phans. That is why you must find your own way. Life is
> not stable. Everything alive is slipping through cracks and
> crevices in time, changing as it goes. Other creatures,
> however, have instincts that provide for them holes in
> which to hide. They cannot ask questions. A fox is a fox,
> a wolf is a wolf, . . . You have learned to ask questions.
> That is why you are an orphan. You are the only creature
> in the universe who knows what it has been. Now you
> must go on asking questions while all the time you are
> changing. You will ask what you are to become. The world
> will no longer satisfy you. You must find your way, your
> own true self.[6]

Man, the cosmic orphan, alone in his understanding, does
not find the universe a friendly place. It is a sphere of predic-

ament. It is the home of man, which he assumes mothers him, only to find it is utterly indifferent to him:

> A man said to the universe:
> 'Sir, I exist.'
> 'However,' replied the universe,
> 'The fact has not created in me
> A sense of obligation.'

Man stands today at the top of a vast scientific edifice in his knowledge of the universe. But the horrifying thing, he discovers, is that it may belong to no one, and that no one is in charge. It is like a ghost town; no one lives there. When there is no vertical dimension to the world, only the straight line of the horizon, then there is no real mystery, no real depth to life, no real height to human aspirations. Crane expresses this in another poem:[7]

> I saw a man pursuing the horizon;
> Round and round he sped.
> I was disturbed at this;
> I accosted the man.
> 'It is futile,' I said,
> 'You can never—'
>
> 'You lie,' he cried,
> And ran on.

Some, like the philosopher Milton K. Munitz, would say there is no reason for the existence of the world. 'Science, in its manifold and endless quest for intelligibility, can never remove the mystery of existence.'[8] Science can only measure the world in its details, facts and comings-and-goings. Yet behind this stance is the hidden assumption that science is still the only source of intelligibility, and that mystery adds no dimension to what can be factually known.

Man faces alienation at another level, when he faces the vastness of the total universe. What is our earth but a tiny speck of dust, one speck in one of hundreds of millions of planetary systems. Our galaxy alone, we are told, has a diameter of about a hundred thousand light-years (reckoning the velocity of light at 186,000 miles per second). How trivialised man has become compared to the compatible dimensions of medieval man when the earth was the centre of the universe and the heavenly space was only four hundred miles above him. Robert Frost, who often contemplated the night sky, puts the problem gloomily:

> Space ails us moderns: we are sick with space.
> Its contemplation makes us out as small
> As a brief epidemic of microbes
> That in a good glass may be seen to crawl
> The patina of this the least of globes.
> But have we there the advantage after all!
> You were belittled into vilest worms
> God hardly tolerated with his feet;
> Which comes to the same thing in different terms.
> We both are the belittled human race,
> One as compared with God and one with space.
> I had thought ours the more profound disgrace;
> But doubtless this was only my conceit.
> The cloister and the observatory saint
> Take comfort in about the same complaint.
> So science and religion really meet.[9]

Since the theologian has to deal with a God so vast, and the astronomer has to deal with a universe so great, it all comes down to the same meaninglessness, argues Frost. The conclusion is:

> There is a limit to our time extension,
> We are all doomed to broken-off careers
> And so's the nation, so's the total race.
> The earth itself is liable to the fate
> Of meaninglessly being broken off.

For Frost, God is mere convention. If the universe has a purpose, it is just purpose, which cannot be deciphered, read or understood. In the title of another poem, he describes it as 'Accidentally on Purpose'. To such artists, there is a size at which greatness begins, and a size at which grandeur begins, but there is also a size at which ghastliness begins. Nature is ghastly.

Man, the cosmic orphan, is alienated in another dimension: his chance occurrence. When man conceives of his own existence as a chance event only, not the choice of human love but the chance affair of nature's child, then he is an orphan indeed. Man is the chance product of a cosmic instant, says the biologist John A. Livingstone.[10] For of all the half billion cells of a single ejaculation, multiplied by innumerable incidences of sexual intercourse, man is the orphan of chance instance. What a crushing defeat this is to his ego, to the stability of his identity, to his search for personhood!

Yet the randomness of human identity was already speculated about a century ago by Darwin's theory of evolution and the fantastic assumptions made by Herbert Spencer. Darwin hit upon the formula 'I know' as a new scientific creed that replaced 'I believe', while his doctrine of the 'Survival of the Fittest' gratified a generation dumbfounded to learn they were 'no longer children of God but members of a brute creation'. His 'Science of Sociology', which Thomas Carlyle called 'that dismal science', declared human life was a social organism which was in evolution of progress, and whose evils could be cured by scientific investigation. What is frightening is that this man influenced profoundly a young girl, Beatrice Webb, who lost her faith in Christianity, finding his mystical creed satisfying. Thus was socialism founded. In the last year of her life (in 1943) she had a vision that suddenly all things had ceased to exist. She wrote in her diary:

> The garden will disappear and all our furniture, the earth and the sun and the moon. God wills the destruction of all living things, man and even a child. . . . we shall not be frozen or hurt. We should merely not exist. . . . What an amazing happening and well worth recording in my diary. But that also will suddenly disappear even if I went on with this endless writing.[11]

Lord Tennyson, who lived disturbed by all the possible chance extravagances of nature, longed for some assurance of the economy of human meaning, which neither Herbert Spencer nor the Fabians could give him:

O, yet we trust that somehow good
Will be the final goal of ill,
To pangs of nature, sins of will,
Defeats of doubt, and taints of blood.

That nothing walks with aimless feet;
That not one life shall be destroyed,
Or cast as rubbish to the void,
When God has made the pile complete.

That not a worm is cloven in vain;
That not a moth with vain desire
Is shriveled in a fruitless fire,
Or but subserves another's gain.

Behold, we know not anything,
I can but trust that good shall fall
At last—far off—at last, to all
And every winter change to spring.

So runs my dream; but what am I?
An infant crying in the night;
An infant crying for the light;
And with no language but a cry.

While Tennyson's human cry was still vocal, the empirical language of our times has stifled it in what has been called 'nothing-buttery'. There is *nothing but* the natural explanation, *nothing but* the mechanical or the material cause of reality, it is argued. The evolutionary reductionist Ernst Haeckel illustrated this concept as early as 1877 when he said:

> The cell consists of matter . . . composed chiefly of carbon with an admixture of hydrogen, nitrogen, and sulphur. These component parts, properly united, produce the soul and body of the animated world, and suitably nourished, become man. With this single argument the mystery of the universe is explained, the Deity annulled, and a new era of infinite knowledge ushered in.[12]

Man is thus also alienated from the real world when he assumes that he has mastered his complexity and removed it of its mystery. Man has therefore to re-understand what Pascal realised with such vision in the seventeenth century:

There are two equally dangerous extremes:
to shut reason out, and to let nothing else in.

3. Protean Man

When man is no longer at home in the world, but placeless in spirit, then he can only be a migrant, an exile, living
uncertainly and experimentally in flux. He is then like Proteus,
the Greek mythic prophet, who could change his form—wild
boar to lion, flood to fire—according to prevailing circumstances. Proteus could not stay, however, in a single form. Today, Protean man is the typical model of our society, interminably
engaged in experiments, fads and fashions. It is the environment engendered by Future Shock, of new experiences, wife
swaps, new drugs and new identities. Homelessness has led to
cosmic placelessness.

One factor contributing to Protean existence has been
the blasting of boundaries. In our own generation, we have
witnessed the bestiality of Auschwitz and the atomic destruction of Hiroshima. The holocaust and nuclear war have introduced new times of cruelty and destruction once thought
unimaginable.

This breakdown of boundaries tempts man to break other
boundaries of human existence, including the disintegration of
the family, the erosion of any sexual standards, and the loss of
authority in society.[13] In place of structure and form, there is
now emphasis on flux. Human identity is seen, not in terms of
fixed moral activity, but as an endless process of self-discovery
and personal fluidity. Instead of clear ethical contours in our
landscape of life, there is moral shifting that embraces situation
ethics. It is as if man is being influenced to leave the seashore
of a bounded world and to become *Homo novus;*[14] a new, technically determined sea-creature that, like a jellyfish, is infinitely
plastic and floats aimlessly between the interfaces of time, tide
and wind in a vast ocean current of amoral possibilities.

A series of processes is accelerating this breakdown of
human structures. First, there is the worldwide sense of what
may be called 'psycho-historical dislocation'. This is the loss of
vital connections with space and time, the loss of a sense of

personal history: roots. Due to increasing mobility, man is increasingly placeless. The standard of human values is subordinated to the dictates of technocracy; 'Organisation Man' falls apart when the value of a person is defined in terms of his income and social role. Then the vast majority of mankind are condemned to being defined as 'nobodies'. The traits of the technological society, where everyone is a technician *(Homo faber)*, caught up in the tyranny of the efficient, suggests a new age. The historian J. H. Plumb has described this as 'the death of the past'. Cut off from the past and isolated by the 'uniqueness' of our contemporary pressures and problems, man is tempted to feel perennially restless. Vital and nourishing symbols of our cultural heritage begin to disappear and to become irrelevant, even burdensome, to the new generation.

Secondly, there is the flood of imagery, produced by the mass-media, that is sweeping us into a chaotic and unassimilable whirlpool of influences. We are overwhelmed by undigested data, with endlessly incomplete alternatives to every sphere of living, and with synthetic sensations for every mood and fancy. If I think faster than I can speak, speak faster than I can act, act more than I have character to assimilate, there is already a basic disjunction within me, which challenges me to live a more integrated, authentic existence. But the extensions of forms and sensations that *techne* provides exacerbate our loss of integrity. The myth of the global village, moreover, assumes that modern man's place in this world is not in a fixed location, but only in space, in placelessness. For everything is now homogenised in universal cultural packages that are dictated to us by the whim of manufacturer and media producer.

Thirdly, there is the tendency of the modern arts to mirror—and indeed anticipate—this spirit of change and flux. The pace of technological exploits, the overcrowding and complexity of factual knowledge, the turmoil of multifluid events, and the heaps of undigested experiences are all generating overload. The seeming boredom and passivity of many youth today is perhaps only the state of unconsciousness we mercifully fall into when we carry too much pain. Beyond that stage further overload eventually leads to an explosion of rebellious rage, to revolt, or to other loss of continuity and coherence.

Perhaps, then, the breakdown of style in literature, the loss of form in the arts, and the atonality of music that we are witnessing today in our culture reflect this tendency towards chaos, much like the sweeping pervasiveness of Noah's flood. In fact, chaos is exploited systematically today with the exploration of the unconscious,[15] free association, and in such movements as the Theatre of the Absurd. Modern writers like Sartre and Beckett allow their thoughts to flow around any boundaries or any concepts of fixity. Thus the medium becomes the message, technique is master, and means rather than ends the rule. Protean man, in such a culture, ends up as *Homo absurdus,* body without soul, message without content, technique without purpose—ultimate absurdity.

4. Man, Destroyer of the Earth

In a world bounded with fixed laws and the natural limits of physical existence, Protean man is yet unwilling to live within his means. He is not a good householder of the *oikos* that is our home on this planet. Unlimited population growth now puts a strain on the earth's limited resources. Our insatiable appetites, which cannot distinguish between basic needs, neurotic wants, and infinite desires, threaten a wholesale collapse of our fragile biological systems, which we call 'ecosystems'. A new limit—that of the sewage capacities of the rivers of the world, and of the air circulation system to absorb our industrial wastes and pollution—is expected to be reached within the next two decades. Never before has *man* threatened the very extinction of his planet; until now it has appeared as if nature threatened man.

Ours, then, is a cancerous society that faces a profound dilemma of abnormal and excessive growth at the expense of the well-being of the whole earth. How do we distinguish growth that is muscular and normal from fat that is excessive, or from cancerous growth that is deadly? We can apply this question to each discipline of man's needs today: to economics, to politics, to education, to technology. Cancer cells proliferate without regard to the well-being of the rest of the body. This metaphor describes the runaway character of so many features of our post-industrial society, pockmarked as it is with slogans such as 'knowledge for knowledge's sake' or 'technique for technique's sake', as well as fevered with a grasping consumerism that reaches out for more and more profits.

There must be limits to growth, since the upward graph of the G.N.P. is on collision course with the slower, cyclical courses of the life-systems and the much slower renewal of fixed geological systems. This growth dilemma is exaggerated by the work-role dilemma of modern man. For if man's neurotic image of his identity is based solely in terms of what he has and what he does, then his insatiable appetite for more of these neurotic wants will inevitably end in the destruction of the world as his home.[16] Such an addiction for more of the same, like that of the alcoholic, only leads to a worsening situation, both for man and for his ecological household.

Some futurists see the next two decades as a period of profound and necessary changes. Man must accept fundamental changes of mind and spirit if there is to be any hope for his future on the earth.[17] 'New birth', 'conversion', being 'born again', are religious terms, but they provide suitable descriptions of this new image of man that naturalism and secularism cannot provide. A pantheist solution, for man to 'get back into nature', is impossible, for man's transcendence over nature has clearly set him on a collision course with the earth's systems of renewal.[18] Man is not just a child of nature, otherwise we would not be facing the environmental mess we are now in.

The Christian doctrine of creation is thus not doctrinaire, a religious faith hopelessly out of touch with contemporary reality. It is literally the only understanding of man and his world that makes sense and which can prescribe the right attitudes to appropriate actions. The prophet Hosea understood clearly how our social and environmental problems are related when a people forget God. The source of all the trouble occurs when disloyalty to the covenant relationship with the Creator God leads logically to the dissolution of natural bonds within family, society and environment.

> The Lord has a controversy [lawsuit] with the inhabitants of the land. There is no faithfulness or kindness, and no knowledge of God in the land; there is swearing, lying, killing, stealing, and committing adultery; they break all

bounds and murder follows murder. Therefore the land
mourns, and all who dwell in it languish, and also the
beasts of the field, and the birds of the air; and even the
fish of the sea are taken away.   (Hos. 4:1–3)

Disloyalty to the creation ordinances of God makes it impossible to 'know God' as a suzerain people. The state of our
environment today is like a cosmic treaty; its covenant has been
broken by its subject people. Instead, man has established himself as the sovereign lord and worshipped nature rather than
nature's God. In Hosea's time this idolatry was to Baal, so that
the prophet voices the Word of God saying: 'It was I who gave
the grain, the wine, and the oil' (Hos. 2:8); not Baal. So Hosea
speaks accurately of such people as living like prostitutes who
break all the rules of valid relationship. They are rightfully
condemned to be stricken, whose 'root is dried up and . . .
[they] bear no fruit' (Hos. 9:16).

THE WORLD OF NATURE

1. The Sentiment of Nature

The Baalism which the prophets condemned is still with
us as naturalism. The counter-cultural revolution exhorts us to
follow the 'new naturalism'. Ecologists like Barry Commoner
tell us: 'Don't mess with Mother Nature.' Perhaps more than
any other form of secularism, the dominance of nature has
tended to eclipse the light of the Creator in the Western world.
So one of the most enduring goddesses of the pantheon of
Western idols has been 'Mother Nature'.

To the Greeks, *physis*, from which we get our word physics, meant 'the beginning', 'the coming-to-be', as an acorn becomes an oak tree. The Romans, notably the Stoics, identified
the world with *natura* (*nasci*, a birth), thus giving an organic
analogy to reality. The union of *physis* and *natura* as 'Nature'
has produced a classical cosmogony that continues to rival biblical creation. Nature has become what the Chinese call 'the ten
thousand things', which the dictionary lists accordingly under
fifteen or more headings in its definitions.

The basic dilemma with nature is that it is only a mirror

that casts a reflection of what is projected upon it. Or to change the metaphor, it is an echo, not a word. So the whole history of Western thought has used and re-used the idea of nature, as R. G. Collingwood has noted, according to the philosophical and religious ideas prevalent at any one time.[19] In the Middle Ages, the Stoic view of nature was adopted by the church uncritically, to be conceived as the servant of God. Later, as the mechanical laws of cause and effect were recognised by the deists within the Newtonian world-view, nature became an independent force, a closed system of cause and effect. (See Appendix C.)

The Romantic movement, first in France, then in England and Germany, sentimentalised her as 'La Belle Nature', man's goddess and teacher.

> First follow Nature, and your judgment frame
> By her just standards, which is still the same:
> Unerring Nature, still divinely bright,
> One clear, unchanged, and universal light.[20]

The sentiment of the poet Pope was innocent enough, considering that gentlemen were re-designing their country estates into landscaped gardens, 'according to nature', in eighteenth-century England. But there accumulated in romanticism four major senses to which appeal was made to the authority of Nature.

1. Nature as an object to be imitated and reproduced.
2. Nature as a system of necessary and self-evident truths.
3. Nature, the exemplar of 'the good', semi-personified in the cosmic order.
4. Nature as naturalism, the real, which promotes self-expression, self-consciousness, freedom from conventions, the quality of the primitive, spontaneous, the completeness of life.[21]

These are the sources that inspire the poets and the writers of the following century with their poems and stories about nature. Thus the poet Schiller, in his *Ode to Joy*, represents mankind as nourished by the breasts of Nature. Francis

Thompson sought this nourishment in his escape from God, but proclaims his disappointment:

> Nature, poor stepdame, cannot slake my drouth;
> Let her, if she would owe me,
> Drop yon blue bosom-veil of sky, and show me
> The breasts o' her tenderness:
> Never did any milk of hers once bless
> My thirsting mouth.
>
> *The Hound of Heaven*[22]

In spite of this disappointment, modern man persists in seeking from nature what he needs of spiritual nourishment and faith. Even the theologian Paul Tillich assures us that the name 'God' does not add anything to what is already involved in the name 'Nature'.

C. S. Lewis, who was himself attracted to Stoicism in his youth, concludes very differently on this subject: 'When it sets itself up as a religion it is beginning to be a god—therefore a demon. . . . Nature dies to those who try to live for love of nature.'[23]

2. Evolutionism

A new shaping of naturalism in the nineteenth century was evolutionism. Although T. H. Huxley clearly foresaw the ethical danger of translating Darwinism—'Nature red in tooth and claw'—into social Darwinism, we needed the bestiality of Nazi 'naturalism' with its theology of blood and its distortion of creation ordinances of 'race' to convince us of the terrible evil of naturalism when its fruit ripened and then rotted in concentration camps.[24] In spite of that, we still find the persuasive theme of evolutionism thrust upon us, both in science and religion. In spite of the tautology of such terms—'the survival of the fittest' = those that 'survive' are the 'fittest'—and the variant biological views of diversification of genetic reproduction, evolutionism has enormous appeal to those who see the world only in terms of flux and novelty, and to those who seek a unitary approach to knowledge. It is an easy, but costly, way of seeing the unity of life.

Teilhard de Chardin would argue for this concept of evolution, even at the cost of re-uniting the biblical revelation on
his own terms:

> Human knowledge is developing exclusively under the
> aegis of evolution, recognised as a prime property of ex-
> perimental reality. So true is this that *nothing can any longer
> find place in our constructions which does not first satisfy the
> conditions of a universe* in the process of transformation. A
> Christ whose features do not adapt themselves to the re-
> quirements of a world that is evolutive in structure will
> tend more and more to be eliminated out of hand. . . .
> if a Christ is to be completely acceptable as an object of
> worship, he must be presented as the saviour of the idea
> and reality of evolution.[25]

Behind this affirmation is his concern for wholeness of vision,
just as pantheism has gripped the faith of millions for thou-
sands of years. The evocation of the whole, its presentiment
and nostalgia, seize man's imagination. But the 'new' God of
evolution cannot give substance and uniqueness to all that is,
and certainly it cannot take human personhood seriously. It
knows nothing of the holiness of God, and it cannot take sin
seriously as the biblical faith does.

3. Objections to Naturalism

The dilemma of naturalism is that in attempting to explain everything within the closed world of Nature, with its
autonomy of thought, it fails to explain anything meaningful
for *human* existence.

In the first place, the reasoning process of man cannot be
explained solely in terms of natural causes. Men do not treat
all their ideas as mere 'feelings' in their heads, induced by
biochemical processes. We assume the validity of reasoning. We
live under the assumption that rational thought is independent
and not interlocked within the interrelated systems of events
we may call 'Nature'. Within each of us there is a realm of
activity that exists independently. The mind is not the brain,
however interrelated the two may seem to be. The human
mind is, in a very real sense, a 'transcendent' entity. It cannot

be explained by recourse to Nature or to evolutionism. As C. S. Lewis has argued,

> The myth [of mindless Evolution] asks me to believe that reason is simply the unforeseen and unintended by-product of a mindless process at one stage of its endless and aimless becoming. The content of the Myth thus knocks from under me the only ground on which I could possibly believe the Myth to be true. If my own mind is the product of the irrational ... how shall I trust my mind?[26]

Thus reason is more than cerebral bio-chemistry. Yet naturalists fail to give sufficient attention to the fact that men actually think.

In the second place, man exercises another transcendent dimension in making moral decisions. If all we say or do is ultimately reducible to the mechanical, where is there room for the 'ought' or 'ought not' that we formulate into ethical behaviour? If the whole moral dimension could be explained fully in naturalistic terms so that 'values' were manufactured out of 'facts', then morality would be reduced to nonmoral categories. But it would be an illusion. If moral judgments are simply reduced to feelings, then there is no good or bad, only the illusion of values. Even the most consistent naturalist does not behave by such reasoning. He is successful as a scientist only when he seeks truth as a value with utmost integrity. He does not really act as if his conscience were the chance product of blind natural forces. Morality, as well as many other personal attributes of human existence, is a signal of the transcendental that distinguishes man from the other creations of the natural world.

In the third place, man transcends the natural world in practical ways. By science and technology he has achieved remarkable independence over against his environment. That is why we now have on our hands the 'environmental issue', so that we fear man's impact on the globe through resource depletion, pollution and other forms of environmental deterioration.

When all meanings of nature are reduced to their basic ingredients, two remain: nature as the totality of all processes and beings, and nature as the counterpart to culture and man's activities generally. This *double entendre* in nature suggests that man cannot be understood merely as a natural being whose home is nature.[27] If man is to be understood at all, it is as a spiritual and natural being whose objectification of the natural realm and moral awareness of the technological impact he is now making upon the physical world deny his inclusion wholly within nature. Rather, nature is the context of, and material for, man's transcendent powers. Nature is the sphere of both his immanence and his transcendence. But 'nature' is not his true home. His actions belie the omnipotence and autonomy of nature.

4. The Vulgar Notion of Nature

Robert Boyle, known as the father of chemistry, and a contemporary of Thomas Traherne whose enjoyment of creation we shall consider later, wrote a critical appraisal of nature after over twenty years of reflection on the matter. 'Nature', he concluded, was 'a licentious word, and one which is detrimental to a fully based faith in the Creator.'

> I have sometimes seriously doubted whether the vulgar notion of nature has not been both injurious to the glory of God and a great impediment to the solid and useful discovery of his work. I am apt to think that the Grand Enemy of God's glory made great use of Aristotle's authority and errors to distract from it. For . . . Aristotle, by introducing the opinion of the eternity of the world, did . . . openly deny God the production of the world. So, by ascribing the admirable works of God to what he calls 'Nature', he tacitly denies him the moral government of the world.[28]

Boyle has several other objections to the concept of 'Nature', in addition to its being worshipped as a semi-deity that detracts from the glory of the Creator. Like 'Fortune', which is a vague notion, 'Nature' is a loose and vaguely understood notion. In the scientific economy of explanation, nature is unnecessary to postulate. Common assumptions about nature have not been investigated nor understood. But above all, Boyle saw nature as a concept dangerous to the faith of the Christian. Significantly, he notes that neither the word nor the notion is to be found in the Hebrew of the Old Testament.[29] Instead, there are repeated warnings against the deification of created things. He quotes three significant passages:

> If I have looked at the sun when it shone,
> or the moon moving in splendour
> and my heart has been secretly enticed,
> and my mouth has kissed my hand;
> this also would be an iniquity to be punished by the
>   judges,
> for I should have been false to God above.
>
> (Job 31:26–27)

> Beware lest you lift up your eyes to heaven, and when you see the sun and the moon and stars, all the host of heaven, you be drawn away and worship them and serve them, things which the Lord your God has allotted to all the peoples under the whole heaven.   (Deut. 4:19)

> Because they exchanged the truth about God for a lie and worshipped and served the creature rather than the Creator, who is blessed for ever! Amen. For this reason God gave them up to dishonourable passions.
>
> (Rom. 1:25–26)

In harmony with these biblical injunctions, Boyle waged his polemic against Nature, so 'that it may induce men to pay their admiration, their praises, and their thanks, directly to God Himself, who is the True and only Creator of the sun, moon, earth, and those other creatures that men are wont to call the works of Nature.'[30]

Boyle's attack on the deification of such concepts as nature, unique in the history of English literature for its extent and explicitness, is consistent with our needs today. Man is not at home in nature precisely because the fantasy of an idol is being imposed upon the reality of man. It is a distortion of the true character of man to fit him into such a framework. Man is only at home in the biblical landscape of creation. There he need not live in alienation and absurdity. There he need not wander like Godot's two tramps, chattering inanities. For there he can learn to listen to the Word of the Creator.

Significantly, little attention was paid to Boyle's book. A century later, the leading thinkers of the Age of the Enlightenment were to further advance the eclipse of creation by offering secular alternatives to the providence of God. In spite of the incompatibility of producer and consumer, said the economic theorist Adam Smith, nonetheless there operates in the marketplace the principle of harmony. In spite of the divergent needs and conditions of the classroom, argued the philosopher Lessing, this same goddess 'harmony' operates in the interest of public education. Likewise Rousseau saw the same secularised providence as operative in the political self-interest of the majority vote to bring about the 'best' government.[31] It is ironic to us today to see how our institutions of capitalism, education and democracy are being questioned and deeply challenged. Like Mother Nature herself, they are founded upon the sinking sands of secularised providence that absolutise creaturely assumptions. No wonder our contemporary artists sense the absurdity of life in our society.

Clearly the technological society is here to stay. But if it is merely an expansion of what we already have, it will drive us into a fool's paradise that is like Godot's wilderness. Our existing trends are on collision course; we cannot hope to survive with more of the same growth. The technical-scientific trip may well end as the trap of the future. We need a profound re-shaping of the landscapes of our minds and spirits to survive. To be at home in the world we need a profound re-shaping of our view of the world. For a technocratic view of man and nature is death: death to man, death to man's world.

NOTES

1   Mary McDermott Shideler, *The Theology of Romantic Love, a Study in the Writings of Charles Williams*, New York, Harper & Brothers, 1962, p. 16.
2   G. L. Prestige, *God in Patristic Theology*, London, S.P.C.K., 1952, ch. XIV, pp. 282–302.

3   Cited in Robert A. Evans, *Belief and the Counter Culture*, Philadelphia, The Westminster Press, 1971, p. 50.

4   C. B. Cox and Arnold P. Hinchliffe (edit.), *T. S. Eliot, the Waste Land*, London, Macmillan Press Ltd., 1972.

5   Samuel Beckett, *Waiting for Godot*, New York, Grove Press Inc., 1954.

6   Loren Eisely, 'The Cosmic Orphan' in *The New Encyclopaedia Britannica*, Chicago, Propaedia, 1974, p. 207.

7   Quoted in Maurice Bassan (edit.), *Stephen Crane*, Englewood Cliffs, N.J., Prentice-Hall Inc., 1967, p. 32.

8   Milton K. Munitz, *The Mystery of Existence*, New York, Dell Pub. Co., Delta Books, 1968, pp. 211–219.

9   Quoted by Howard Mumford Jones, *Belief and Disbelief in American Literature*, Chicago, University of Chicago Press, 1967, pp. 133, 134.

10   John A. Livingstone, *One Cosmic Instant*, Toronto, University of Toronto Press, 1973, p. 60.

11   Kitty Muggeridge and Ruth Adam, *Beatrice Webb, a Life, 1858–1943*, New York, Alfred A. Knopf, 1968, pp. 38–39 and p. 255.

12   Quoted by Loren Eisely, 'Science and the Sense of the Holy', *Quest*, March/April 1978, p. 70.

13   R. J. Lifton, *Boundaries*, C.B.C. Lectures, Toronto, C.B.C. Publications, 1967.

14   Fred and Anne C. Richards, *Homo novus, the New Man*, Boulder, Colorado, Shields Publishing Inc., 1973.

15   Erich Kahler, *The Disintegration of Form in the Arts*, New York, George Braziller, 1967.

16   William Leiss, *Limits to Satisfaction*, Toronto, University of Toronto Press, 1976.

17   Wyllis W. Harman, *An Incomplete Guide to the Future*, Stanford, Calif., Stanford Alumni Association, 1976, p. 6.

18   Frederich Elder, *Crisis in Eden, a religious study of man and his environment*, New York, Abingdon Press, 1970, pp. 21–61, describes the inclusionist position.

19   R. G. Collingwood, *The Idea of Nature*, Oxford, Clarendon Press, 1965.

20   M. H. Abrams, *The Poetry of Alexander Pope: a Selection*, Northbrook Pub. Co., 1954, p. 10.

21   Arthur O. Lovejoy, ' "Nature" as Aesthetic Norm', *Modern Language Notes*, 42, 1927, pp. 444–450.

22   Quoted from *The Collected Poetry of Francis Thompson*, London, Hodder & Stoughton, 1913, p. 52.

23   Clyde S. Kilby (edit.), *A Mind Awake*, New York, Harcourt, Brace & World Inc., 1969, p. 202.

24   Richard Gutteridge, *Open thy Mouth for the Dumb!* Oxford, Basil Blackwell, 1976.

25   Teilhard de Chardin, 'What the World is Looking for from the Church of God at this Moment', *Christianity and Evolution*, London, Collins, 1971, p. 212.

26   C. S. Lewis, 'The Funeral of a Great Myth', *Christian Reflections*, Grand Rapids, Eerdmans, 1967, p. 89.

27   Gordon D. Kaufman, 'A Problem for Theology: the Concept of Nature', *Harvard Theological Review*, 65, 1972, pp. 337–366.

28   Robert Boyle, *A Free Enquiry into the Vulgarly Received Notion of Nature, made in an Essay*, London, The Royal Society, 1682, p. 6.

29   Ibid., p. 49.

30   Ibid., p. 134.

31   Paul Tillich, 'The Enlightenment and its Problems', in *Perspectives on 19th and 20th Century Protestant Theology*, edit. Carl E. Braaten, London, S.C.M., 1967, pp. 24–70.

CHAPTER TWO

The God Who Creates

We all sense there is a basic disharmony today between man and his environment. Our 'technocracy', that is to say, the modern apperception of a man-made, man-ruled society and a man-shaped universe, is not sustainable on a permanent basis with the natural world on which we depend for our survival. That is why we call it 'the environmental crisis', as we have seen. Yet it seems innate in man to see the connection he must have with the land. In Chinese thought, for example, Taoist nature mysticism has emphasised the need for harmony between man and his world. 'Feng-shui' was the art of adapting the living and the dead so that they would be in tune with the cosmic breath that frames and maintains the world. For physical changes also had moral consequences, so that conformity to nature was happiness and nonconformity led to disaster. In contrast to technocracy, which is modern and wholly man-centred, this alternative, ancient view of mankind may be called 'ontocracy' since ontology has to do with the essence of things, with being. As we have already seen, the sentiment of nature that has discoloured the reality of so much Christian thought in the Western world is another form of ontocracy.

A great deal of thought is being given today to ways in which technocracy can somehow be welded together with traditional forms of ontocracy, so that the technocrat and the ecologist, for example, can, like the wolf and the lamb, lie down together in millennial pastures. It is the imagery of what Leo Marx has called 'the Machine and the Garden', of technology and the paternal idyll in North American society.[1] As the Spanish philosopher Ortega y Gasset said sarcastically:

The new man wants his motor-car, and enjoys it, but he believes that it is the spontaneous fruit of an Edenic tree. In the depths of his soul he is unaware of the artificial, almost incredible, character of civilisation and does not extend his enthusiasm for the instrument to the principles which make them possible.[2]

However, several great American novels have sensed the incongruity of the two realms. In *The Great Gatsby* (1925), F. Scott Fitzgerald saw it producing a landscape of ashes.

About half way between West Egg and New York the motor road hastily joins the railroad and runs beside it for a quarter of a mile, so as to shrink away from a certain desolate area of land. This is a valley of ashes—a fantastic farm where ashes grow like wheat into ridges and hills and grotesque gardens, where ashes take the form of houses and chimneys and rising smoke and, finally, with a transcendent effort, of men who move dimly and already crumbling through the powdery air. Occasionally a line of gray cars crawls along an invisible track, gives out a ghastly creak and comes to rest, and immediately the ash-gray men swarm up with leaden spades and stir up an impenetrable cloud, which screens their obscure operations from your sight.[3]

This hideous, man-made wilderness is a product of the technology that gives Gatsby his wealth, but none of his possessions can give him the quality of life to which he aspires. A pastoral landscape cannot be harmonized with man's acquisitiveness.

THE QUEST FOR HARMONY

1. Technique and Nature

In a recent novel, Robert M. Pirsig's *Zen and the Art of Motorcycle Maintenance*, the attempt is renewed to weld together ontocracy with technocracy. The author tells us to discount any strict relationship between Zen Buddhism and motorcycles, but in following the archetypal symbol of 'the way' from East to West, the two systems are in fact united. The narrator is an ex-philosophy professor who takes his son Chris across the American continent on a motorcycle trip. They are accompanied by two friends—the Sutherlands—part of the way. It is a pilgrimage towards 'Center', where he seeks to reconcile nature and machine, representing the basic dualities. His instinct tells him he must unite them, and he uses every power of Western rationality to do so. It is crucial to do so, since he represents an entire culture that yearns to see them integrated.

Before the journey's end the Sutherlands have parted company with him, for, representative of the counter-culture, they are using the motorcycle only as an escape from the city into the country, to nature, but they show no responsibility for their machine:

> I disagree with them about cycle maintenance, but not because I am out of sympathy with their feelings about technology. I just think their flight from and hatred of technology is self-defeating. The Buddha, the God-head, resides quite as comfortably in the circuits of a digital computer or the gears of a cycle transmission as he does at the top of a mountain or in the petals of a flower. To think otherwise is to demean the Buddha—which is to demean oneself.[4]

In contrast to their romanticism, the narrator would be a mechanised centaur, who speaks of steel as taking shape in man's mind. Man and machine must be in tune with each other, and this is an art of choices where we must go beyond absolutist thinking to combine reason and feeling, technology and art. Basic to this 'art' is one indispensable term: Quality. The search for its meaning is the preoccupation of the second half of the book. Quality is the Tao, the sense of harmony with the universe, 'the great central generating force of all religions'. He also gives it the name 'gumption'.

> I like the word 'gumption' because it's so homely and so forlorn, and so out of style it looks as if it needs a friend and isn't likely to reject anyone who comes along. . . . I like it also because it describes exactly what happens to someone who connects with Quality. He gets filled with gumption. The Greek called it *enthousiasmos*, the root of

'enthusiasm', which means, literally, filled with *theos* or God, or Quality. See how that fits? ... Gumption is the psychic gasoline that keeps the whole thing going. . . . In nondualistic maintenance gumption isn't a fixed commodity. It's a variable, a reservoir of good spirits that can be added to or subtracted from. Since it's a result of the perception of Quality. . . .[5]

In quest of Quality or 'gumption', the narrator returns to the land of Phaedrus, who had in his dream made a map of a route across a mountain for which he had sacrificed everything. So the narrator and his company attempt to relocate the route. Crossing the first big mountain he says, 'I am a pioneer now, looking onto a promised land.' Like Phaedrus, he enters 'the high country of the mind' where 'one has to become adjusted to the thinner air of uncertainty, and to the enormous magnitude of questions asked, and to the answers proposed to those questions'.[6] He finds that one has to re-think mountains particularly; so imbedded are they in our symbolism of achievement and of ego-climbing. Indeed, he finds more Zen in the valleys. Thus the narrator attempts to map out transcendent realities where the rubber meets the road. He looks for myths as the force beyond logic for the needs of individual knowledge in the modern world of the machine, which can then be offered to the whole culture.

What Pirsig failed to recognise is that not only are technocracy and ontocracy incompatible with each other, but they are clearly incompatible with theocracy. This whole motorcycle saga is man-centred, man-operated and man-directed.

Technique, as the social prophet and lawyer Jacques Ellul has called the whole obsession with technology, shares with Nature closed views of reality. They are closed worlds, cut off from the roots of their potentials. It is not their structure that enables them to be what they are. The abilities of man on the one hand, and of the Creator of the universe on the other hand, lie behind their apparent realities. The appalling mindset of the technocrat is that he assumes the technical milieu is autonomous in terms of values and ideas, that it is self-determining, and that the accumulation of means without direction towards ends is its momentum. It will advance relentlessly like a juggernaut unless *all* men are shown

... that Technique is nothing more than a complex of material objects, procedures, and combinations, which have as their sole result a modicum of comfort, hygiene, and ease.... Man must be convinced that technical progress is not humanity's supreme adventure.... As long as man worships Technique, there is as good as no chance that he will ever succeed in mastering it.[7]

Likewise Nature, as we have seen, is a fantasy if it is not related to its Creator. As C. S. Lewis has said:

Only Supernaturalists really see Nature. ... To treat her as God, or as Everything, is to lose the whole pith and pleasure of her. Come out, look back, and then you will see ... this astonishing cataract of bears, babies and bananas: this immoderate deluge of atoms, orchids, oranges, cancers, canaries, fleas, gases, tornadoes and toads. How could you ever have thought that this was ultimate reality? How could you ever have thought that it was merely a stage set for the moral drama of men and women?[8]

2. The Kingship of God

We must not take nature too seriously, in place of God, nor may we treat nature with less seriousness than as the creation of God. To enjoy this proper harmony between man and the world we need 'theocracy', God's rule in the world. This is the meaning of the landscape of creation: that God is King. This affirmation alone enables man to live in an authentically open world, open to the nature and needs of man as a person. For the rule of God implies the intersection of earth and heaven, time and eternity, human responsibility and divine grace. This is the antithesis of the existential anguish and absurdity of the closed world depicted in *Waiting for Godot*, as well as in *Zen and the Art of Motorcycle Maintenance*.

Unlike faith in nature or in technique, which require no other authority than themselves, faith in creation requires a prior acknowledgement of faith in the Creator. And prior to any faith in the Creator, there must be faith in the transcendent Lordship of God. He is not Creator and, therefore, Lord; He is first Lord and then Creator. As the Apostles' Creed states: 'I believe in God the Father Almighty, Maker of heaven and earth. . . .' Our prior knowledge of the creation is not what first determines whether we accept or reject the Creator. Rather, the acceptance of the will of God, knowing Him as subjects and creatures first—this is how to live properly in His world.

Theologians have often argued that the children of Israel first experienced redemption, learning thereby to know the subsequent reality of the whole creation of God. Clearly I cannot affirm 'I believe in creation' unless I have first experienced the faith to say 'I believe in the Creator'. Moreover, creation is not a comprehensible reality; it cannot be mastered by the human mind. Rather it masters us, as a stance we must take of dependence upon the Creator for everything. For we are no more capable of comprehending creation than a character in a story is capable of standing outside the plot of a book to describe the motive and plan of the author.

Getting inside the miracle of creation is an impossibility for us.

> No, He is too quick. We never
> Catch Him at it. He is there
> sooner than our thought, our prayer.
> Searching
> backward, we cannot discover *how*
> or get inside the miracle.
>
> Even if it were here and now
> how would we describe the just-born trees
> swimming into place at their green creation,
> flowering upward in the air
> with all their thin twigs quivering
> in gusts of grace? or the great
> white whales fluking
> through crystalline seas
> like recently inflated balloons? Who could
> time the beat of a man's heart
> as the woman comes close enough to fill
> his newly-hollow side? Who will
> diagram the gynecology
> of incarnation, the trigonometry of trinity?

or chemically analyse wine
from a well? or see inside
joints as they loosen, and whole limbs
and lives? Will anyone stand beside
the moving stone? and plot the bright
trajectory of the ascension? and explain
the tongues of fire
telling both heat and light?

Enough. Refrain.
Observe a finished work. Think:
Today—another miracle—the feathered
arrow of my faith may link
God's bow and target.   Luci Shaw

The most ardent literalist has no idea of the process by
which God still performs miracles, nor indeed how the King
of creation brought the universe into being. Thus the Bible
does not defend any particular picture or 'world-view'. The
story of creation must therefore be distinguished from all the
theogonies, cosmogonies or cosmologies—ancient or modern.
Genesis one is not a primitive account of *how* the universe
began, but about *who* brought all things into being. The attitude of 'how-it-all-began' is the product of deistic views that
would speculate about how the phenomenal world began and
was then left alone to run its own course. Rather, the kingship
of God is that He still rules. He still 'upholds all things by the
Word of His power'. In His general as well as His special providence, God has not abdicated the moral governorship of the
universe to the hypotheses of men.

God is no King if He only originated creation and then
has left it to unwind like a clock. The Creator is behind all
physical processes, all reproductive capacities, all principles of
harmony in the universe. God's activity therefore does not come
in as an extra. As Professor MacKay has said, 'If God is active
in any part of the physical world, He is in all. If the divine
activity means anything, then *all* the events of what we call the
physical world are dependent on that activity.'[10] If so, then in
principle there can be no conflict between faith and science.
Conflict will arise only if God is assumed to be merely the God-

THE GOD WHO CREATES

of-the-gaps, whose activities are circumscribed to the miraculous while science studies the 'normal' or 'natural' events. If the Creator is Lord of all events, taking ultimate responsibility for everything, even evil, then the term 'natural' will not mean self-explanatory, but that fixed and stable state of processes in the universe of which God is the Ruler and Maintainer.

Creation thus can never be a rival hypothesis to the latest scientific theories, since God has given man the faculty of intelligence to develop science as well as regulate the structure of reality he can perceive. The mind of man and the nature of reality are fit together by the mind of the Maker. Sometimes the biblical analogies of creation are expressed in human language, for various Hebrew words are used to describe what He has done. He 'makes' (*asah*, Gen. 1:7, 31; 2:4); He 'fashions' like a father (*yatsar*, Gen. 2:7, 8, 19; Jer. 1:5; Hos. 4:13); He 'forms' (*qana*, Gen. 14:19; Ps. 139:13; Prov. 8:22). But the word *bara* is used uniquely of God's creation (Gen. 1:1, 21, 27; 2:3, 4) to stress its absolute distinctiveness. Significantly, it is used fourteen times in the book of Isaiah, and there the prophet uses it both of creation and of re-creation or redemption. Indeed, the prophet speaks of creation within the context of God's plan of salvation, a theme we shall consider later. Likewise Jeremiah venerates Yahweh as both redeemer and (re-)creator.

Scholars have tended to see the concept of God as Creator as a late motif of the Old Testament. Yet clearly the worship of Yahweh is traceable to remote antiquity. As the chronicle records: 'To Seth also a son was born, and he called his name Enosh. At that time men began to call upon the name of the Lord (Yhwh)' (Gen. 4:26). Later we have in the book of Exodus a revelation that is pivotal to the structure of the entire book and all that follows in the history of Israel. At the burning bush, Moses asks God to declare His name; to reveal who He really is. God says to Moses, 'I AM WHO I AM' (Exod. 3:14). This brings into focus the root meaning of the Hebrew word *hyh*, to be.[11] This, then, is not a tautology, for the phrase 'I am the one who is' expresses the identity of the Creator ('I am'), while 'is' expresses His existence. To be more precise, God claims to be 'The Being', 'I am the One Who Is'. The dynamic, effective being of the Creator is thus affirmed as the eternally effective

Yahweh, the Creator. The verbal meaning of *qal* is both 'I am' and 'I shall be', thus expressing the unconditional existence and sovereignty of God over the present and the future. In the context of Moses and his people, God thus promises Moses 'I am and remain present, and always will be present with you'. Yet man's needs are never enough to define the mystery of God, so the title could also be interpreted 'I will be what I will be'.

The implication for the Old Testament theology of the Creator, then, is that God, who is the Lord of history, the redeemer of His people, and who has pledged Himself in covenant with Israel, has a sure and steadfast testimony in doing so, for He is the Creator, and His covenant is already founded on His continual faithfulness in creation. His name signifies, 'I cause to be what comes into existence'—all things, all the time. The prophets based their words upon this grand assurance that Yahweh is 'the Lord of hosts', that is to say, the all-powerful and irresistible King of creation. Thus Amos says that 'He who forms the mountains and creates the wind' is 'the Lord, the God of hosts, that is his name' (Amos 4:13). Likewise 'He who made the Pleiades and Orion, and turns darkness into morning' is the Judge (Amos 5:8). The Lord God of Hosts is the one who controls the rise and fall of the Nile, so vital for Egypt's powerful civilisation, as well as all the 'waters of the sea' (Amos 9:5, 6). This title, 'Lord of Hosts', is thus the theological basis of so much prophetic utterance, being used 59 times in Isaiah, 76 times in Jeremiah, 24 times in Malachi and 52 times in Zechariah. Ezekiel repeats 70 times another pregnant phrase, 'I am Yahweh', to indicate that God, faithful in creation, is also faithful in covenant with His people.[12]

The implication of this is that only those who depend upon God every day of their lives, 'in whom they live, and move, and have their being', so that they recognise every breath they breathe as God-given and God-sustained, can worthily call God their Creator. Christians have failed to see profoundly enough that God cannot be Redeemer unless He is Creator, so that we see redemption creatively, and see creation redemptively. To live within self-contained world-views so as to view reality speculatively is to be blind and deaf to the reality of the voice of the Creator. 'Technocrats' do not need God, for they depend upon their techniques. 'Ontocrats' do not need God, for they rely upon nature. Only 'the poor in spirit' can affirm God's reality, for they listen to the Word of God.

CREATION BY THE WORD

1. The Word in the Ancient World

That union between man and the world whose harmony modern man still yearns to have, as we have seen in Pirsig's novel, was sought in the ancient world in the magic of the word. For to the ancients the word did not merely convey a meaning. It was also dynamic; it was thought to possess a power that extended beyond the realm of the mind into the spatial and material world. Thus in the Babylonian creation epic *Enuma Elish*, Marduk gives proof of his divine power by calling an object into being by his word of command and then letting it vanish again. In Old Egyptian cosmogony, Ptah, the god of the universe, used his creative power with the aid of 'heart and tongue', that is, by means of his word.[13] The powers of blessing and curse in the ancient world were also dynamic.

However, there are fundamental contrasts between the significance of the creative word in the pagan world, and that of the Bible. In the former it is the power of magic, power inherent in the word itself, just as their concept of sanctity was viewed as inherent in the thing itself. In this sense, the modern power of technique is also magical, and the technocrats today are our magicians. In contrast, the biblical revelation is that the power of words is in their sources, so that when God speaks, the potency is not in the words uttered but in the Spirit of God who is so expressed.

A second contrast lies in the temporal manifestation of the magical word, where God's Word is continuous. In the creation narrative of Genesis one, the phrase 'God said . . . and it was so' constantly recurs, that is to say, the continuance of the created thing is guaranteed by the God who speaks. That is why we need to re-assess the close relationship between creation and providence. The Creator is not a deist who makes a machine and then leaves it to operate unaided. Creation continues as a contingent series of endless miracles of His grace. Behind the being of all existence is the continuing, sustaining Word of God. Martin Luther emphasises this point in his commentary on Genesis one:

> When you hear this saying *and God spake*, beware that you do not think that it is a passing saying such as we men speak. Know that it is an eternal saying which is spoken from eternity and continues to be spoken. As little as God's being ceases, so little ceases that speech without which the creature would not enjoy his existence in time. But it continues to speak and goes on without interruption for no creature can maintain his own existence. Therefore, so long as the creature exists, so long will the Word also exist: so long as the earth bears, or is able to bear, so long that speech will continue without intermission. . . . That means that all creatures in their life and work without intermission are acted upon, and maintained by, the Word.[14]

Thus the writer to the Hebrews speaks of Christ, in whom God has finally spoken to us, who 'upholds the universe by His Word of power' (Heb. 1:3). Therefore, warns the apostle Peter, those who 'deliberately ignore this fact, that by the Word of God heavens existed long ago, and an earth formed out of water and by means of water', will suffer the same judgment as those who did not live in the efficacy of God's sustaining providence. Instead they perished in a flood of chaos. 'By the same word the heavens and earth that now exist have been stored up for fire, being kept until the day of judgment and destruction of ungodly men' (2 Pet. 3:5–7). Denial of the life-giving Word of creation only unleashes chaos and judgment. To deny the active Word of God now is to cut the nerve of belief in the Creator, who is still actively sustaining all things now. For 'man does not live by bread alone, but . . . man lives by everything that proceeds out of the mouth of God' (Deut.

8:3). Man's natural existence is wholly dependent upon the Word of God; this is one of the most profound realities man can ever know.[15]

2. The Word That Creates

In Genesis one, light and the rest of God are key principles that unify the creation week that man is about to witness. On the first day of the week light is called into being so that man may see the acts of God. By enlightening all that the Creator has made, God has given things a creaturely light by which they are made intelligible and invite our understanding of them. It is the light of God that continues to shine through the refractions of man's darkening spirit of rebellion, so that 'in His light do we see light'. Rest is also needed at the end of creation week, to enjoy all that God has perfectly accomplished. The one—light—is a symbol of the revelation of God's grace, the other—rest—is a prerequisite for the actualisation of God's grace. The modern mind that sees only an impersonal universe of 'nature' can only see mechanical causation as the *raison d'être* of existence; it is dehumanised. But the biblical perspective is that behind all reality is the personal transcendence of God, which implies that we should see the world as the effects of the Word of God, the expression of His will and purpose.

The church has often been misled, I believe, by too much emphasis on the doctrine of 'creation out of nothing' (*creatio ex nihilo*). As we shall see later (see Appendix A), this was an emphasis which, while it expresses in a form of shorthand the transcendence of the Creator, tends to turn our attention towards how the creation was formed, and to speculate as to the nothingness from which it was formed. Creation by the Word (*creatio per verbum*), in contrast, is consistently biblical, being often reaffirmed in the Bible. Even the scripture which is often used as a proof text of *creatio ex nihilo*—'God . . . calls into existence the things that do not exist' (Rom. 4:17)—focuses upon the call of God, His Word. Thus the Psalmist declares:

> By the Word of the Lord the heavens were made,
> and all their host by the breath of His mouth.

> For He spoke, and it came to be;
> He commanded, and it stood forth.   (Ps. 33:6, 9)

Likewise the Psalmist declares that the Creator 'determines the number of the stars, He gives to all of them their names'. 'He sends forth His Word' and the ice melts, and 'He makes His wind blow, and the waters flow' (Ps. 147:4, 18). 'He commanded and they were created' (Ps. 148:5). Isaiah expresses the same sentiment:

> Lift up your eyes on high and see: who created these? He who brings out their host by number, calling them all by name; by the greatness of His might, and because He is strong in power not one is missing.   (Isa. 40:26)

When God laid the foundation of the earth, and spread out the heavens, they stood forth together (Isa. 48:13). Thus it is wholly consistent to find this central truth of Scripture: 'By faith we understand that the world was created by the Word of God, so that what is seen was made out of things which do not appear' (Heb. 11:3).

In Genesis one it is impressive to see how the whole narrative of creation is determined by and focused upon the Word of God:

1. *Announcement of the Command*
   'And God said' (10 times: Gen. 1:3, 6, 9, 11, 14, 20, 24, 26, 28, 29).
2. *Word of Command*
   'Let there be' (6 times: Gen. 1:3, 6 [twice], 14 [twice], 15).
   'Let there be gathered' (Gen. 1:9).
   'Let the dry land appear' (Gen. 1:9).
   'Let the earth put forth vegetation' (Gen. 1:11).
   'Let the waters bring forth swarms of living things' (Gen. 1:20).
   'Let the birds fly' (Gen. 1:20).
   'Let the earth bring forth living creatures' (Gen. 1:24).
   'Let us make man' (Gen. 1:26).
   'Let them have dominion' (Gen. 1:26).

3. *Formula of Accomplishment*
   'and there was' (Gen. 1:3).
   'And it was so' (6 times, Gen. 1:7, 9, 11, 15, 24, 30).
4. *Act of Execution*
   'And God made' (3 times, Gen. 1:7, 16, 25).
   'God set' (Gen. 1:17).
   'God separated' (2 times, Gen. 1:4, 7).
   'God created' (4 times, Gen. 1:21, 27 [three times]).
   'I have given you' (Gen. 1:29).
5. *Formula of Appreciation*
   'light . . . good' (Gen. 1:4).
   'it was good' (5 times, Gen. 1:10, 12, 18, 21, 25).
   'very good' (Gen. 1:31).
6. *Subsequent Word*
   'God called' (5 times, Gen. 1:5 [twice], 8, 10 [twice].
   'and God blessed' (2 times, Gen. 1:22, 28).
7. *Reference to the Day*
   'And there was evening and morning, one day' (Gen. 1:5).
   number of day (5 times, Gen. 1:8, 13, 19, 23, 31).

Each deed of creation is accomplished by the Word. God's will is spoken, and with His speech the deed is done. The Word is the deed. The Hebrew word *amar*, or the creative Word, has a great diversity of meaning.[16] It calls attention to subject-object relationships so as to focus on specific realities. When it is used here in Genesis one it emphasises the creative command of God, the pledge of God to sustain what He has brought into being, and the revelation of God as the Creator. Thus, in this passage the creative command of God is such that His imperative and indicative are one. God speaks and it is done ('. . . and it was so'). Power is also given to each of His creatures to reproduce, to sustain, to diversify 'according to its kind', whether on land or sea or in the air. God created all the natural processes and all the structural principles for the maintenance of the universe. All the ordering principles are God's providential care of what He has commanded into being. This reminds us that God's command to us personally is always God's provision for us, so that He never commands where He does not also provide for the command's fulfilment. As Abraham discovered on Mount Moriah, God commanded him to make a sacrifice, but He also provided the lamb for the burnt offering. The same principle holds in creation. Nothing within creation lies outside the providence of God. He wants all things to actualize their potential. Everything points beyond itself to a directed end, from which all the processes receive their meaning and purpose, in a miraculous unfolding of coherence in all things. Thus the astronomer Jeans could see 'the universe looking more like a great thought than like a great machine'. He added:

> Mind no longer appears as an accidental intruder into the realm of matter; we are beginning to suspect that we ought rather to hail it as the creator and governor of the realm of matter—not of course over individual minds, but the mind, out of which our individual minds have grown, exists as thoughts.[17]

As the creative command, whose demands are fulfilled by His provisions, there is imputed power, promise and blessing. In this is revealed the character of the Creator. Because God is good, He saw that all that He had done was good. Likewise, as we shall see later, the righteousness, the justice and the wisdom of God are reflected also in the moral ordering of creation. Thus all the creative works of God reflect upon His character, revealing who He is. Creation is also revelatory of God, since His Word imparts the ability for God to be heard and understood. God expresses Himself as a revelatory Creator, so that the apostle affirms: 'Ever since the creation of the world His invisible nature, namely, His eternal power and deity, has been clearly perceived in the things that have been made' (Rom. 1:20).

Robert Browning in his poem *Unfaith and Faith* invites the sceptic to throw overboard his dogmas, and the poet will accompany him.

> And now what are we? unbelievers both,
> Calm and complete, determinately fixed
> Today, to-morrow and for ever, pray?
> . . . Just when we are safest, there's a sunset-touch,
> A fancy from a flower-bell, someone's death,
> A chorus ending from Euripides,—

And that's enough for fifty hopes and fears
As old and new at once as nature's self,
To rap and knock and enter in our soul,
. . . There's the old misgivings, crooked questions are—
This good God,—what he could do, if he would,
Would, if he could—there must have done long since:
If so, when, where and how? some way must be,—
Once feel about and soon or late you hit
Some sense in which it might be after all,
Why not 'The Way, the Truth, the Life'?[18]

Yes, says the Psalmist, 'the heavens are telling the glory of God;
and the firmament proclaims His handiwork' (Ps. 19:1). Then
he proceeds to show that there is mystery in the utterance of
creation.

Day to day pours forth speech,
and night to night declares knowledge.
There is no speech, nor are there words;
their voice is not heard;
yet their voice goes out through all the earth,
and their words to the end of the world.   (Ps. 19:2–4)

What can this mean in creation, that there is speech yet silence,
declaration yet muteness? Is it not that creation is the language
of the Creator, but it is not a language man can naturally master
and understand? God the Creator is recognisable in all the
handiwork of the universe, but not describable in human terms;
it is not saving knowledge for man. But in the second half of
the Psalm (19:7–14), our attention is drawn to the specific revelation of God in the *Torah* or Law, which is the only way man
can know the Creator.[19] For God has broken through the silence of creation to speak specifically to man in mighty acts of
redemptive grace in the history of mankind, to reveal Himself
as Lord of both space and time. For the man of faith, trusting
in the living reality of God, creation does bear witness to the
Creator, but only because first of all God has become known
in our hearts and minds by responsive trust and obedience to
His saving grace. Thus the hymn-writer Isaac Watts could sing:

The heavens declare thy glory, Lord;
In every star thy wisdom shines;
But when our eyes behold thy Word
We read thy name in fairer lines.

Once man knows God, then he can look upon nature with new eyes, as creation, and bring God back into His world, so that He is not worshipped as a worldless God but as Creator of everything.

THE MYSTERY OF CREATION

When we therefore approach the language of creation in such passages as Genesis one, we take the stance Pascal took when he asked, 'Who has put me here?' What is the meaning of my existence? To 'ask about the beginning', argues Bonhoeffer, 'is the innermost impulse of our thinking; for in the last resort it is this that gives validity to every true question we ask.'[20] Yet to ask about the beginning is to drive man beyond himself. For as man is a creature within space and time, and 'the beginning' also involves the beginning of space and time, it becomes inconceivable to know the beginning. Such thinking collapses even though man's spirit may drive him on to ask and ask again about it. The question of 'the beginning' drives us either to God or to despair. God used such shock therapy in His dealings with Job:

> 'Where were you when I laid the foundation of the
>   earth?
> Tell me, if you have understanding.
> Who determined its measurements—surely you know!
> Or who stretched the line upon it?
> On what were its bases sunk, or who laid its
>   cornerstone,
> When the morning stars sang together, and all the sons
>   of God shouted for joy?'   (Job 38:4–7)

And in Isaiah (40:12, 21, 22) we read:

Who has measured the waters in the hollow of his hand
and marked off the heavens with a span,
enclosed the dust of the earth in a measure
and weighed the mountains in scales
and the hills in a balance?

Have you not known? Have you not heard?
Has it not been told you from the beginning?
Have you not understood from the foundations of
the earth?
It is He who sits above the circle of the earth,
and its inhabitants are like grasshoppers;
who stretches out the heavens like a curtain,
and spreads them like a tent to dwell in.

No infinite amount of time—even the twenty billion years now being postulated for the 'Big Bang' hypothesis for the origin of the universe—nor any infinite amount of space, can help us to conceive the ineffable mystery of the Creator and His eternity of being. When we talk of God as 'Creator' and of 'knowing Him', we are thus introducing a qualitative difference that no amount of scientific data can either prove or disprove. It is an altogether different way of knowing. Yet with simple majesty the writer of Genesis one outlines this mystery of creation.

First, he speaks of an unargued cause: God.[21] 'In the beginning God created the heavens and the earth' (Gen. 1:1). This declaration is both the title and the prelude to all that follows. No proof of God is given, nor can it be given if He is the Author of all that is. No more can we prove His existence than the character of a story can step outside the book and 'prove' the existence of the author of the book. He lies outside the realm of possible investigation. He is not subject to anything, to any principle, any power, for *Elohim*, the transcendent God, is the Creator of all things. Likewise His creation is inconceivable in its fullness, so that while we may know something of earth, He is also Creator of 'the heavens', whose sphere is inscrutable to mortal man. The verb *bara*, 'to create', is deliberately used here, indicating also that all analogies using human metaphors—make like a potter, create like an author, shape like a sculptor, compose like a musician—fail, for how is God said to 'create'? For in the sense of His transcendent power He brings all into being out of nothing.

Secondly, the writer speaks of an indefinable era: the absolute beginning of all things. It is this that shapes time as a linear progression between the beginning and the end. But what does it mean to speak of 'the beginning' of time? This is where human language fails us, for time makes it impossible to think of an absolute beginning 'in time'. That is why, unless we live in the light of eternity as well as time, man lives in a closed system of thought, as the Greeks and many others have done since then.[22] An evident warning against such a Greek view is voiced in Ecclesiastes 3:11. God 'has made every thing beautiful in *its* time'—just as God saw that His creation 'was very good' (Gen. 1:31); 'also He has put eternity into man's mind', that is, in man God has set *His* time. The world is not eternal, but man is privileged to have fellowship with the Eternal God.

The framework of six days of creation is therefore 'its time', the appropriate time for every created thing. But this does not in any way confine God the Creator within the continuum of space and time as Isaac Newton and many Christians since then have envisaged. P. J. Wiseman has pointed out that to confine God literally to six days of creative activity is to demean the mystery of God.

> How unworthy of God has been the idea that this record of Creation was ever intended to teach that, at sunset, the Almighty God turned aside from creating the world and resumed it at sunrise! Evenings and mornings have to do with the inhabitants of this planet earth. . . . Is it legitimate to think of the God of heaven, when creating, being unable to continue because of the timing of the earth upon its axis, or by its movements in relation to the sun? These things affect man's time, not God's. As the creation Psalm (139:12) says, 'Darkness hideth not from Thee, but the night shineth as the day; the darkness and the light are both alike to Thee.' But of man it says (104:23), 'Man goeth unto his work and to his labour until evening'.[23]

What then was God doing in these six days? He was speaking to man, revealing what He said to bring creation into being. The present tense is used throughout the narrative: 'God saith'. A statement of command to all creation, it is also a statement of revelation to man. Among Babylonian and Canaanite creation narratives there are descriptions of a seven-day literary framework, which indicate that it was used to describe the completion of great events.[24] The use of colophons has also illuminated our understanding of the literary framework of Genesis 1:1–2:4. A colophon is a literary device formerly placed at the end of a book or narrative, and identifies what has been said beforehand; nowadays we put the title, printer's name and date at the beginning of the book. Scholars have recognised Genesis 2:4 as a colophon of the preceding narrative. The title is the phrase 'These are the generations [or history] of the heavens and the earth when they were created'. The datum given is 'In the day that the Lord God made the earth and the heavens' (Gen. 2:4). 'In the day' is not a contradiction of the 'six days' previously described but means 'when' or 'at the time' when the creation took place.

The recording of this fundamental narrative on six tablets used the six days of creation symbolically as a possible literary framework. The linkage and sequence of each tablet could be recognisable by the phrase 'day one', 'day two' and so on to 'day six', together with the repeated phrase, 'And there was evening and there was morning'.[25] It is also mysterious that the day should commence with the sunset, not the sunrise. Cassuto and other textual scholars assume this reckoning of the new day with the sunset was an earlier, nomadic tradition.[26] The practice in Israel was to count the start of the Sabbath or a holy day of festival with the sunset. Perhaps behind this practice, however, is the theological affirmation that the day—every day—begins with God the Creator and not with the natural agency of the sun.

Thirdly, Genesis 1:2 describes the earth, 'without form and void' and of inscrutable constitution, for it was formless (*tōhū*) and empty (*bōhū*). This prelude does, however, point to the direction creation will take: it will be formed and it will be populated. We read, 'darkness was upon the face of the deep'. These are symbols of deeper realities, still to be revealed in the illumination of light, 'deep' in their mystery and obscurity.

However, 'the Spirit of God', which is synonymous with the Word of God, assures us that an unlimited power is present, sweeping God's omnipresence and creative power over all 'the waters' (which might suggest chaos), but even chaos is under the Creator's control. For from the beginning God is the moral governor, who creates by acts of separation—binding all things into specific, structural realities—and by acts of reproduction—the source of all fertilisation, population and reproduction. This prelude sets the theme for the following six days of creation.

GOD "FORMS" in the midst of formlessness (tōhū)	GOD "FILLS" in the midst of emptiness (bōhū)
Day 1 Division of light from darkness (1:4)	
Day 2 Division of lower waters from upper waters (1:7)	
Day 3 Division of lower waters from dry land (1:9); creation of vegetation (1:11)	
	Day 4 Creation of lights in the sky (1:16)
	Day 5 Creation of water, animals and birds (1:21)
	Day 6 Creation of land animals and man, and the provision of food (1:29)

GOD FINISHES CREATION
on the seventh day (2:1–3)

Two significant motifs characterise creation. First of all, God provides a framework, a structuring of reality by acts of separation.[27] The writer describes these in physical terms, but as we shall see later, the physical structure of creation also reflects upon the moral structuring of reality. Man therefore can know the creation intelligently in terms of laws and boundaries. Man lives also in a moral creation, with moral laws and boundaries built into creation as basic creation ordinances. Secondly, while we may need to distinguish, for logical reasons, between *creatio per verbum* and *creatio continua*, between creation at the beginning and the general providence of God, yet providence in terms of the natural processes of replication, reproduction and growth is built into creation by God's grace. This is consistent with the awareness that God's commands are also God's provisions, to fulfil His demands of creation.

All this is a denial of the technocratic world, and of the ontocratic world, which the motorcycle mystic, Pirsig, attempted to bring together. Man is not the maker of all things, nor can life be anything but absurd when he attempts to live in a closed world that excludes God. For only 'In the beginning God . . .' can form the background to the specificities of the world. By the Creator's transcendence a real world exists. By His Lordship it is kept from chaos.

THE LANGUAGE OF CREATION

As we have seen, how God created is unimaginable, but numerous figures of speech are used in the Old Testament.[28] Heaven is spread out like a metal mirror (Job 37:18), or stretched out like a tent (Isa. 40:22; 44:24). Earth is based on pillars (Zech. 12:1; 1 Sam. 2:8), and made fast (Ps. 93:1; 96:10). The stars, too, are set and fixed (Ps. 8:3; Jer. 10:12). Thus the phenomenal world is described matter-of-factly, according to appearances, but they are all related to the work and activity of God.

There are no evidences of secondary causation, for everything is attributed to the creative acts of God. He sends the rain (2 Sam. 21:10) or withholds it (Deut. 11:17; 1 Kings 8:35). He covers the heavens with clouds (Ps. 147:8; Isa. 50:3). He causes the wind to blow (Ps. 78:26). Abstract conceptions of space and time, nature and the cosmos are all alien to the Hebrew mind, since the sovereignty of God is absolute and nothing exists without Him. Hence God is pivotal to the whole Hebrew understanding of reality: without Him nothing was made that has been made. Moreover, the biblical authors do not consider the beauty of created life around them, nor the expanse of sky and sea and mountains, as proofs or evidences of the Creator's handiwork, for they are believers already. They make no attempt to prove the existence of God from the created world. Rather, the world is the arena of God's self-disclosure. 'The heavens are telling the glory of God, the firmament proclaims his handiwork' (Ps. 19:1).

Thus the language describing creation is not concerned with theories about natural phenomena other than to assert constantly that God is behind them all. One looks in vain for data on the theory of relativity, evolution or quantum physics. Scientists can only work with pre-existing matter, but 'we understand', says the writer to the Hebrews, 'that the worlds were framed by the word of God, so that things which are seen were not made out of things which do appear' (Heb. 11:3). Scientific explanations are out of place since they can deal only with secondary causation; the biblical writers speak only of divine, *fiat* creation. Likewise, the language of the Bible is that of appearances, arising out of observation—'dewfall', 'sunrise', 'sunset'—and the heavenly bodies are noted only as sun, moon and stars. Fish are either great or small, animals are domesticated (cattle) or wild (beasts of the field). This is popular language, with no attempt made to examine physical phenomena with the scientific mind-set of modern man.

Various scholars have tried to define the literary genre of the first chapter of Genesis.

1. *Myth*—The Old Testament scholar Hermann Gunkel first drew attention to presumed similarities between the Babylonian epic of *Enuma Elish* and the Genesis account.[29] This old idea of the mythic character of Genesis is largely rejected by modern scholarship on at least two counts: the lack of literary evidence, and the clear intent of the biblical narrative to discount the myths of the surrounding pagan world in polemical challenges that we shall discuss later. Moreover, myth does not take either time or space seriously, whereas the whole thrust

of the Bible is to take time and space very seriously, as creations of God that serve His purposes. The historic faith of Israel and Christianity is incompatible with the mythic mind.

2. *Saga*—The theologian Karl Barth has substituted saga for myth as the literary device to be used in analysing Genesis one.[30] That still leaves the suspicion that saga is not any different from myth. How seriously can it take the reality of God's creation? Is it not all lost in the vagueness of man's imagination?

3. *Eschatology*—Two other German scholars, Oscar Cullmann[31] and Claus Westermann,[32] have spoken of the eschatological character of God's reality between primal history and end history, of Alpha and Omega. Again, this can push aside the reality of God's creative deeds into 'never-never land'. It may not take seriously enough the actual existence of this world, in which theological scholars dispute and argue their points. Creation may still be relegated to 'mythological language'.

4. *Parable*—An interesting suggestion, first made by Alan Richardson and followed through more thoroughly by Donald Evans,[33] is that parable is the genre of the creation stories. Since parable is extended metaphor, it illuminates an inner meaning which calls for a response from the hearers. The call for involvement in faith is important in parabolic language, but this suggestion has a significant demerit: it does not take seriously enough the actuality of the deeds of God in creation. Clearly the creation narrative does matter in all its details, even though there is an elusive, mysterious structure to its framework and theological intent beyond the clear announcement of the transcendence and the immanence of the Creator in all creation. 'Parable' fails to stress the actuality of God's creation.

5. *Aetiology*—Karl Adam, another German scholar, has suggested that the genre of Genesis 1–2 can be understood as 'historical aetiology'. Aetiology means that the cause of something is inferred from what one sees around one, at the present time. As the writer observed the universe, he attributed all to the Creator, God. This is a commendable explanation, except that there does appear a distinct difference between the creation stories of Genesis 1 and 2, a difference of genre and of purpose.

The Two Creation Narratives

Genesis 1:1–2:4	*Genesis 2:5–25*
God as Sovereign (Elohim)	God as Personal Being (Yahweh)
Creation by divine fiat	Creation by divine craftsmanship
Aetiological descriptions (general, matter-of-fact description of all creation)	Allegorical narrative (specific story about man's creation)
Diagrammatic schema of six days of creative acts	Pictorial representation of man's creation
Progressive creation in six days	Punctiliar act of creation in one day (Gen. 2:5)
God alone the agent of creation	God and man in creative harmony (Gen. 2:5b, 8, 19)
Adam = male and female	Male prior to female
Transcendent view of God, who, with His world, is to be enjoyed by man in sabbath rest.	Anthropomorphic view of the world as realm of human stewardship and responsibility
All seen as 'good', for it is God's world.	Human choice entails the possibility of seduction.

In these two accounts of creation, the transcendence and the immanence of the Creator are juxtaposed. God relates to the whole universe as the author of it all, and yet He is uniquely in communion with man, as the creature He has set in dominion over the earth as His vice-gerent. The language and genres are appropriate to these two contexts of creation.

6. *Polemical Intent of Creation Narratives*—While the unique character of the creation narratives in Genesis 1–2 may make it impossible to categorise them into one particular literary tradition without distorting their theological character as the revelation of God (like the two tables of the Law received by Moses), we can trace a polemical intent.[34] Ancient historical research has now compiled over 5,000 tablets or fragments of the literary skills of the Sumerian civilisation (4th–3rd millennia B.C.) whose naturalistic polytheism affected all the later

cultures of the ancient Near East.[35] We now realise that their myths of creation were not merely entertainment for their peoples, but by magical recitation they sought to uphold the structuring of reality as they conceived it. This they did at great religious festivals. We also realise that the inspired biblical writers borrowed the imagery of these myths, but not their theology. They did so polemically, to contradict the false views of reality held by these pagan peoples.

Basic to biblical polemic is that the *Torah*, the Word of God, is set over against myth. There is no magic that has innate powers, which by recitation and incantation in solemn religious rites can keep the world going. Instead, the biblical writers affirm it is all created and sustained by the Word of God. Hence Genesis one is a great paean of praise to the creative power of God's *Torah*. Divine revelation is not magic, moreover, for it is sustained, influencing the believer's whole life—body, soul and spirit. So it gives no place to the credulous imagination, to superstition and to curiosity. Its intent is not mere information, but moral reformation of character before God.

Secondly, God is one God, whereas all the ancient myths are polytheistic. There is no one ultimately in charge of reality in the pagan world. Instead, the gods are rivals and upset the *status quo* in their quarrels; fate ultimately is inscrutable. A polemic in Genesis 1:3, 14 is that light is created before the luminaries, just as the days of creation begin with the sunset, for God is not bound by and does not emanate from natural forces such as the sun. Even the polemical avoidance of naming the luminaries is deliberate; they are just 'great lights', candelabra set in the sky, without the terrifying powers of fate men ascribed to them. The writer adds laconically and almost parenthetically that God made 'the stars also', as if to deny any primary potency in astrology. They do not control the fates of man; God does.

Thirdly, the eternal and sovereign Creator denies any reality to theogony or to theomachy. There is no strife, no struggle, no rival powers that resist creation by the *fiat* of God's word and will: 'God said . . . and it was so.' Nor can there be any causal origin of God: 'In the beginning God . . . .' And so Genesis one knows nothing of the primordiality of matter, nor the cyclical nature of time. Matter and time are both the creation of God. Likewise the great fish God made in Genesis 1:21 are created (*bara*). The word *bara* is used only three times in the narrative, each time for a unique act of God (Gen. 1:1, 21, 27). The writer of Genesis applies this term deliberately to the great sea monsters. They are not independent, mythological sources of chaos, as venerated in Canaanite and other myths.[36] Indeed, as His creatures, God plays with them (Ps. 104:26) and commands their praise (Ps. 148:7).

Finally, there is the polemic concerning the creation of man, which we shall consider in more detail in the next chapter. Suffice it to say here that in the biblical account God makes man distinct from Himself—not the blood of a slain god mingled with dust but taken from the dust of non-being, to be created in His own image. In the Babylonian texts of the *Enuma Elish* and the earlier *Atrahasis Epic*, man is created merely to relieve the gods of their hard labours. The gods depend upon man to provide for their food. In contrast, in the Genesis narratives man is no afterthought based on the primordial principle of violence. Rather, man is viewed as the pinnacle of created beings, the fulfilment of all else. Instead of being a slave, man is God's viceroy, God's 'lieutenant', with environmental responsibility as steward of the earth (Gen. 1:28). All seed-bearing plants and fruits are *man's* to domesticate for *his* food needs (Gen. 1:29), since God has no need of sustenance by anything that He has created.

Into man's mortality there is breathed the transcendent spirit of God, to enjoy God's Word and to have personal relationship with his Creator. That is why we have the creation narrative—not as magic by which to uphold the world and attempt to integrate it, as Pirsig tries, but in order to live godly lives before His covenant friendship. So Jesus said:

> No longer do I call you servants, for the servant does not know what his master is doing; but I have called you friends, for all that I have heard from my Father I have made known to you. You did not choose me, but I have chosen you and appointed you that you should go and bear fruit and that your fruit should abide.
>
> (John 15:15–16)

NOTES

1 Leo Marx, *The Machine in the Garden*, London, Oxford University Press, 1964.
2 Ortega y Gasset, *The Revolt of the Masses*, New York, W. W. Norton, 1932, p. 89.
3 F. Scott Fitzgerald, *The Great Gatsby*, New York, Charles Scribner's Sons, 1925, p. 79.
4 Robert M. Pirsig, *Zen and the Art of Motorcycle Maintenance: an Inquiry into Values*, New York, Morrow, 1974, p. 26.
5 Ibid., p. 296.
6 Ibid., pp. 265, 93, 245.
7 Quoted by Denis Goulet, 'A Pride of Prophets on our Technological Future', *Worldview*, March 1978, p. 35. See Jacques Ellul, *The Technological Society*, New York, Vintage Books, Random House, 1964, for one of the most significant critiques of this subject in modern literature.
8 C. S. Lewis, *Miracles*, London, Collins, 1947, ch. 9.
9 Luci Shaw, *The Secret Trees*, Wheaton, Illinois, Harold Shaw, 1976, p. 56.
10 Donald MacKay, *The Clockwork Image*, London, Inter-Varsity Press, 1974, p. 57.
11 G. H. Parke-Taylor, *Yahweh: the Divine Name in the Bible*, Waterloo, Ontario, Wilfrid Laurier University, 1975, p. 51.
12 Ibid., p. 70.
13 Gerhard von Rad, *Old Testament Theology*, London, S.C.M., 1975, vol. 1, p. 143.
14 Quoted by Gustaf Wingren, *The Living Word*, London, S.C.M., 1960, pp. 72–73.
15 Walther Eichrodt, *Theology of the Old Testament*, London, S.C.M., 1967, vol. 2, pp. 74–75.
16 See *Theological Dictionary of the Old Testament*, edit. G. J. Botterweck and Helmer Ringgren, Grand Rapids, Eerdmans, 1974, vol. 1, pp. 328–345.
17 James Jeans, *The Mysterious Universe*, Cambridge, Cambridge University Press, 1937, p. 137.
18 Quoted from *The Faber Book of Religious Verse* (edit. Helen Gardner), London, Faber and Faber, 1972, pp. 258–259.
19 Bernhard W. Anderson, *Out of the Depths*, Philadelphia, The Westminster Press, 1974, pp. 109–110.
20 Dietrich Bonhoeffer, *Creation and the Fall*, London, S.C.M., 1959, p. 13.
21 A helpful summary of Genesis 1 is given in the lectures by David Ewert, 'Creation from a Biblical Perspective', circulated privately, Fresno, California, 1976.
22 Arnold Ehrhardt, *The Beginning*, Manchester, Manchester University Press, 1968, pp. 17–27.

23 P. J. Wiseman, *Clues to Creation in Genesis* (edit. Donald J. Wiseman), London, Marshall, Morgan & Scott, 1977, p. 136.

24 The New Media, *Bible Times*, vol. 1, no. 1, 1976, p. 3.

25 P. J. Wiseman, op. cit., pp. 143–168.

26 U. Cassuto, *A Commentary on the Book of Genesis*, part 1, Jerusalem, Magnes Press, 1961, pp. 28–30.

27 See Paul Beauchamp, *Creation et Separation*, Paris, Aubier Montaigne, 1969, for a structuralist approach to the understanding of Genesis one. But the author goes too far in not looking beyond this one principle for the understanding of creation.

28 Luis I. J. Stadelmann, *The Hebrew Conception of the World*, Rome, Biblical Institute Press, 1970.

29 This is well rebutted in Alexander Heidel, *The Babylonian Genesis*, Chicago, University of Chicago Press, Phoenix Books, 1963.

30 Karl Barth, *Church Dogmatics* (G. W. Bromiley and T. F. Torrance, trans.), Edinburgh, T. & T. Clark, vol. 3, part 1, pp. 81–94.

31 Oscar Cullmann, *Christ and Time*, London, S.C.M., 1962.

32 Claus Westermann, *Beginning and End in the Bible*, Philadelphia, Fortress Press, 1972, pp. 30–31.

33 Donald Evans, *The Logic of Self-Involvement*, London, S.C.M., 1963, pp. 242–251.

34 Gerhard F. Hasel, 'The Polemic Nature of the Genesis Cosmology', *Evangelical Quarterly*, 46, 1974, pp. 81–102.

35 See the excellent article on 'Creation Myths' by Bruce K. Waltke, in the *Tyndale Family Bible Encyclopedia*, Wheaton, Illinois, Tyndale Press, 1979.

36 Mary K. Wakeman, *God's Battle with the Monster*, Leiden, E. J. Brill, 1973.

CHAPTER THREE

After the Seventh Day

We have seen that the landscapes of the mind project upon the landscapes of the world. We have a choice of what we see: nature or creation. Likewise, we have seen that either God is the Creator of all things, or else we live with a worldless god, whose place in the scheme of things is never clear. Now we have to look further at ourselves and see why man has such a propensity to turn paradise into an animal farm, why he is constantly messing up the environment he lives in, and worse still, so at emnity with his fellow man. What is the meaning of his immanence in the world, and at the same time of his transcendence over the world?

Today we are confused by two contrary views of man. On the one hand, man is a creature, bound to his environment in which he breathes, is fed and interlinked with the physico-chemical processes of life on earth. It is tempting to lift up all these pulsating, interdependent systems of the biosphere and call it one organism, of which man is but a part. The Greeks exulted in this view, worshipping Dionysus as the god of the Thracian countryside, the god of fertility and the energy of nature. Dionysian man exalts sentiment over mind, ecstasy over order, the senses and the unconscious over the reflective and the rational.

On the other hand, man is creative. His immanence in the world is apparently contradicted by his transcendence over the world. The Greeks assumed that man's transcendence lay in his reason, his intellectual capacity to 'surge up' in the world, to build other worlds of culture beyond the natural and, by his technologies, to subject the laws of nature to his own wishes.

Is man therefore to be thought of more as a creator than as a creature? This is a crucial question for our age. The Greeks in their classical age of intellectual achievement envisaged Apollo as this god of achievement, who champions the autonomous life and the goal of self-achievement. He is the god of man the craftsman, and the Apollonian way is obvious today in our technological society. Technological and scientific man gains the power to distinguish, clarify and gain control by knowledge and reason.

As for Apollonian man, Voltaire's gibe is unfortunately full of bitter truths: 'After God created man in His own image, man rendered Him in his own image.'

These two models of man express elements that occur in any culture since they represent order and chaos, fixity and spontaneity, discipline and ecstasy, domination and responsiveness in the two faces of Apollonian and Dionysian man.[1] We may summarise these two ways of living as follows:

Apollonian Man	*Dionysian Man*
Man the maker, *Homo faber*, is the moulder and manipulator of his environment	Man the dancer, *Homo ludens*, responds to the immediate givenness of life
Will and intellect dominate	Feeling and sensation are central
Values are translated as action; authenticity is aggressiveness and masculinity	Values are discovered in wonder and acceptance; authenticity is passion and femininity
God is encountered in deism, in order, deed and action	God is defined as pantheistic, in the power of being all, in flux, and in the depths of experience
Life is lived consciously	Life is authenticated by the unconscious

Western civilisation has oscillated in a zigzag course between these two models. In times of stability, perhaps the Apollonian model has dominated, while today in the counter-culture, with social upheaval and dislocation of familiar patterns, the Dionysian way is becoming obvious. Yet the Dionysian way of life is based on the Apollonian, just as Pirsig seeks to combine technocracy with ontocracy.

As we shall see, man has a double creation mandate. He has been created in the image of God, to have dominion and to rule as vicegerent of the world (Gen. 1:28). He is also to be fruitful and multiply, and to enjoy a relationship with the Creator. It is the distortion of this role of stewardship and of relationship with His Maker which leaves man, as Pope said:

> Created half to rise, and half to fall,
> Great lord of all things yet a prey to all;
> Sole judge of truth, in endless error hurled;
> The glory, jest and riddle of the world![2]

However, it is typical of our age that modern man is deaf to his own predicament. That is why modern writers like Flannery O'Connor use the grotesque to depict the contemporary situation. 'To the hard of hearing you shout; to the almost blind you draw large and startling figures,' she has said.[3] So all her characters are 'displaced persons', because the world too is out of joint. But to depict the ordinary only conceals this, so her characters have to be shown blatantly grotesque. She is particularly concerned about Apollonian man today. In her novel *The Violent Bear it Away*, Rayber is the unforgettable intellectual, the impersonal secular rationalist. He is almost literally a mechanical man with 'two small drill-like eyes' that bore out of soullessness as if to capture the souls of others. They are eyes that look like 'something human trapped in a switch box'. He wears an electrical hearing device, referred to as 'the machine', a 'metal box . . . joined by a cord to a plug in his ear', which makes Tarwater wonder if 'his head ran by electricity.' Tarwater asks Rayber, 'Do you think in the box . . . or do you think in your head?' Indeed, his guts are in his head, and the old man warns Tarwater that if Rayber dominates his thinking:

> the first thing he would do would be to test your head
> and tell you what you were thinking and how come you

were thinking it and what you ought to be thinking instead. And before long you wouldn't belong to yourself no more; you would belong to him.[4]

Apollonian or Dionysian, who is man? The origin of man becomes profoundly important to help us find out who he is today.

THE ORIGIN OF MAN

It is widely assumed that man's origins determine his present significance. That is why *Roots* has aroused such a phenomenal interest. Doesn't man's ancestry determine so much of his nature and his needs? Since Darwin's views assumed man's origin from the apes, it is thought that a sub-human past leads to a less than human present. Certainly some Christians take this stand.[5] But we have already discussed how the problem of origins is complicated, whether it is conceived empirically or theologically. The absolute origin of the universe is inconceivable, for we cannot conceive of the meaning and the process whereby God created space and time and all matter *ex nihilo*; we are not intended to by such a declaration! Creation therefore has to be a statement of faith, not an empirical deduction. We have a similar problem in relating to the origin of man.

We have some empirical evidence from the studies of fossil man that establish the presence of hominids one, two or even three million years old. Physical anthropology has sought to trace biological linkages in the skeletal forms of *Ramapithecus, Paranthropus, Australopithecus, Homo habilis, Homo erectus* and *Homo (sapiens) neanderthalensis*. Linkages remain uncertain scientifically.[6] But this whole evolutionary approach is bedevilled, not only by fragmentary anatomical understanding, but by the reductionistic approach that assumes a skeleton is a person. The origin of dead bones is a poor guide to the character of a living person. True, the early Palaeolithic period reveals that man was a stone-using creature who hunted big game; the middle Palaeolithic period shows that Neanderthal man used axes, while the upper Palaeolithic period reveals that *Homo sapiens* had burial cults that reflected concern for the after-life.[7]

But the origins approach to man still leaves us with vast ignorance concerning the nature of man as man.[8] This approach cannot help us explain why man, unlike all other animals, is one genus and one species, unique as no other creature is unique.

The biblical account takes a relational approach to the creation of man and gives a theological definition of how man relates to his Maker. The Bible is not really concerned with man's physical origins, but with his character before God, which in turn defines his uniqueness before all other created things. It tells us man is made from dust, which our mortality clearly reveals; thus our burial services are observed with the words 'dust to dust'. To say man is derived from the hominids is not to say anything more radical than the biblical description of man's dusty origins. But what the Bible has to say of man's relationships is revolutionary in relating a true understanding of his nature and responsibility.

A person, however, has a specific history. He is born, lives and dies. To regard the story of Adam and Eve as a myth is to shatter both the consistency and meaning of man as the agent of the events of history. Man today *is* responsible for sin, although he is also caught up in the groundswell of past evil, as 'the sins of the fathers are visited upon the children'. We therefore hold two truths in tension. Sin is a given element in life. Yet it is my responsibility. Too often Christians have talked loosely of the 'Fall' as a chronology of man as he once was—perfect—and man as he is now—depraved. The story of Adam and Eve is not a beautiful story of 'once upon a time'; it is about ourselves, how we are *now*. This present tense is given in Gen. 2:24 in the context of Adam and Eve. 'Therefore a man leaves his father and mother and cleaves to his wife, and they become one flesh.' This is a present reality.

At the same time, the historicity of Adam and Eve and the Fall has to be taken seriously, otherwise we are not in tune with the biblical writers. Luke, in his genealogy of Jesus, records Adam as historical along with the rest of the biblical characters (Luke 3:23–38). Likewise, Paul tells the Athenians that God 'made from one every nation of men to live on all the face of the earth' (Acts 17:26). He also declares that 'sin came into the world through one man' (Rom. 5:12). In this chapter, the apostle speaks of 'one man' eleven times, seven times referring to Adam, and four times to Jesus Christ. Paul clearly assumes Adam was as historical as Jesus Christ, who was actually born in Bethlehem in the reign of Caesar Augustus (cp. also 1 Cor. 15:21–22). Just as evolution is an approach that involves man in 'processes' but gives him no uniqueness as historically eventful, so myth may convey meaning but without the framework of space and time. The Bible speaks of both realities, of man's individual uniqueness and his personal responsibility, as he is caught up in the events of history.

1. Man, as the Creature of God

The true humanity of man is dependent upon God, not man. In other words, man is most truly understood in terms of theology, not anthropology. The latter may deal with the evolutionary schema concerning man's physique, or with the diversity of his racial origins, languages and customs. But the Bible alone confronts us with the direct issue: What is man? Four times this is asked (Job 7:17; Ps. 8:4; 144:3; Heb. 2:6). In Psalm 8 in particular this is set forth in the context of the joyful recognition of Yahweh's universal sovereignty:

> O Lord, our Lord,
> How majestic is thy name in all the earth.

Man as man is conceivable only within the context of the sovereign will and grace of the Creator. Man as man does not depend upon anything inherent in man, argues the Psalmist. For what is man compared with the majesty of the heavens— why should God pay any regard to man? Yet before man's head swells up too quickly over his status in creation, the Psalmist adds that God's glory above the heavens is chanted by babes, who cannot articulate any form of speech!

This is to say that God does not need man's innate abilities to manifest His glory. His glory is His mercy, revealed in His unmerited favour towards His creature man, to whom He gives all the special status man has in creation. What gives glory to God is therefore not man's strength and natural abilities, but his weaknesses, like 'babes and sucklings' wholly dependent upon the Creator. It is in his creatureliness that man is man. As the Russian philosopher Nicholas Berdyaev has said, 'God is more concerned about man's humanity than man is.'

It is a biblical principle that natural origins do not define our humanity in its spiritual dimensions. Within churches today, there are those who assume they are naturally Christians, *naturally* because they were christened at birth, enrolled in the church register and active in church affairs. The apostle Paul speaks against such an assumption when he says: 'For not all who are [genealogically] descended from Israel belong to Israel, and not all are children of Abraham because they are his descendants' (Rom. 9:6–7). Likewise John the Baptist says, 'Do not begin to say to yourselves, "We have Abraham for our father" [because they had been physically circumcised], for I tell you, God is able from these stones to raise up children to Abraham' (Luke 3:8). Can we therefore be 'naturally' human beings without the grace of God?

Left to ourselves, 'the fate of the sons of men and the fate of beasts is the same; as one dies, so dies the other. They all have the same breath, and man has no advantage over the beasts; for all is vanity. All go to one place; all are from the dust, and all turn to dust again' (Eccl. 3:19–20). 'Man cannot abide in his pomp, he is like the beasts that perish' (Ps. 49:12, 20). The biologist Dobzhansky has spoken graphically of the dust of our mortality:

> The aggregate volume of all the genes in the sex cells which produce the contemporary world population (of 4 billion) probably do not exceed the volume of a vitamin capsule. How precarious that this tiny mass contains all the biological heredity of the living representations of our species and the material basis of its future.[9]

Beyond our dusty mortality, man has a somewhat precarious distinction from the animals. Significantly, he was created on the sixth day, when the animals also came into being. The well-known ethologist W. H. Thorpe has said:

> Forty years or so ago, psychologists and moralists used to list a number of ways in which animals are clearly differ-

ent from man. It was said animals cannot learn; animals cannot plan ahead; animals cannot conceptionalise; animals cannot use, much less make tools; it was said they have no language; they cannot count; they lack artistic sense; they lack all ethical sense.[10]

We know that all these assertions are either wrong or at least debatable. Most of these differences are differences of degree. They do not really define the uniqueness of man. So ethology has become a good stick with which to beat the natural pride of man. There is a sense in which the Bible 'out-Darwins' Darwin concerning the origin of man. Darwin said man came from the monkeys; the Bible says man comes from the dust. So it is not Nature that has determined man's natural evolution as a cultural being: it is God. God alone keeps man from relapsing into the state of animality. Man without God—as the Oriental despot Nebuchadnezzar discovered—finds his kingship relapsing into the state of a beast of the field.

If God created the whole universe by the Word of His power, it is appropriate that man's unique dignity in creation should be the address of God spoken in grace. This is the theme of Psalm 8. Man is simply the creature that Yahweh relates to graciously, in remembrance and care. Man has been made the partner of Yahweh's earthly reign, so that in his transcendence over the rest of creation man evidences the immanent rule of God. Without God, man quickly falls into animality, as George Orwell shows in *Animal Farm*.

There is the road to animality in naturalism. 'Vive la vie naturelle', we are exhorted, for this is the pulse beat of humanity. So, 'be natural'. 'Let the hot blood course through our veins.' This mystique of 'the natural' leads to paganism.

There is the road to animality in aestheticism or hedonism. Man in discovering a reality beyond himself, and his instincts, is tempted to assume that what pleases him and gives comfort to him should be his guiding principles. The sexual obsession of our age reflects this philosophy. What is more beastly than pornography?

There is the road to animality in materialism. Our economic philosophy of 'dog eat dog' and 'the survival of the fittest', in the jungle warfare of seeking fat and fast profits, does

not engender an ethos of humane tolerance and love of neighbour. Materialism does not produce socialism, otherwise Marxism would not seek in vain for the creation of the 'New Man'
to bring about the revolution necessary for Utopia. The tiger
of human selfishness is only made more powerful in a materialistic society.

Thus it is our human experience *now* that man is not
man 'naturally' by evolution.[11] It is by election, by the free,
sovereign grace of God, his Maker, that man is man.

2. *Man, as the Image of God*

Man as man implies sovereignty—sovereignty over his
environment, over other creatures, over himself. Man's self-
consciousness, his sense of uniqueness, his conservation of
memory and culture, his tool-making ability, his capacity for
thought and speech, the capacity he has to think abstractly and
have self-knowledge—all evidence his sovereignty. He is unique
also in his search for truth, in his ethical aspirations, and in
his concern for moral values. That man can know God but
can corrupt these God-like attributes must be recognised before man can be truly understood. Otherwise man is constantly
deceived by his own powers, and disappointed by his own
weaknesses.

As we have seen, Psalm 8 emphasises that human mon-
archy is grounded, not in human power, but in Yahweh's gracious sovereignty alone. God has caused man to have dominion,
and God continues to crown man with the insignia of such an
office.

> Yet Thou hast made him little less than God,
>   and dost crown him with glory and honour.
> Thou hast given him dominion over the works of Thy
>   hands;
>   Thou hast put all things under his feet.
>
> (Ps. 8:5–6)

No limits and no guidelines are set to man's rule, other
than the implicit understanding that the question 'What is Man?'
is addressed to God and that it is God's sovereignty upon which
man depends for his rule. In this spirit Solomon at the com-

mencement of his rule could dedicate the temple saying: 'But who am I, and what is my people, that we should be able thus to offer willingly? For all things come from Thee, and of Thine own have we given Thee. . . . All this abundance that we have provided . . . comes from Thy hand and is all Thine own' (1 Chron. 29:14, 16). All a man can do and give, in his self-transcending powers, is only possible because of the sovereignty of God's grace.

In the Genesis passages dealing with the *imago dei* (Gen. 1:26–27; 5:1; 9:6), there is also an implicit polemic that, unlike the myths of the ancient Near East in which the king alone is the god's deputy, all mankind is granted the status of kingship. Man, who is but dust—non-being—is enthroned by God to have identity and rule.[12] Indeed, under the theocracy all men are responsible as God's deputies.

The interpretation of Genesis 1:26–27 in terms of human dominion over creation has again been brought to attention by the environmental crisis. Some argue that this monarchical model of man is precisely what has bred human despotism over the earth, while others argue that it only re-enhances the fullness of human responsibility.[13] As D. Cairns notes in his study, throughout history church leaders have given diverse interpretations of the *imago dei*,[14] especially when theologians have attempted to separate an understanding of 'image' and 'likeness'.

'Then God said, "Let us make man in our image, after our likeness" ' (Gen. 1:26). Is the 'image' the natural aptitude man has, despite the Fall, while the 'likeness' is what can only be supernaturally regained after the Fall? This medieval distinction was rejected by the reformers. Calvin believed the 'image' is still in all men who are sustained by the Word, recognising their being in the glory and goodness of God. Luther saw the 'image' as God's intention for man, restorable to believers, but attainable to man not by nature and reason, but only by faith.

The theologian E. Brunner has argued that a distinction should be made between 'image' as formal and as material.[15] Formally, all men, in spite of the Fall, still have superiority in creation, though this is understood not only in terms of the concept of human dominion, but also in the sphere of human responsibility. Man is a being subject, and responsible in freedom, to God. Formally, sin does not infringe upon the image; materially, man has completely lost the image, for he is a sinner through and through. Karl Barth criticised Brunner's distinction between the formal and the material image, suggesting that man's capacity to relate to God in the formal image introduces the innate possibilities of natural theology without the gift of God's grace.[16] Brunner answered that without freedom and responsibility man cannot be activated by the exercise of faith that responds to the grace of God. Clearly, then, the 'image' does entail awareness of man's unique status of responsibility.

This aspect of the *imago dei* as human responsibility is reinforced by the context of the phrase in Genesis 1:26. Unlike the creation of other creatures of whom it is said, 'And God said, "Let there be" . . . and there was', the creation of man is introduced by the plurality of the majestic fullness and responsibility of God: 'Then God said, "Let us make man in our image". . . .' This suggests a deliberate counselling of divine 'persons', and the responsibility involved. Clearly, then, this reflects upon the responsibility man experiences. In his exercise of freedom he responds to God and finds his unique status. Biblical man is essentially a commanded being, whose sense of obligation provides him with dignity and significance. Unlike Greek man, who is above all a rational being, biblical man is a being of whom demands are made. His central problem is not, 'What is being?', but rather: 'What is required of me?'[17]

There is a third aspect, however, implicit in the *imago dei*: man as a relational being.[18] In Genesis 1:27 we read, 'So God created man in His own image, in the image of God He created him; male and female He created them' (cp. Gen. 5:1). As Karl Barth emphasised, the 'image' is one of relationships: The relationship between male and female, e.g., points to the fact that man alone is not man. He is only a man when he is confronted with the 'Thou' before his 'I'. This in turn is a reflection of the eternal relationship within the Trinity, of God's 'I' and 'Thou'.

The image is twofold: vertically, man has been created to relate to God in fellowship; horizontally, man has been created to share with man in friendship. That man and woman were created as complementary helpmeets reflects on man's inability to live alone. Man has been created for personal existence, towards God and fellow man, the former providing the resources to demonstrate this realistically and practically to the latter. As the spirit needs the body, so man needs his relationship with God as well as his relationship to man to exhibit his full nature. For man was created in love, to be a being of love. How different, then, is man's life from the instinctive and natural life of the animals.

3. Man, as a Cultural Being

Significantly, man is created as the finale of creation. All is completed, and God sees it is all good. The seventh day, therefore, speaks of a completed world in which man is placed to enjoy richly all that God has done. This is the beginning of man's existence: to 'enjoy God forever', as the *Shorter Catechism* expresses it.

From a human perspective, we might think of the cosmic forces God released at creation. We see the mighty Pacific Ocean caught up in its endless motion of winds and currents, or the solar wind relentlessly pouring forth its thermal heat, or the expansion of the universe itself racing outward from its initial explosion. Has the Creator Himself been caught up in these infinite dynamisms of power? Will He, like 'Organisation Man', for ever be on the treadmill of His own making? Clearly, the reality of the Sabbath rest denies this. In the sovereignty of His grace, He rests, and amazingly He purposes to rest in His fellowship with man.

It is as if all the bounded structures of the six days of creation, measured as they are by evening and morning, are focused upon and determined by the climax of this day of rest. It is 'a day' unlike all other days, for it has no bounds of evening and morning. It is limitless in its celebration of God's satisfaction with the goodness of creation, and above all with God's communion with man. It is as if the seventh day was designed for fellowship between God and man in the enjoyment of God's world. Man, like God, is a relational being, given the capacity to rest, to take time off, to live reflectively, playfully, adoringly, in the praise and adoration of his Maker. This, then, is the dignity of man. He is the worshipper of God.

Within our culture we have become caught up in a neurotic work ethic instead of an authentic leisure-work ethic. To absolutise the work of our hands and minds is not only idolatrous, but it gives man the false identity of *Homo faber*, as if man without God could make anything at all.

'Be still, and know that I am God' (Ps. 46:10), declares the Lord. In the rhythm of the week the Sabbath provides the starting point at which we can set our priorities clearly. Our significance, our identity, can only be in God. We commence the workaday world on Monday morning, giving work its authentic significance as a human mandate under God. But if work is the parasitic activity from which I extract my significance, then as a 'workaholic' I am no different from the poor alcoholic who lives on the bottle instead of in authentic personal relations. Solzhenitsyn describes a middle-aged woman surgeon in *Cancer Ward* in terms of *what* she is, rather than *who* she is. Strip her of her profession as a surgeon, and then who is she? No one! The creation narrative in Genesis thus emphasises that man is not defined by what he gives to his culture, for he gives significance to his culture and his works by who he is.

Moreover, the Latin word *cultura*, from which we derive our word 'culture', implies cultivation, not creation. Human 'creativity' is an idolatrous idea that needs a proper understanding. 'The Lord God took the man and put him in the garden of Eden to till it and keep it' (Gen. 2:15). A gardener is not a creator, he is a cultivator of the given realities of air, sunshine, rain, soil and plants. Likewise, man can be 'creative' only through the rearrangements he can make, whether it be with words as a writer, with musical notes as a musician, with paints and canvas as an artist, or with the laws of nature as a scientist. Man creates nothing. He simply re-arranges, re-fashions, re-designs the given realities of creation. Man merely has the ability to enjoy the fruits of God's creation, not to exercise god-like powers of creation by and for himself.

Man was also given the cultural mandate to 'name' the animals. In Semitic thought, naming implied the ability to learn the inner secrets or essence of an object, just as man has such powers in science today. Man's power to so 'name' the animals was notably set in the context of his recognition of his own relational needs. He found no helpmeet in such knowledge.

This creation ordinance teaches man that there are levels of knowledge, so that the I-it world of objective reality is not to be confused with the I-you realm of personal relationships. This is the confusion of spirit that Pirsig, Rayber and many other people today exhibit—seeing man as a thing: a sex object, a tool for production, an object of scientific investigation.

THE FALL OF MAN

If, then, we are aware of levels of knowledge, which we confuse to our peril, there are also limits within which man's cultural abilities are set. In Paradise man was created to exist only in a state of the knowledge of good. Paradise was the state of being after the sixth day, when man was introduced to the rest of God. The rest of God was dwelling in the goodness of God. Paradise was acceptance of all the goodness of creation, from the hand of a good Creator. Paradise and Sabbath were thus the realms within space and time in which man celebrated the goodness of God. For Paradise was the realm where man knew only good, for there was nothing but good to accept and to cultivate. Dwelling in the Sabbath was resting in the reality of a finished creation that was 'good', indeed 'very good', since man could explore and articulate, as the priest of creation, praise to God on behalf of all creation.

At this juncture Charles Williams has deep insight into the nature of the fall of man. He speaks of 'the Adam', man and woman, who existed each in his or her own right, separate yet interdependent. Their union reflected the interdependence they had with the world of creation, and their mutual dependence upon God. Together they reflected their Creator, with real, if limited, powers. 'Some possibility of opposite actions there must be', argues Williams, 'if there is to be any relations between different wills.'[19] God therefore pointed out to the Adam the tree of the knowledge of good and evil. The Creator allowed them as responsible creatures the freedom of choice. Such freedom 'is the only method by which He can praise His creatures; if they are not to be allowed to choose, neither can they enjoy His will nor He theirs'. The Adam could choose to know the good or something other than the good.

They knew good; they wished to know good and evil. Since there was not—since there never has been and never will be—anything else than the good to know, they knew good as antagonism. All difference consists in the mode of knowledge. They had what they wanted. That they did not like it when they got it does not alter the fact that they certainly got it.[20]

The change in their manner of knowing inevitably produced a change in their landscape. Their inscape of the spirit was no longer good, so their landscape was no longer Paradise. Their separation as two people, male and female, now opened them to hostility as well as harmony. Their bodies continued to be the same as God had made them, but an ugly guilt of spirit made them see their bodies shamefully, so that they made aprons—not for each other but for themselves. They now blamed each other, their children killed each other, and with the speed of cancer the whole universe was diseased. In place of coinherence, there was disharmony, separation, dissolution.

It was only by the grace of God, which is also His providential judgment, that man and woman were then banned from seizing the ultimate source of god-like powers, the fruit of the tree of life, of immortality. As it is, *techne* has been misused by man to extend himself, as an axe does the physical abilities of one's hand, or a computer one's mental attributes, or an organisation one's social presence. So today, man's fall into evil is exacerbated by the technological projections of his cultural shadow. He has not only made 'aprons' to cover his shame, but hydrogen bombs as well. This highlights the terror of the fall of man. Modern writers are also profoundly concerned about this.

William Golding is one such writer who sees man as inescapably a being 'who manufactures evil the way a bee makes honey'. In his novels *Lord of the Flies*, *Free Fall* and *Pincher Martin* he traces progressively man's pessimism and determinism, the inevitability of human evil and the loss of human freedom to choose. But one of the elements missing is the universality of creation. *Lord of the Flies* is set on an island, with typical British insularity, like Sir Thomas More's *Utopia*, Shakespeare's *Tempest* and Defoe's *Robinson Crusoe*. *Martin Pincher* is the story of a shipwrecked sailor perched on a rock. *Free Fall* describes the state of mind of a prisoner in an isolation cell of a concentration camp. Progressively our culture is no longer able to see the world as God's world, for Paradise has shrunk to Utopia, 'no place'. Consequently, the sense of mystery is lost too, so that man is left ultimately with only the mystery of death, of evil, of nothingness.

In *Lord of the Flies*, Golding tells the story of the hell man inevitably makes of paradise. A party of schoolboys crash-lands on a desert island. At first they are dazzled by the wonders of the paradise they are so free to enjoy. Three of the boys walk along the beach. 'A new kind of glamour was spread over them and the scene, and they were conscious of the glamour and made happy by it. They turned to each other, laughing excitedly, talking, not listening. The air was bright. . . . Ralph, faced by the task of translating all this into an explanation, stood on his head, and fell over.' They climb the mountain, see the circular horizon of water and recognise it as an island. 'This belongs to us,' they boast. 'Eyes shining, mouths open, triumphant, they savoured the right of domination. They were lifted up: were friends. . . .'[21]

What the boys do not realise is that savouring this right of domination over natural objects like a mountain view or an island paradise leads to changes in their own character. It degenerates into the desire of some boys to dominate the others. The eating of the forbidden fruit gives man power to see things both as objects of delight for their own sake and as instruments of evil. Adam and Eve used the trees of Paradise, no longer to enjoy openly but to hide behind, to obstruct the openness and communion that once existed between man and God. God's world now consisted of objects corrupted for purely self-directed ends. Likewise, the boys in *Lord of the Flies* take a piece of rock, once an object to be admired for its beauty, and use it as a murderous weapon to kill. As Ruth Etchells has observed of this novel:

> The safe ordinariness of everyday objects, therefore, takes on a new dimension of threat or menace in some way

connected with what individuals can become, and beneath this what human beings *are*. And so existence in
the world *as a human being* becomes inescapably, terribly,
dangerous. 'I'm afraid of us,' says Ralph, the central character, as the true nature of their predicament becomes
clear to him.[22]

As fear and distrust seize them all, they react by asserting
their separate identities, making futile efforts to build a corporate society out of their individual needs. At the end of the
story, two of the boys have been murdered by their compan-
ions, three have disappeared, and all that are left suffer the
guilt and knowledgeable grief of the dark depths of their own
hearts. The island is scorched like dead wood. Paradise without,
as a human habitat, as well as paradise within, as a state of
mind, is irrevocably lost. Their love of nature has degenerated
into paganism, even into cannibalism. For they have lost their
individual identities in their regression into savagery.

Golding is interested in that point of human achievement
where man's creativity turns sour, and instead releases irrational desires to hurt, destroy and kill. These destructive impulses do not seem material; there is no reason for them. Yet
they are always concomitant with human achievement when
man forgets God the Creator. Then the awe and mystery of
reality, of dependence upon God, give way to the spirit of pride,
domination and self-seeking mastery. Is then 'the rise of civilisation' another name for 'the fall of man'? This seems clearly
so in the narrative of Genesis: of Cain who 'built a city'; of
Jubal who 'was the father of all those who play the lyre and
pipe'; of Tubal-cain, who 'was the forger of all instruments of
bronze and iron' (Gen. 4:17, 21, 22). Man's progressive self-
consciousness about achievement is also his fall.

THE REALITY OF SIN AND EVIL

As we have seen, man's mandate to be the kingly cultivator of
the good things of creation has seduced him to be both Apol-

lonian and Dionysian. Man is unhappy because he has lost his
kingship, and he is absurd because he has lost his dependence
upon God. The radical contradiction of his being makes him
a stranger in a strange world, just as Cain wandered in the
land of Nod, the place of no home. As the song puts it:

> People are strange
> When you're a stranger,
> Faces look ugly
> When you're alone. . . .

Whether he realises it or not, the depth of man's alienation is seen in relation to his kingly origin. As Pascal asks: 'Who
is unhappy at not being a king, except a deposed king? All
these miseries prove man's greatness. They are the miseries of
a great lord, of a deposed king.' Likewise Kierkegaard says:
'The greatness of man is great in that he knows himself to be
miserable.' It is the *imago dei* that encourages man to see himself as a sinner. Without this perception man's conception of
sin and evil can only be expressed in terms of absurdity.

Apart from the biblical understanding of sin and evil,
there can only be three basic explanations of the rationale of
evil: naturalism, dualism and monism. (These are discussed in
Appendix A.) They may distinguish general consequences of
evil, such as famines, earthquakes, tidal waves and other natural
disasters, from evils that may befall an individual. But sin is a
meaningless concept without the awareness of a personal Creator God. The consciousness of forbidden fruit, of legitimate
claims upon one's life, of revolt against God—these are pre-
requisites for a sense of sin. A low view of man, of his origins,
therefore will engender a low view of sin.

Thus, unlike all other religious and philosophical systems
of the world religions, the Bible views sin in terms of violated
personal relationships, and stresses the need for a reorientation
of life so radical that it requires new birth, conversion, pardon
and return to bring about a remedy for sin. For the pervasiveness of sin is such that only by death to the old life can
man authentically relate to God in newness of life. Two aspects
of sin may be distinguished. What is called 'original sin' may

better be called 'radical sin', since it goes back to the roots of man's existence and origins. Individual sin is continuing to live in reversal of one's role as the image-bearer of God, to be man-as-if-he-were-God.

Man assuming and behaving as if he were God is man in revolt, rebelling against the rule of God, and against the limits imposed by God. This is known as *pesha* in the Hebrew, and bears such imagery as infidelity, adultery, refusal to listen, hardness of heart, stiffness of neck, all associated with rebellion and pride. It is assertion over others, over the creation and over the Creator. It is also associated with *chattat*, i.e., missing the mark, going astray, failing to conform to the creation ordinances of God. It implies also the symbol of *awan*, in which divergence from order, deviation from the straight road, leads to confusion, disorder and lostness. There is the perversion of what is good, in knowledge and action. It is also acquisition, selfishly, so that the desire to have what we cannot have leads only to envy, jealousy, suspicion and lovelessness towards each other. Thus the human condition is described as *shagah*, the situation of being astray, in a radical state of alienation.

The biblical story is not concerned, then, with the origin of evil so much as the beginning of man's responsibility. The origin of evil is lost in a wider mystery of freedom for man to choose, and to be responsible. As Alan Paton has reflected:

> I cannot ever conceive that life could have meaning without suffering. There would certainly be no music, no theatre, no literature, no art. I suspect that the alternative to a universe in which there is suffering, in which evil struggles with good and cruelty with mercy, would be a universe of nothingness, where there would be neither good or evil, no happiness, only an eternity of uninterrupted banality.[23]

Man was not created and thereafter bound to a choiceless existence. Clearly there is no place for dualism in the biblical narrative (see Appendix A). The tree of the forbidden fruit is God's creation; the serpent that tempts Eve is one of God's creatures. The objects man uses as instruments of terror and destruction are within God's creation. Whence then evil? The silence of Scripture is simply that there is 'the mystery of iniquity', as the apostle calls it. Set in juxtaposition are the affirmations Isaiah makes:

> He did not create it a chaos,
> He formed it to be inhabited.   (Isa. 45:18)

> I form the light and create darkness:
> I make weal and create woe:
> I the Lord do all these things.   (Isa. 45:7)

God uses even disorder to provide for human freedom, for God is God. God has accepted the terrible, awesome implications of evil within His creation, as the responsibility only God can take and for which only He can provide a remedy. So the triumph of God over evil is based upon the character and reality of God Himself. Without such a faith, world structures and world foundations crumble into chaos, as the faiths of the ancient civilisations have shown. How sharply contrasted they are to the biblical faith in the Creator God may be seen from a survey of Egyptian serenity, Babylonian neurosis and Greek tragedy.[24]

1. Egyptian Serenity

The Old Testament speaks of 'the wisdom of the Egyptians'. It was a stable power, self-confident and self-sufficient. It was the hydraulic civilisation par excellence, based on the Nile, 'where thou waterest the land with thy foot'. Understandably, the Egyptian took his cosmic orientation from the south, where the Nile's source lay. The words 'south' and 'face' were synonymous, as were the 'north' and 'back of the head'. That is, the Egyptian faced the south, and attributed life to the east, where the sun rose, and death to the west, where the sun set. There was a strong sense of symmetry in Egyptian life; the creative principle of *Ptah* operated through mankind as the conceptive heart that thinks, and the creative tongue that commands. The Pharaoh looked upon himself as a god, confident of acting as the representative of the gods in the land of Egypt.[25]

Like the technological society today, the faith of the Egyptians was an easy faith. It was hedonistic, carefree and optimistic—at least in its heyday. But its sense of confidence lacked introspection and therefore the deep intellectual and emotional enquiry concerning good and evil. Free from anxiety, it was apathetic to great spiritual explorations. Its golden age and its norms lay in the past, after creation commenced on the hillock above the receding flood waters. Pragmatic and materialistic, the Pharaohs could not conceive the after-life to be any better than this life, so they extended into the after-life all the accoutrements of their mortal life. Easy pleasures, many songs and bright sunlight predisposed the Egyptians to live technically, like many today. But the serenity of its people has given us no great literature on the problem of evil, as in North American society today.

2. Babylonian Neurosis

The Egyptian pyramids still stand, while the ziggurats of Mesopotamia 'have become heaps', as the Old Testament prophets predicted they would be. The contrast is fitting, because the mood of the Babylonian civilisation was altogether different: insecure, self-despairing, distrusting, with human rulers who did not rival the divine status of the Pharaohs; indeed, they had to be re-enthroned annually at the spring festival. The flood season and the waters of the Euphrates–Tigris were more uncertain, the floods more dangerous and exposure to hill-raiders and salinisation of the delta lands made life all the more precarious.

Unlike Egypt, the cosmic order cannot be taken for granted. So creation has to be celebrated annually at the spring equinox, and much human ingenuity is required for the endless ritualistic appeasements of the gods.[26] There is no stabilising principle like the Egyptian *Maat* or cosmic justice. In its theogonies (i.e., creation of the gods), it is implicit that chaos is anterior to order, and that the reality of evil is primordial and co-extensive with the generation of the divine.

But order is only possible through the further use of evil, so that in the creation of man a criminal act is performed. In the slaying of a god, whose blood was mingled with dust, lies the origin of mankind. Mankind hopes to survive, not because good prevails over evil ultimately, but because, hopefully, not all the gods are angry with mankind all the time. The gods need man as a master needs a slave, and in the quarrels of jealous gods, man can hope for some protection from these cosmic bullies, in the chance event that one god may defend him as his patron.

Towards the end of Babylonian civilisation, passivity and resignation to despair intensified cynicism and the relativism of all values. In the literature of absurdity, such as the *Dialogue of Pessimism* between a master and his slave, the conclusion is that whether one does good or evil makes no difference: it will not be remembered in times to come.

> 'Slave, agree with me!' 'Yes, my lord, yes!'
> 'Now then, what is good?
> To break my neck and thy neck,
> to fall into the river—that is good!'[27]

The world with all its vanity has only one good, as Camus' *Outsider* understood, exposing his 'heart open to the benign indifference of the universe': to die. And so, too, Babylonian society collapsed internally, dissolved by its own intrinsic anxieties that were based on an ultimately insecure theology of creation.

3. The Greek Tragic Vision of the Cosmos

Epics like that of Gilgamesh, who is known to have been king of Uruk c. 2700 B.C., indicate that epic tragedy as a literary genre had extensive roots in the ancient Near East long before the rise of Greek tragedy. Through Babylonia, not Egypt, the heroes of Gilgamesh, Enkidu and Humbaba share the same universe of evil and suffering as the gods and mortals of the Homeric Hymns, Hesiod's *Theogony* and the *Odyssey*. On a corner of the known earth, between the unknown waters of the Ocean and the Abyss, men asked the same questions of life and death, creation and salvation. Sailing the Aegean and Mediterranean seas, a particular type of hero developed, Ulysses-like, whose courage and personal love of adventure bred a special style of leader who pitted himself against the elements of sea and wind. The epic of Goliath, the Philistine challenger of the Israelite faith, manifests this style of leader (1 Sam. 17).

Behind the origin and character of Greek tragedy, with its high seriousness in matters concerning human survival, human suffering and human freedom, the question was why man was for ever torn between good and evil, freedom and necessity, truth and deceit. Are the causes of his suffering in blind chance, the evil designs of the gods or within himself? Why is truth so elusive and goodness so perishable?[28]

Greek theology is based on all the previous assumptions of Babylonian experience. Evil is assumed to be a primordial reality, chaos pre-exists creation. There is no distinction between the divine and the diabolical, but the awareness of this is veiled from man. Thus Homer in the *Iliad*, led astray by the darkening of the mind, expresses the theme of human impotence through his blindness. The Homeric hero is led astray in such feebleness in the midst of hostile, transcendent powers. This blindness is attributed perhaps to Zeus, or to *Moera* or to the fates. Such is the 'lot' of mankind. Evil is inseparable, loss is irretrievable, suffering is inevitable. Moderation is the only recourse left for man to follow in the midst of the jealousies of the gods. The truly tragic element is that the overpowering force of evil is confronted by puny man, who has the freedom to halt the juggernaut only momentarily. Ultimately the human spirit is crushed, and inevitably destroyed.

In sharp contrast to these paradigms of reality, which are still with us, received either optimistically, or with resignation, or with a heroic spirit, the biblical view of evil describes it as not intrinsic to the world. For God is good, and He created a good world. 'And God saw everything that He had made, and behold, it was very good' (Gen. 1:31). Chaos and evil are not anterior to God or His creation. Consequently, God takes responsibility for all things, as the prophet Isaiah recognises (Isa. 45:5–7, 18–19).

God created man to be free: free to have dominion over the world, free to respond and to be obedient to the Creator. His freedom lies in obedience; not freedom *from*, but freedom *for* God. For man is wholly dependent upon God, and so, unlike the animals, his nature is defined in relational terms, not by instinct. This freedom is the source of man's responsibility. In this context sin is the impairment of man's relations with God, for which man is responsible, even though the existence of evil is still a mystery, its origin unknown to man.

But God's righteousness points to His sovereignty over evil, with the assurance that evil is neither the beginning nor the end of God's purposes, for He created all things good. And He will take responsibility for the removal of all evil. In such faith, man need neither despair nor be passive. He will then see a different landscape from those who believe evil is a primordial principle of reality—the landscape of creation.

NOTES

1   Sam Keen, 'Manifesto for a Dionysian Theology', in *The New Theology*, Martin E. Marty and Dean G. Peerman, edits., No. 7, London, Macmillan, 1970, pp. 79ff.

2   M. H. Abrams (edit.), *The Poetry of Alexander Pope: A Selection*, Northbrook, Illinois, A. H. M. Publishing Corp., 1954, p. 57.

3   Quoted by Carl Skrade, *God and the Grotesque*, Philadelphia, Westminster Press, 1974, p. 87.

4   Ibid., p. 90.

5   Philip E. Hughes, *Christianity and the Problems of Origins*, Philadelphia, Presbyterian and Reformed Publishing Co., 1964, p. 37.

6   Wilfrid le Gros Clark, *Man-ape or Ape man?*, New York, Holt, Rinehart & Winston, 1965.

7   E. K. Victor Pearce, *Who was Adam?*, Exeter, Paternoster Press, 1969. He argues that Adam is the innovator of the New Stone Age, but this begs the question why Upper Palaeolithic man had this spiritual interest in the after-life, if he pre-dated Adam.

8   The origins approach forces us to either scientific or philosophical approaches *per se*, for Scripture is silent about that approach. See D. Gareth Jones, 'Man in the context of evolutionary theory', in Carl F. H. Henry (edit.), *Horizons of Science*, New York, Harper & Row, 1978, pp. 36–62.

9   T. Dobzhansky, *Mankind Evolving*, New Haven, Yale University Press, 1962.

10 W. H. Thorpe, *Animal Nature and Human Nature*, New York, Doubleday, 1974, p. 271.

11 No attempt is made in this work to deal with evolution as a scientific approach to biological knowledge. That is a scientific issue. What is attacked here is evolutionary humanism, a metaphysical faith that views man as only a natural product of materialistic processes.

12 Walter Brueggemann, 'King in the Kingdom of Things', *Christian Century*, 10 Sept., 1969, pp. 1156–1166.

13 See James Barr, 'The Image of God in the book of Genesis— a study in terminology', *Bulletin of the John Rylands Library*, 1968, pp. 11–21.

14 David Cairns, *The Image of God in Man*, London, S.C.M., 1953.

15 E. Brunner, *Man in Revolt*, trans. Olive Wyon, London, Lutterworth, 1947.

16 Karl Barth, *Church Dogmatics*, trans. G. W. Bromiley and T. F. Torrance, Edinburgh, T. & T. Clark, 1958, vol. III,i, pp. 181–206; III,ii, pp. 44–45.

17 A. J. Heschel, *Who is Man?*, Stanford, Stanford University Press, 1965, p. 74.

18 David J. Clines, 'The Image of God in Man', London, *Tyndale Bulletin*, vol. 19, 1968.

19 Charles Williams, *He Came down from Heaven*, London, Faber & Faber, 1956, p. 201.

20 Ibid., p. 21.

21 William Golding, *Lord of the Flies*, New York, Capricorn Books, G. P. Putnam's Sons, 1959, pp. 25, 26.

22 Ruth Etchells, *Unafraid to Be*, London, Inter-Varsity Press, 1969, p. 26.

23 Alan Paton, 'Why Suffering?' in *Creative Suffering—the Ripple of Hope*, Boston, Pilgrim Press, 1970, p. 15.

24 A suggestive study of the distinctions made in the nature of evil in the ancient world in the book of Paul Ricoeur, *The Symbolism of Evil*, New York, Harper & Row, 1967.

25 Henri Frankfort *et al.*, *Before Philosophy*, London, Penguin Books, 1949. This is a useful comparative survey of both ancient Egypt and Babylonia.

26 Thorkild Jacobsen, *The Treasures of Darkness, A History of Mesopotamian Religion*, New Haven and London, Yale University Press, 1976.

27 N. K. Sandars, *Poems of Heaven and Hell from Ancient Mesopotamia*, Harmondsworth, Eng., Penguin Books, 1971.

28 See the article on Greek tragedy in the *New Encyclopaedia Britannica*, London/Chicago, Encyclopaedia Britannica, 1947, Macropaedia, vol. 18, pp. 582–584.

CHAPTER FOUR

Understanding the Creator

The biblical doctrine of creation seems an insuperable obstacle to the minds and the emotions of many today. For one thing, man inhabits a shrinking planet within an expanding universe. For another, Christianity is no longer called upon to render legitimate moral and social order in our culture. Today we live in an efficient society, not a moral society. But no religion can solemnise the symbols of our time—computers, cars and tape-recorders. If the world has shrunk, so too has the relevance of faith for many. Not only do we live in the godless world of secularism, we also tend to worship a worldless god. With the divorce of man from God, and the alienation of man from creation, we live with two basic challenges. How can we live faithfully before the Creator in a godless world? How can we live convincingly with a worldless God?

William Golding in his novel *Free Fall* describes the loss of freedom of a prisoner-of-war in a concentration camp as he reflects in solitude upon all his past life. He remembers his schooling: 'Somewhere, some time, I made a choice for freedom and lost my freedom. . . . There, somewhere there? Back among the flowers and smell of cloakrooms, among the exercise books and savage emotions, back among the rewards and penalties. . . ?' Sammy Mountjoy questions the making of his worldview. 'The star's light reaches us millions of years after the star is gone, or so they say, and perhaps it is true. What sort of universe is that for our central darkness to keep its balance in?'[1] He is virtually an orphan, since 'I never knew my father,' and his mother was a whore. So he was fostered. At school he was educated to live in two worlds, two worlds that never met—a religious world taught by Miss Rowena Pringle, and a rationalist world taught by Nick Sholes, the science teacher.

'People are the walls of our room, not philosophers.' The beauty of Miss Pringle's cosmos was vitiated because 'she was a bitch'. Nick's stunted universe was 'irradiated by his love of people'. 'She would lift curtains' to show the Bible, 'full of wonder and importance', only to spoil it all with silly plausibilities of explaining it away. Nick's world was an innocent paper world, where 'matter can neither be destroyed nor created', a world that 'was not enveloping'. 'There was no place for spirit in his cosmos and consequently the cosmos played a huge practical joke on him.' For it was 'not science but poetry that filled him and us', loving people selflessly and kindly, so that he was the homeland for all people, not his dreary rationalistic universe of cause and effect. Both the incompatibility of these two worlds, and the inconsistency with which they were both taught, meant that neither could be integrated. 'We crossed from one universe into another when we came out of her door and went into his. We held both universes in our heads effortlessly because by the nature of the human being, neither of them was real. Both systems were coherent . . . ,'[2] but neither could be inhabited.

At the end of his reflection, Sammy Mountjoy wanted to visit both his old teachers. He wanted to tell Nick Sholes, 'you did not choose your rationalism rationally. You chose because they showed you the wrong maker.' In his youth, Nick had been taught a caricature of God, as a tyrant. Now Nick lay dying, before whose presence Sammy could only be silent and feel his own nothingness. In his reverie he then visits Miss Pringle to exchange a ministry of forgiveness, but in ten seconds such a thought had evaporated before the artificial world she lived in, utterly and wholly; 'there was a plaster rabbit sitting by a plaster bird-bath'.[3] He could not communicate a single thought to her.

OBSTACLES TO BELIEF IN A PERSONAL CREATOR

The challenge that Golding's Sammy Mountjoy presents us with is profound. We are reminded of the dilemma that faced

Naaman the leper after he had been cured by Elisha the prophet. He asked for forgiveness for the time when he would have to go back into the house of Rimmon, with his master the King of Syria, to bow there in worship to his false god. So he asked for two mule-loads of Yahweh's earth, that he might spread it in his courtyard and thereon lay his prayer mat, and always have a *locus standi* before Yahweh (2 Kings 5:15–19). Is that how we compromise our restricted place, where we stand, under the Creator, in an otherwise secularised world that does not acknowledge the Creator of all things? How small is our area of freedom when we know and live in the light of the Maker of Heaven and Earth? Is that how we stand under His glory?

1. Pragmatism

Clearly, the first obstacle to belief in a personal Creator is that creation and natural science are two walls with no connection, no bridge between them. It seems that objective knowledge of the world of things erases the shadow of the observer from the picture. So to conceive of the universe as caused by a personal God appears to be just too ridiculous to be true, that is, to be 'scientifically' true. Mathematics, physics and chemistry enjoy spectacular success, precisely because the personal dimension is eliminated. So how can we believe in a personal God at all when dealing with a universe that makes us sick with its spaciousness?

Moreover, the logical, mechanical approach to reality has given us precise, concrete powers over the material world. Science and technology tend to reinforce each other, as self-sustaining and self-contained explanations of reality. First, deism in the eighteenth century, and now, existentialist theology in the twentieth century, shrink before the triumphalism of the modern scientific spirit, so that the man of faith appears to have no more than Naaman's two mule-loads of Yahweh's earth in hostile territory. What the English scholar Willey has called 'cosmic Toryism'—that God is the logical necessity of philosophers, the First Cause, or that religion is the need of society—has not been an adequate bulwark against the spirit of secularism.[4] It has, in fact, played into its hands. For if the ultimate explanation is rational, then man himself is the master of reality. That is why intellectualism holds such a powerful appeal for modern man: it feeds human pride with a sense of self-sufficiency and self-achievement. But the reduction of creation to mechanical laws eliminates the need of the presence of deity.

The cosmic vanity of man is that he can project his own desires upon the universe—like the screen of the drive-in theatre—and see reflected what he wants to see. Watch a child at play and see how he personalises his whole environment by talking to the things around him, convincing himself that they are all on his side. Likewise, man projects onto reality the characteristics of life he wishes to possess. To predict, to control, to master the universe, technological man thus determines that only causality rules the universe.

But man finds that to conquer the moon and to walk there, he has to turn himself into a machine. He has to keep company with other intelligent machines to escape from the earth's gravity. He further discovers that to intoxicate his mind with logic and mathematics, he must empty his head of truth. Thus the evolution of the machine results in the devolution of man.

Man's desire for mastery plays many tricks upon his spirit. The seventeenth-century philosopher René Descartes assumed that man ought to become the 'master' and possessor of nature through the natural sciences and thus fulfil his destiny in creation. This he described as his 'redemption';[5] and the restoration from the Fall was made possible by scientific achievement. Likewise, Francis Bacon, the early scientist of the same century, assumed that the restoration of the *imago dei* in man was through scientific understanding of nature, by 'the restitution and re-investing [in great part] of man to the sovereignty and power . . . which he had in his first state of creation'.[6] This fatal misunderstanding of Scripture, that fallen, sinful man could ever force a mandate to exercise self-development through science instead of through the forgiveness of God's grace, has brought us to the issue of the environmental crisis today. It has led us to the unrestrained domination and exploitation of the creation. If man cannot control his own *hubris*, how then can he possibly control his family, his society, his world? Thus even men of faith like Descartes and Bacon have shown us that their interpretations of Scripture may need to be corrected and re-focused.

2. *The World: a Closed or Open System?*

A misconception of creation for many Christians is that it is a rival theory to those of the geological and biological sciences, especially on the issue of the origins of the earth. Scientists affirm the need for millions of years of evolution, while the mature creationist will speak of the 'six days'. If creation is then only about origins, it comes into conflict with natural science. So even Christians will tend to be indifferent about a doctrine that seems bizarre in comparison with the findings of modern science. This is a tragic misunderstanding, for it tends to fragment the faith of the believer into three pieces: creation, which deals with the past; redemption, which is one's major preoccupation in the present; and the *eschaton* in the future, about which wild speculations may be encouraged. No wonder such a view of religious faith fails to convince Sammy Mountjoy and his kind. It is like Naaman transporting his two mule-loads of Yahweh's earth into secular territory.

In more sophisticated debate, two philosophers once argued on empirical and religious terms about the meaning of creation. The Christian, Donald M. MacKinnon, emphasised that creation has much less to do with origins than with the language of dependence.[7] Creation *is*, and not merely *was*. The central meaning of the biblical words for 'create' is divine activity, regardless of when the 'creating' is said to have taken place. This then opens up the possibilities for creation to be conceived of in an open system of thought. The secular philosopher Antony Flew was worried about the language used concerning creation, for it used the vocabulary of the finite about something—God—that was by definition infinite. Thus secularists often feel that Christians are using analogical language fraudulently, to express infinite reality in finite terms: how much is literal, and how much is not? Professor MacKinnon's reply, which is central to the understanding of the doctrine of creation, is that we believe it only 'in Christ'. Why so? Because 'in this riddle of Christ's life, lived, and Christ's death, died, we see through a glass darkly the infinite boundless love, love without condition, translated into terms of the finite and the bounded.'[8] Christ is the basis on which finite language can be used about the infinite, for 'the Word was made flesh', as we shall consider later.

It is, therefore, a tragic mistake when well-meaning Christians build up their views of creation solely on the grounds of scientific speculations or rebuttals to them, and overlook the fact that the doctrine of creation is a Christian doctrine about Christ, revealing the character of God as covenant maker with His creation.

Thus, when we say the doctrine of creation is 'open', we mean:

(1) that it has various possibilities for unpredictable change
(2) that its future is not wholly determined by the present state
(3) that it is open to relationships with other systems or doctrines of thought
(4) that the final condition will be different from the original state.[9]

All this is based on the mercy of God. Predictably, in a closed moral system God visits 'the iniquity of the fathers upon the children to the third and fourth generations of those who hate me'. But what is immeasurable, unpredictable, is that God's mercy is 'unto a thousand generations' (Exod. 20:6). This means that since 'God so loved the world', He operates creation with an open system that included the Incarnation. Who could have conceived that reality by reading only Genesis one? Psalm 104 might have added some pointers to it, but it would still not have been anticipated. Likewise, since God loves man, he still lives in a creation that is 'open' to the ways of God, for 'eye has not seen, nor ear heard, neither hath it entered into the heart of man the things which God hath prepared for those that love him' (1 Cor. 2:9).

We may cite those examples of how our secular world is being broken into by new attitudes towards the reality of transcendence. First of all, since the 1950s the researchers of radio astronomy have supplied increasing evidence for the origin of the universe through an initial explosion of matter, the 'Big Bang' hypothesis, over against a cyclical view of eternal existence. At a recent meeting of the American Association for the Advancement of Science, the astrophysicist Robert Jastrow admitted the intellectual embarrassment of facing the insurmountable Beginning.

> Scientists cannot bear the thought that there is an important natural phenomenon which they cannot hope to explain, even with unlimited time and money. Scientists hold that every effect has its cause. But every item of evidence that might have given a clue to the cause of the great explosion was destroyed in that holocaust. The sense of cause is violated by a Beginning. . . . known laws of physics cannot be valid under circumstances which we cannot now discover. . . . When something like that happens, the scientist has really lost control.[10]

That is to say, he has lost control of boxing in reality within a closed system. It is as if scientists, after scaling Himalayan mountains of scientific achievement, make the final assault on the last summit to witness the ultimate vista of reality, only to find a group of theologians already there, grinning as they say: 'I told you so!' It is not very nice.

It is, in fact, impossible to pursue the end of human thought without encountering mystical elements at every turn. That is why we have to utilise, in a study of this kind, not only the more rational systems of theological persuasion, but also the insights of poets and writers. Such too is the experience, for example, of the neurologist who finds that the mystery of the mind transcends all the available anatomical facts of the brain. So too, the programmed instruction of the genetic code implanted in DNA is forcing genetics to face new mysteries of life. Any physical research, if probed deeply enough, ends up as metaphysical enquiry. How wise was Pascal who, recognising this, said: 'The final stage of reason is to recognise that there is an infinity of things beyond it. It is but feeble if it does not see so far as to know this.'[11]

In the sphere of social life, the sociologist Peter Berger has spoken of 'signals of transcendence' in his book *A Rumour of Angels.*[12] The human exercise of judgment, play, humour, faith, hope and love, all point, argues Berger, to a moral structuring of reality beyond the immediate needs of human customs and cultures. They point to a structured underpinning of life, upon which all human existence depends.

These are indicators of the mystery of transcendence, beyond atoms, molecules and cells, that should keep our minds open and our spirits receptive to the realms of wonder and awe. If modern man finds creation difficult to believe, it is not because it is irrational, but perhaps, like Miss Rowena Pringle, because we are not prepared to live radically enough in our dependence upon God to make our faith in the Creator credible enough for other people to accept. Perhaps then, like the seventeenth-century poet, we have to begin with ourselves:

> . . . since no creature comprehends
> The cause of causes, end of ends,
> He who himself vouchsafes to know
> But pleases his creator so.
>
> Sidney Goldolphin—*Hymn*[13]

3. Miracles and the Supernatural

Naturalism, as we have already seen, is like a California smog that obscures the reality of the Creator. He is still there, but we do not see Him because our minds are fixated by the cause and effect relationship of an autonomous Nature. Miracles—if we can believe in them at all in such a system of thought—are then unusual events that erupt through our causal system in inexplicable ways. Miracles defined in this way reduce God to what Professor C. A. Coulson called the god-of-the gaps;[14] not a very satisfactory god to trust because fresh scientific discoveries will continue to erode into his territory, which is only a territory ascribed to him by human ignorance, not a vital faith. The modern god-of-the-gaps is a superstition which shows no improvement upon Naaman's 'two mule-loads of Yahweh's earth'.

It also diminishes our credence in the Creator if, in His use of miracles, we envisage Him only as a wonder-worker, a magician. Human magicians we can understand, but why a cosmic magician overriding His own laws in a world that He has made? Is this not pointless, if He is the Creator of all?

The real issue is the nature of transcendence—of God's rule over creation. In the biblical world this is affirmed; in the Greek world it is denied. To the Greeks, the *kosmos* was an orderly structure, based upon cause and effect, linked to the innate power of things in themselves, to nature. To the Hebrews, *creation* was expressive of the will and Word of God, whose consistency did not depend on the Greek idea of *physis*, but upon the moral character of God. The Old Testament Israelites never questioned the reality of God. They simply questioned what God was doing, and why He was doing it. Creation, the Exodus, the Conquest—these were the deeds of God. As the life-giver, God was sought therefore in both psalms of lament and imprecatory psalms. The secondary causation of physical phenomena was never conceived to have importance (see pp. 61–62). In such a realm of faith in the Creator, ordinary day-to-day existence was as miraculous as the big events in the life of an individual or the mighty deeds of Israel's national existence. The yearly harvest of the peasant, the multiplication of his flock and the increase of his children were all as miraculous as the great event of Exodus and deliverance. So creation was not so much a physical universe as it was the language of God (Ps. 19:1–6).

Two major issues did affect Israelite faith. First, by what name was God called; that is to say, what was God's character? Secondly, how did one know one was in fellowship with God? These two issues were raised in Elijah's challenge to the priests of nature, of Baal, on Mount Carmel. The miracle of Elijah's sacrifice revealed he knew the name of God—Yahweh—and he, the prophet, was vindicated in his relationship to Yahweh (1 Kings 18).[15]

When we come to the New Testament, miracles are a prominent feature of the ministry of Jesus. Rarely, however, is the word 'miracle' rendered 'wonder' (*thaumasion*). Instead, the miracles in the Gospels are commonly described as 'power' (*dynamis*) or 'sign' (*semeion*).[16] That is to say, the miracles of Jesus are not those of a wonder-worker, but are evidence of His character: the Co-Creator who, as the Infinite, lived finitely in this world. His miracles—of healing, of providing food, of destruction in judgment—are all consistent within creation, as the Creator's providence. Wisely, C. S. Lewis calls these miracles of 'the old creation', that is to say, they are consistent with the regularities of the physical world as we see and know them.[17] But Christ also came to inaugurate the new creation—in redemption—and so He sees other miracles like the resurrection of Lazarus and His own resurrection appearances as belonging to this character of His ministry as 'new creation'. In other words, the miracles in the Bible are all consistent with the character of God. It is His *faithfulness* in His covenant with Adam, Noah, Abraham and Israel that is the basis for the uniformity and consistency apparent in the creation, not the mechanical laws of cause and effect, for God made and upholds these laws. He is their Maker. Thus the ultimate *locus* of consistency is not in matter, but in the personal; in the character of a God who 'cannot deny Himself'. With this guiding principle we can, of course, ask whether some events that previous generations of Christians have assumed were miracles, really were so. A good example is the incident in which God is supposed to have held the sun still for Joshua. Do we really believe it is consistent with the character of God the Creator to have created so radical a dislocation of the whole stellar system, and to have left no trace of the event in the further history of the universe? What would be the point of doing so? The issue is not, could the Creator have done so—clearly He could—but why do so? It is likely that our Hebrew translation is at fault,[18] and that what Joshua actually commanded is:

> Be eclipsed, O sun, in Gibeon,
> And thou moon in the Valley of Aijalon!   (Josh. 10:12)

The faith of Joshua, in the expression of such a prayer, was in the Creator who rules the universe. That is the essence of prayer, absolute trust in the goodness, faithfulness and sovereignty of the Creator, who responds to faith and prayer by continuing to be consistent with His own character of righteousness and love.

In modern physics, a deterministic world-view has had to be abandoned, not because quantum physics is more difficult than the old views, but because of the new views that matter is not intrinsically deterministic. It might seem that this would engender a more receptive attitude to the place of miracles and of the supernatural than previously. This is unlikely, because the new forms of science are still statistically determinate, and violations of these will still be viewed with distrust.[19] The issue therefore remains—either there is awareness of transcendence, of the need of God in the human heart, or there is no place given to Him.

For the Christian, who sees in the Incarnation the miracle that envelops all other miracles, all life is miraculous, for all of life is lived under the transcendent light and life of God. But it is not miracles as such that impress the Christian; they have their place as satellites do to the sun. It is the reality of Jesus Christ, the bringer of the rule of God into every area and dimension of life, that is the wonder of wonders. In Him, indeed, is evidence of the glory of God. Miracles, then, are presented in the Gospels as evidential proofs of the goodness and the power of God. But the cardinal miracle was, and is, Jesus Himself. It is in encounter with Jesus today, says John Wesley, that

> The change wrought by the Holy Spirit in the heart is the equivalent to all outward miracles, as implying the self-same power which gave sight to the blind, feet to the lame, and life to the dead.[20]

In understanding the reality of miracles, the Christian sees them not as 'a suspension of nature', as if God acted arbitrarily on such occasions, but as evidence that God can and does act with new and surprising means. It is not only the novelty of surprise, but of the greatness of God's power. 'Is anything too hard for Yahweh?' was God's reply to Sarah's laugh at the time of motherhood (Gen. 18:14). What is impossible in human life is possible with God. So we may see miracles as signs of good things to come, when God will make all things new, when sin shall be no more. Then we shall see that there are potentials in creation that have been inhibited by evil, which will then be released. God, then, does not work against 'nature', but He will finally release it from its bondage to decay and fulfil its fullness of promise.

THE GOODNESS OF THE CREATOR'S PROVIDENCE

1. The Good Creation

> The world is charged with the grandeur of God.
> It will flame out, like shining from shook foil;
> It gathers to a greatness, like the ooze of oil
> Crushed. Why do men then not reck his rod?
> Generations have trod, have trod, have trod;
> And all is seared with trade; bleared, smeared with toil;
> And wears man's smudge and shares man's smell:
>   the soil
> Is bare now, nor can foot feel, being shod.
>
> And for all this, nature is never spent;
> There lives the dearest freshness deep down things;
> And though the last lights off the black West went
> Oh, morning, at the brown brink eastward, springs—
> Because the Holy Ghost over the bent
> World broods with warm breast and with ah! bright
>   wings.

Gerard Manley Hopkins
God's Grandeur[21]

This poetic sense that in the created world 'there lives the dearest freshness deep down things', reflects on the goodness of God's creation. In spite of man's exploitation of the earth, beyond the stark bareness of the eroded soil, beyond even the more ominous 'smell' impregnated with man's evil presence, creation still holds the heart of things in freshness. Miracles are one way in which God's providence is manifest, but the deep beauty of the world is another way in which it is daily revealed. But the poet is aware that this is not a mechanical, deterministic or innate goodness, 'because the Holy Ghost over the bent world broods'. It is a bent world, it groans in travail, says the apostle (Rom. 8:22), yet the providential care of the Holy Spirit over it, as at the beginning of creation (Gen. 1:2), continues.

It should not surprise us that nature should be so venerated by many as a source of spiritual uplift and romantic delight. Without awareness of God, the worship of Nature is understandable, as evidence of a deep sense of resonance in man to its beauty. What sights, smells, sounds, touches and tastes fill our being with delight: the naturalness of a butterfly, the silhouette of individual trees, the grandeur of alpine ranges, the daily horizon of sky and sea; the smell of new-mown hay, the fragrance of a rose, the scent of wet earth after rain; the sound of the sea, the babble of a brook, the call of a bird; the texture of a leaf, the feel of wood, the sponginess of moss; the crispness of an apple, the lingering flavour of a strawberry, the taste of spring water. Yet we make idols of creaturely things unless we see the handiwork and sustaining providence of the Creator in all these delights. For none of them is invested with self-existence. God sustains them all.

Some theologians speak loosely of God's providence as continuous creation (*creatio continua*). Karl Heim even says: 'We may say with justice that the universe, as it now appears, is created each instant out of nothing, just as in the first day of creation.'[22] To take this seriously would be to conceive of the world as perpetually falling into nothingness, and constantly being called back into existence by fresh acts of creation. In contrast, the Scriptures speak of the stability and actuality of the original creation:

Of old Thou didst lay the foundation of the earth.
(Ps. 102:25)

Will you question me about my children,
or command me concerning the work of my hands?
I made the earth,
and created man upon it;
it was my hands that stretched out the heavens,
and I commanded all their host.   (Isa. 45:11–12)

Yea, the world is established; it shall never be moved.
(Ps. 93:1)

Likewise in the New Testament, several times the phrase is reiterated: 'From the beginning of the creation' (Matt. 19:4, 8; Mark 10:6; Heb. 1:10; 2 Pet. 3:4). There is profound consistency in the biblical affirmations that there is no doctrine of continuous creation. As the theologian Charles Hodge argued succinctly a century ago, there are five reasons why there is no biblical doctrine of continuous creation:

(1) It destroys all continuity of existence.
(2) It effectually removes all evidence of the existence of an objective external world.
(3) It denies the existence of secondary causes, for God is sole agent.
(4) There can be no responsibility and no sin.
(5) It merges as a system of thought into pantheism.[23]

What providence means, therefore, is that the Creator sustains and rules over what He has already brought into being in the initial creation. This emphasis Calvin saw so clearly:

> That the providence of God, as it is taught in Scripture, is opposed to fortune and fortuitous accidents. . . . Not a sparrow of the least value falls to the ground without the will of the Father (Matt. 10:29). Certainly, if the flight of birds be directed by the unerring counsel of God, we must be constrained to confess with the prophet that, though 'He dwelleth on high', yet 'He humbleth Himself to behold the things which are in heaven and in earth' (Ps. 113:5, 6). [Thus Calvin adds] We admit not the term *fate*. . . . *Fortune* and *chance* are words of the heathen, with the signification of which the minds of the pious ought not to be occupied.[24]

Creation, as we have seen, is an open system, open ultimately to the goodness and sovereignty of God. It is therefore a view incompatible either with Fate, as Calvin recognised, or with chance, as Jacques Monod the biologist has argued in his popular book *Chance and Necessity*[25] (see Appendix B for a discussion of this book). For the goodness of the world cannot be contained within a closed system.

It is commonly overlooked that while the problem of evil in providence is a problem for the believer in a good and sovereign God, the problem of good in the world challenges the non-believer. From whence comes good if not from God? The problem may be stated as follows:

> The world is a complex of closed systems (physical, chemical, biological), each self-contained, but interacted upon

by the others. For there is no final cause, no ultimate purpose, merely the cyclical.

Man, however, experiences 'the Good', the Tao, some ultimate, indefinable but real awareness of quality to life.

As 'the Good' is not deducible from, nor the product of, those self-contained material systems, since it is the naturalistic fallacy to confuse facts with values, the source of good must lie outside these physical systems.

Therefore, the world as a system of self-contained interactions is not the totality of reality, for one reality must be added, namely 'the Good'. What then is this ultimate reality that encloses 'the Good'?[26]

A common way to deal with this issue is to refuse recognition of such an ultimate reality. Science, it may be argued, can never deal with the question 'why', because it leads to the infinite. This either forces all explanations to be incomplete, as when Pirsig talks about that having 'gumption' (see p. 43), or else reality is sealed off, as Monod does, by the assumption that all living things have innate desires to live. Theodicy, that is, the justification of the ways of a good God to men in a world of evil, is thus essentially a Christian problem. But the origin and nature of good is a real problem for the non-believer if all of life merely originated from the nastiness of the material world, where cancer cells, liver flukes, killer whales, floods, hurricanes and earthquakes are all part of nature.

2. *The Sustenance and Rule of the Creator*

The emphasis we have made that creation is an open system allows for the reality of good, for as the Psalmist declares: 'O taste and see that the Lord is good!' (Ps. 34:8). Or as Jesus said, 'No one is good but God alone' (Mk. 10:18). Creation, too, is an open system, because there can be no self-containment within it. Even the enchanting world of 'coinherence' that Charles Williams celebrates, as a system of interdependent entities, could possibly be misinterpreted to give the impression that this principle is itself innate to nature.[27] At bottom, all assumptions about substances as things in themselves, that is, as deifying creatures, display the Greek influence of investing creatures with self-existence. This is not the case in the world of the Bible. Instead, the Scriptures emphasize total dependence upon God:

> For of Him, and through Him, and unto Him are all things.   (Rom. 11:36)

> He is before all things . . . for in Him all things were created. . . . All things were created through Him and for Him.   (Col. 1:16, 17)

> Thou art the Lord, Thou alone; Thou hast made the heaven, the heaven of heavens, with all their host, the earth and all that is on it, the seas and all that is in them; and Thou preservest all of them.   (Neh. 9:6)

> Thou openest Thy hand, Thou satisfiest the desire of every living thing.   (Ps. 145:16)

Psalm 104 bears marvellous testimony to the sustenance of the Creator. The Psalmist concludes: 'These all look to Thee, to give them their food in due season' (Ps. 104:27). Such was the pledge of the covenant God made with creation, and renewed with Noah: 'While the earth remains, seedtime and harvest, cold and heat, summer and winter, day and night, shall not cease' (Gen. 8:22). Daily, then, we are reminded in the rhythms of life, of the seasons, of the faithful providence of God.

Traditionally, theologians have distinguished between the general providence of God in all creation, and the special providence of God in history. God not only provides for the birds, the fish, and all the realities of our ecosystems. He also sustains each thing in its uniqueness. The 'is-ness' of each object is sustained by God, who is the 'I am that I am'. Without God, such aesthetic sense of fitness, of uniqueness—of every blade of grass, every hair upon our head—would be frightening.[28] The burning bush was not consumed because with that vision Moses heard the voice of Yahweh, the God of the covenant, who declared 'I am that I am'. If, then, God sustains the uniqueness of all things, within the interdependence of creation, how much more, said Jesus, we are worth. 'Fear not, therefore; you are of more value than many sparrows. So everyone who acknowledges me before men, I also will acknowledge before my Father who is in heaven' (Matt. 10:31, 32).

When we speak of the rule of God in providence, we are expressing even more specifically the action of God in the world. God's rule, however, is incomprehensible, acknowledges the Psalmist:

> Thy way was through the sea,
> Thy path through the deep waters;
> Yet Thy footprints were unseen.   (Ps. 77:19)

Likewise the apostle exclaims:

> O the depth of the riches and wisdom and knowledge of God! How unsearchable are His judgments and how inscrutable His ways! For who has known the mind of the Lord, or who has been His counsellor?
>   (Rom. 11:33, 34)

Because God's rule is incomprehensible, it is also invincible. Some twenty-five of the psalms, both in the theophanies of storm and in the so-called enthronement psalms of praise, celebrate the power of God's rule.

> Mightier than the thunders of many waters,
> mightier than the waves on the sea,
> the Lord on high is mighty!   (Ps. 93:4)

> The Lord reigns; let the peoples tremble!
> He sits enthroned upon the cherubim; let the earth
>   quake!   (Ps. 99:1)

As creation came into being by the Word of God, so He continues to rule by His Word. Thus in Psalm 29 we are reminded, 'The voice of the Lord is upon the waters', 'the voice of the Lord breaks the cedars' of Lebanon. Then, like a gathering dust storm, 'the voice of the Lord shakes the wilderness'.

The Psalmists celebrate the everlasting rule of God: 'The Lord will reign for ever' (Ps. 146:10). He is, says the apostle, the King, eternal (1 Tim. 6:15).

By these affirmations, men of faith celebrated that man

had a meaningful existence. Just as friendship implies more than mere proximity, so creation implied more than the ubiquity of God. God's people were aware of His friendship, His *chesed*, a marvellous word that indicates His lovingkindness, His steadfast love, His faithfulness,[29] because of the covenant He has made with the earth in creation, and with man in redemption. The prophet Jeremiah perceived that God's name is *chesed*, and that this is written in the heavens.

> If I have not established my covenant with day and night and the ordinances of heaven and earth, then I will reject the descendants of Jacob and David my servant.
> (Jer. 33:25, 26)

But God has not done so. For Jeremiah also reports:

> Thus says the Lord, who gives the sun for light by day and the fixed order of the moon and the stars for light by night, who stirs up the sea, so that its waves roar—the Lord of hosts is His name. 'If this fixed order departs from before me,' says the Lord, 'then shall the descendants of Israel cease from being a nation before me for ever.'
> (Jer. 31:35, 36)

3. The Creator-Redeemer

The providence of God is obscured in the world, however, by evil. As the poet reminds us, it is a 'bent world'. The apostle speaks of the 'groaning' of the entire creation; man too groans inwardly for the adoption of sonship, as cosmic orphans (Rom. 8:22, 23). We cannot begin to decipher what this groaning means, for it is by definition inarticulate pain. Could it mean the frustration of the language of creation, created by the Word of God, yet whose 'voice is not heard' (Ps. 19:3), not intelligible to man, who is intended by God to be the priest of creation? Does it include the insensibility of man to the suffering of animals, so that even a theologian like Cardinal Newman could assert: 'Man owed duties to his fellow men; but he owed no duties to the lower animals'?[30] Could it point, argues Karl Heim, to the law of polarity that enthralls all reality with profound cosmic discordance?[31] Could it be that creation groans until participatory knowledge covers the earth, so that not only is matter known mechanically, but life-forms are known 'biologically', man is known 'relationally' and the Creator is known 'creaturely' by man?

The ancients called the understanding that is appropriate and adequate to the thing to be known *adaequatio*.[32] There is thus a hidden metaphysic in the exercise of understanding. Clearly, we can have no comprehension of the Creator, of standing over Him; we can only have understanding of 'standing under' Him in an appropriate, 'adequate' stance. That is why Augustine could say, *Crede ut intelligas*, 'Believe that you may understand'. If I lack faith appropriate to the relationship, no degree of objectivity will save me from missing the point. So Jesus could say of the hearers of His parables: 'seeing they do not see, and hearing they do not hear, nor do they understand' (Matt. 13:13). How then do I know the provident God, so that I see the wonders of His ways in creation?

Today in the church there is little understanding of the Creator. The doctrine of providence is not often discussed. For two events have affected modern man in the last century. First, the rise of Darwinism in the period 1859–70 dealt a seemingly mortal blow to Providence. In place of the rule of God in creation which Paley and others had seen, the real cause of things now seemed random, impersonal and mechanical. Yet a remarkable recovery of the idea of Providence developed from 1870 to 1930 with the new ideas of 'cosmic progress', so that evolution was now harnessed to a secularised variant of Providence—the idea of progress. Post-Darwin theology, argues Langdon Gilkey, became 'Providence centred'.[33] Then came the Depression, the Second World War and the holocaust, and Providence was once more in demise, apparently collapsed by Auschwitz, the silence—yes, say some theologians, even 'the death of God'. The violent irruption of evil, the nihilism of many spirits, the loss of faith in a technological society, the sheer confusion of lifestyles, the sense of autonomous man— all undermine the deep sense of the providence of God expressed in the Bible. Can the language of faith restore to us the reality of God as Creator in the closing decades of the twentieth century?

Like the exiles of faith who experience the wilderness that Isaiah lived in, can we anticipate that participation in the knowledge of God of which he speaks, when 'the earth shall be full of the knowledge of the Lord, as the waters cover the sea'? For today, like Matthew Arnold, we mourn that retreat of the 'Sea of Faith' in its

> melancholy, long, withdrawing roar, . . .
> down the vast edges drear
> and naked shingles of the world.

Arnold's only compensation was human love.

> Ah, love, let us be true
> To one another! For the world which seems
> To lie before us like a land of dreams,
> So various, so beautiful, so new,
> Hath really neither joy, nor love, nor light,
> Nor certitude, nor peace, nor help for pain;
> And we are here as on a darkling plain
> Swept with confused alarms of struggle and flight,
> Where ignorant armies clash by night.
>   Matthew Arnold—*Dover Beach*

Before the exile, the Israelites, as we have seen, had a rich treasury of psalms that breathed the reality of creation faith. But significantly Isaiah added to that faith in 'the Book of Comfort' a strong affirmation concerning the Creator-Redeemer (Isa. 40–55).[34] Here, as emphatically as anywhere in the Bible, the prophet assures us that Creator and Redeemer are one. There may be the collapse of old traditions, faulty theologies, incongruities between faith and substance, but Israel is encouraged to fear not, for the Creator-Redeemer is still present in the world, and therefore still with His people.

> But now thus says the Lord, He who created you, O
>   Israel,
> He who formed you, O Jacob:
> 'Fear not, for I have redeemed you;
> I have called you by name, you are mine.

When you pass through the waters I will be with you;
and through the rivers, they shall not overwhelm you;
when you walk through fire you shall not be burned,
and the flame shall not consume you.
For I am the Lord, your God.'   (Isa. 43:1–3)

Time and again in these lyrical songs of hope, the prophet
reminds the people that the Creator who made all things is
also their personal Redeemer. 'I, I am the Lord, and besides
me there is no saviour' (Isa. 43:11).

This does not mean that Israel, or we ourselves, can view
the providence of God in such a way as to give us an advantage,
whether we think of the calm waters of the North Sea during
the Dunkirk exodus in 1940, or any concept of a favoured
nation. Amos makes that clear in his closing chapter.

The Lord, God of hosts,
He who touches the earth and it melts,
     and all who dwell in it mourn,
and all of it rises like the Nile,
     and sinks again, like the Nile of Egypt;
. . . Did I not bring up Israel from the land of Egypt,
and the Philistines from Caphtor
and the Syrians from Kir?   (Amos 9:5, 7b)

Yes, He is the Creator, but He is also the Lord of history, of
the events behind the Exodus. But there can be no national
pride about that, for He was also the sovereign Lord behind
the migrations of the Philistines and of the Syrians. We must
understand the providence of God as Creator-Redeemer in
terms other than self-centredness, pride and nationalism.

Jesus Christ is the embodiment of the providence of God.
He is the lamb promised to Abraham, 'the lamb slain from
before the foundation of the world'. A decisive event was
needed, for another decisive event had already taken place.
Man, created in the image of God to relate to God the Creator
with unique dignity, had 'fallen', that is, fallen out of line with
the development willed by God for man, and through man for
the whole earth. As representative man, God came, incarnate,
both to bear the judgment of His own holiness and to be the
Judge. It is this dual role which Christ undertook, as Judge

and judged, as the suffering God and victorious Redeemer. Jesus Christ is the embodiment of the faithfulness of God, for He came, says the evangelist, 'full of grace and truth' (John 1:14), that is, the grace of steadfast love, and the truth that is loyal to reality as God has purposed. His Incarnation is the embodiment and fulfilment of the faithfulness of the provident Creator.

Thus the providence of God is essentially a Christian doctrine. For it is 'in Christ' that we can develop a sense of dependent faith. Then we can 'consider the lilies of the field, how they grow' (Matt. 6:28). Beneath the night stars Jesus daily prayed, so that His disciples begged Him to teach them how to pray, in dependence on the Father. In the wilderness Jesus was tempted to be a magician, to use miracles like turning stones into bread. Dostoyevsky in the passage on the Grand Inquisitor has taught us superbly that in the three temptations Jesus showed us that divine miracles are not magic, that divine mystery transcends understanding but not conscience, and that divine authority is not tyranny but love.[35] This then is the bridge between the two worlds Sammy Mountjoy never experienced, the bridge between the Creator and the creature: Jesus Christ, in whom all things hang together. The apostle says, 'I live by the faith of the Son of God' (Gal. 2:20). We too can live on the basis of Christ's relationship between heaven and earth, between God and man, between the Creator-Redeemer and our need.

4. Come, Creator Spirit

We have titled this book 'I Believe in the Creator', yet we cannot define the Creator. There are many things we may say about Him, as we have seen. If by 'defining God' we mean comprehending Him, clearly this is an impossibility. This was the mistake made by M. Laplace, who went to present a copy of his treatise on astronomy to Napoleon. The latter said to him, 'M. Laplace, they tell me you have written this large book on the system of the universe, and have never even mentioned its Creator.' Laplace drew himself up proudly, and replied: 'Sire, I had no need of any such hypothesis.' Of course he did not, if he was thinking only scientifically. Charles Darwin did not need God either in his hypothesis of natural selection, nor did Feuerbach in his psychological theory of God as wish-idea. The reality of the Creator is of a higher order of knowledge than that of science; He must be if He created our minds.

The conviction of God the Creator, says the apostle, is like the light that illuminated creation at its beginning: 'For it is the God who said, "Let light shine out of darkness", who has shone in our hearts to give the light of the knowledge of the glory of God in the face of Christ. But we have this treasure in earthen vessels, to show that the transcendent power belongs to God and not to us' (2 Cor. 4:6–7). In Jesus of Nazareth, the light of God has shone supremely and fully into the life of humanity. The Word of God that created all things penetrated into the being of a Man who was completely receptive to it, and who is the Word of God. In Jesus Christ, 'the Word became flesh and dwelt among us'.

We think also of chosen spirits, men like Francis of Assisi and women like Mother Teresa, whose awareness of the Creator-Redeemer has been so profound. We therefore cry, 'Come, Creator Spirit' and fill our hearts with a deeper understanding of Your presence, for the renewal of our worship and witness. For we live on this side of Pentecost, beyond the death of Good Friday, in the risen life of Easter morning. That unique relationship within the triune God—Father, Son and Holy Spirit—is now, in the Son, made available to man.

'Come, Creator Spirit' is a prayer that our spirits may be truly creative, truly of the Creator. As such, creativity is cooperation with God, seeking to bring order out of chaos, discovering the harmony of the universe, being open to the will of God, who is 'able to do exceeding abundantly above all that we ask or think'. It is a prayer to the Holy Spirit to let man be man, entirely dependent upon the Creator, and help us see God as God in all His Godness. Yet this prayer also transcends all attempts to seek the gift of the Holy Spirit for selfish gain. Rather, it is a prayer to see that God is not limited in His acts by the weaknesses and foolishness of man.[36] It is life lived fully in this confidence in God. As the Spirit brooded over that *tōhū bōhū*, formless and void, so too He broods 'with warm breast and ah! bright wings' over man's contemporary nihilism. We pray, therefore, for the Holy Spirit, in open surrender to the absolute creativity of the Creator.

It behooved God to be Man in Jesus Christ, to give to man by His Holy Spirit the power to be an appropriate creation—sons of God. As at the Creation, God has now done a new thing by the Incarnation, the beginning of the New Creation. As a result the Holy Spirit not only gives being to all created things, but He comes to man as the energy of Christ's life, death and Risen Power. Therefore, 'if anyone be in Christ, he is a new creation'. With the coming of the Holy Spirit at Pentecost, a cosmic event has taken place that can break the spell of man's sinful tendency to destroy, to create chaos, to introduce nothingness. That is why we can have no understanding of the Creator unless the light of the Holy Spirit that first shone at creation also shines in our broken and empty hearts.

NOTES

1   William Golding, *Free Fall*, London, Faber & Faber, 1959, pp. 8–9.
2   Ibid., pp. 202, 210–213, 226.
3   Ibid., pp. 250, 252.
4   Basil Willey, *The Eighteenth Century Background*, London, Chatto & Windus, 1974.
5   Quoted by William Leiss, *The Domination of Nature*, New York, G. Braziller, 1972, p. 49.
6   Francis Bacon, *The New Organon*, in *The Works of Francis Bacon*, edit. J. Spedding *et al.*, vol. IV, pp. 247–248. See also Laurence Berns, 'Francis Bacon and the Conquest of Nature', *Interpretation*, vol. 2, 1978, pp. 1–26.
7   Antony Flew and D. M. MacKinnon, 'Creation' in *New Essays in Philosophical Theology*, edit. Antony Flew and Alasdair MacIntyre, London, S.C.M., 1955, pp. 170–186.
8   Ibid., p. 184.
9   Jürgen Moltmann, 'Creation and Redemption', in *Creation, Christ and Culture*, edit. Richard W. A. McKinney, Edinburgh, T. & T. Clark, 1976, p. 124.
10 Quoted in the *Washington Post*, Feb. 8th, 1978.

11   Blaise Pascal, *Pensées*, edit. Louis Lafuma, New York, John Dent, 1960.

12   Peter I. Berger, *A Rumour of Angels*, Garden City, N.Y., Doubleday, 1969.

13   Quoted in Helen Gardner (edit.), *The Faber Book of Religious Verse*, London, Faber & Faber, 1972, pp. 146–147.

14   See the article by Richard H. Bube, 'The failure of the God-of-the-Gaps', in *Horizons of Science*, edit. Carl F. H. Henry, New York, Harper & Row, 1978, pp. 21–35.

15   J. P. Ross, 'Some Notes on Miracle in the Old Testament', in *Miracles*, edit. C. F. D. Moule, London, A. R. Mowbray, 1965, pp. 43–60.

16   C. F. D. Moule, 'The Vocabulary of Miracle', ibid., pp. 235–238.

17   C. S. Lewis, *Miracles*, New York, Macmillan, 1947, pp. 159–196.

18   Robert Dick Wilson, 'Understanding the Sun Stood Still', in *Classical Evangelical Essays in Old Testament Interpretation*, edit. Walter C. Kaiser, Jr., Grand Rapids, Baker, 1972, pp. 61–65.

19   M. Hesse, 'Miracles and the Laws of Nature', *Miracles*, edit. C. F. D. Moule, op. cit., pp. 33–42.

20   Quoted by A. M. Ramsey, *Christianity and the Supernatural*, London, Athlone Press, 1963, p. 5.

21   Quoted from Helen Gardner, *The Faber Book of Religious Verse*, London, Faber & Faber, 1972, p. 288.

22   Quoted by G. C. Berkouwer, *The Providence of God*, Grand Rapids, Eerdmans, 1974, p. 60.

23   Charles Hodge, *Systematic Theology*, New York, Charles Scribner's Sons, 1901, vol. 1, pp. 579–580.

24   John Calvin, *A Compendium of the Institutes of the Christian Religion*, edit. Hugh T. Kerr, Philadelphia, The Westminster Press, 1939, pp. 33–34.

25   Jacques Monod, *Chance and Necessity*, New York, Vintage, 1971.

26   Bernard L. Ramm, *A Christian Appeal to Reason*, Waco, Texas, Word Books, 1972.

27   Charles Williams was inspired in his ideas on coinherence by G. L. Prestige, *God in Patristic Theology*, London, S.P.C.K., 1952.

28   Madeleine L'Engle, *A Circle of Quiet*, New York, Farrar, Straus, and Giroux, 1972, p. 8.

29   Nelson Glueck, *Hesed in the Bible*, Cincinnati, Hebrew Union College Press, 1967.

30   Quoted by John Passmore, 'The Treatment of Animals', *Journal of the History of Ideas*, XXXVI, 1974, p. 203.

31   Karl Heim, *The World, its Creation and Consummation*, trans. Robert Smith, Edinburgh, Oliver & Boyd, 1962, pp. 101–118.

32   E. F. Schumacher, *A Guide for the Perplexed*, New York, Harper Colophon Books, Harper & Row, 1977, p. 39.

33   Langdon B. Gilkey, 'The Concept of Providence in Contemporary Theology', *Journal of Religion*, XLIII, 1963, pp. 171–192.

34 Carroll Stuhlmueller, *Creative Redemption in Deutero-Isaiah, Analecta Biblica*, Rome, Biblical Institute Press, 1970.
35 Fyodor Dostoyevsky, *The Brothers Karamazov*, London, Penguin Books, 1958, vol. 1, pp. 295–305.
36 T. F. Torrance, *Theology in Reconstruction*, Grand Rapids, Eerdmans, 1965, pp. 240–259.

CHAPTER FIVE

This Is My Father's World

Many of our contemporary writers and dramatists are concerned about the unreality of language. In his films, Ingmar Bergman likens the silence of God and the loss of human communication to the cold stillness of the Icelandic landscape.[1] George Steiner, as a craftsman of the word, is concerned like many others in his profession about 'the retreat of the word' as a vehicle of communication.[2] Marshall McLuhan has differentiated between 'hot' and 'cool' vehicles, which are more or less participatory forms of communication.[3] Samuel Beckett, as we have seen in *Waiting for Godot* and other of his plays and novels, is deeply concerned about this loss of language, with the resulting depersonalisation of man. Iris Murdoch, the novelist, too, has said: 'We can no longer take language for granted as a medium of communication. Its transparency is gone. We are like people who for a long time looked out of the window, without noticing the glass—and then one day we began to notice this too.'[4] Our window onto reality is language, but how clear is that window? That is the issue. Our world-views are like frost on the windowpane: they distort, obscure and fog our understanding of reality (see Appendix C).

THE LIVING WORD

We are living in a time of verbal explosion. We are deluged by words, in bulletins, in data collecting, in advertisements, in books, in the promises and slogans of politics, in the mishmash of news. There is talk but not deeds, information but not in-

120

sight, promises but not fulfilment, words not events. For the words of unreal people mean nothing; they are what Beckett calls 'quaqua'.

Iris Murdoch ponders this issue in her book *The Word Child*. It is the life story of Hilary, an alienated, parentless child, fostered in a violent world, who narrates curiously over the days of his creation, the drama of his life. He discovers the world of scholarship, and in this way he saves himself. 'I discovered words and words were my salvation. I was not, except in some very broken-down sense of that ambiguous term, a love child. I was a word child.'[5] He used violence as a kind of magic in a loveless world. We need, however, something to stand on, something that does not yield. 'When I understood grammatical structure I understood something which I respected and which did not yield.' His adoration of words took him to Oxford, where he became eventually a Fellow of a college, until disaster overtook him in a deliberate car crash that killed his lover. The resignation that followed marked the beginning of the rake's progress into alienation.

At the end of the novel, Hilary admits he 'had been turned silently out into the desert; there was no one now to whom I could speak at all of the things which were hourly and minutely devouring my heart'. He goes into the church where T. S. Eliot had been a church warden, St. Stephen's in London. He looks at Eliot's memorial tablet and asks: 'How is it now with you, old friend, the intolerable wrestle with words and meanings being over?' Yet there lingers in Hilary's heart 'a lively gratitude for words, even for words whose sense I could scarcely understand',[6] for clearly he cannot relate to *people*—he is a word child, not a love child. The irony of his life is that even though he reads many languages, he fails to communicate—on holiday abroad, in a civil service job that is only bureaucratic, and with people who seek to love him when he cannot return their love. He 'was unfit for ordinary life'.

What Iris Murdoch cannot communicate—for she is a self-confessed atheist—is that the source of all language is the Word of God. In her lecture, 'The Sovereignty of Good over other Concepts', she wrestles with the issue we have already discussed (see p. 108), the source and character of good. 'But', she says, 'I can see no evidence to suggest that human life is not something self-contained.'[7] Yet self-containment is the death of man, and of his language. As Jacques Ellul has argued, however, this does not mean human language is fated to talk only about God and to be a preaching instrument! That would be absurd.[8] It was this approach that turned Hilary off as a boy to 'low evangelical' Christianity, which was 'over-lit, over simple, covertly threatening'. What it does mean is that language only creates and communicates at the level at which it is rooted. It cannot say or give more than the source it came from. Hilary was only a word child, not a love child, so he could not communicate love. Unreal language is only the communication of unreal people. People are unreal if their environment is unreal. The world is unreal if God is unreal. Ultimately, if there is no Creator who speaks all creation into being, there is no being, no word.

We have already stressed the central importance of the biblical revelation of creation by the Word of God. We need not apologise for taking divine revelation so seriously. If God really is God, the Creator and sustainer of all things visible and invisible, and the world is as intelligible as science celebrates it to be, then God is the Source, too, of all rational order, of all communication. If God really is God, the Creator of us all, then He is not only intelligible and communicable, but He actively reveals Himself in speech and cognition. Built into Hebrew thought and language is the word *davar*, which implies the reality of creation as word-object-event and the unity of command and object, word and thing, that lies behind all reality, the God who creates as He speaks. The irony of 1 Kings 18 is that idols do not speak, they do not create (cf. Isa. 40:19–20; 44:9–20). Their silence is that of non-existence. 'O Baal, answer us! But there was no voice, and no one answered' (1 Kings 18:26).

So when words are not related to those who speak ('Remember from whom you have learned these things'), and things are not integrated to the inner coherence of reality, they fall apart. John Donne voiced this in 1610 when he saw the Ptolemaic universe being destroyed, to be replaced in that same century with the Newtonian world-view (see Appendix C). W. B. Yeats rephrased the same alarm when he saw, with the First World War, the collapse of the neat universe:

Things fall apart; the centre cannot hold;
Mere anarchy is loosed upon the world,
The blood-dimmed tide is loosed, and everywhere
The ceremony of innocence is drowned;
The best lack all conviction, while the worst
Are full of passionate intensity.

W. B. Yeats—*The Second Coming*[9]

But the Bible shows far more profoundly that when language is not based on creation, all communication is blocked in the silence of God and the babble of men.

Significantly the first time *davar* is used in the book of Genesis (Gen. 11:1), it is already blocked speech, all humanity being already a conglomerate of the closed speech of *Homo faber*. Mankind had then one language (*sapha*), whose etymology indicates a limit or frontier already imposed on the closed world inhabited by rebellious man. The previous chapters trace the development of blocked communication against the reality of creation in chapter one. After the Fall, Adam and Eve talk but there is no meaningful dialogue, only monologue. Eve has forgotten the first person plural intrinsic in *Adam* when she exclaims, 'I have gotten a man'—not 'we' (4:1)—and 'God has appointed for me another child'—not 'us' (4:25). She has forgotten the language of Paradise where she first spoke to the serpent in innocence: 'We may eat of the fruit of the garden' (3:2). Human communication and therefore community is fractured because of doubt concerning the Word of the Creator: 'Has God said?' (3:1).

The breakdown of this vertical dimension of the Word leads only to dissolution between Creator and creature. Adam and Eve 'hid themselves'. Cain lied over the slaying of his brother: 'I do not know'. The voice of Lamech is the voice of vengeance and murder (4:23). In the silence of God that follows, there can only be judgment (6:13). Yet He speaks to faithful Noah (7:1; 8:15), through whom blessing is promised (9:1); for God remains true to His mercy, in spite of the faithlessness of man. Juxtaposed with God's creation (1:1) there is man's attempt to set up his own kingdom—Babel (10:10)—based on the materials he *has* (11:3b), not what he should enjoy under the Creator. His 'one language' is the speech of pos-

sessiveness, of pride in manufacturing out of created realities—
clay and bitumen. The building of his tower, 'reaching into
heaven', was like Western man's enterprise in building 'world-
views', a self-existing universe of human achievement. Just as
Babel was destroyed in its own confusion, so we live without
any coherent world-view, in the babel of pluralism. When man
no longer heard the Word of God, then he no longer heard
his neighbour, for his words were for himself, to himself, about
himself. How right Miss Murdoch is when she says, 'We can no
longer take language for granted'.

Today, as in the days of Samuel, 'the word of the Lord
was rare . . . ; there was no frequent vision' (1 Sam. 3:1). Yet
Hannah, though 'her voice was not heard', was given a child,
Samuel, whose name means, 'I have asked him of the Lord'.
And Samuel listened to God's voice: 'Speak, Lord, for Thy
servant hears' (3:9). That was why he became a prophet, to
proclaim the Word of the Lord. Juxtaposed with Samuel was
Saul, who in his disobedience, when he 'enquired of the Lord,
the Lord did not answer him' (28:6). Incongruously, Saul, the
prophet-without-a-word, received no word from the Lord
(14:37), and eventually he sought magically, as our generation
seeks technically—both inside and outside the church—to hear
a word from the Lord (28:11). As André Neher has shown in
his suggestive study *The Exile of the Word*,[10] the whole prophetic
ministry of the Old Testament is set within the context of the
Silence of God, over against the chatter of men, when man
forgets the reality of the creative Word.

In contrast, there are the true prophets who depend upon
'every word that proceedeth out of the mouth of God'. There
is Abraham, who confesses: 'I have taken upon myself to speak
to the Lord, I who am but dust and ashes' (Gen. 18:27). As
dust, he is non-being, but the word—God's word—becomes a
verb that actualises so that his life becomes the speech of God.
There is Moses, who confesses, 'O Lord, I am not eloquent
. . . slow of speech and of tongue. . . .' Then the Lord said to
him, 'Who has made man's mouth? . . . Is it not I, the Lord?
Now therefore go, and I will be with your mouth and teach
you what you shall speak' (Exod. 4:10, 11, 12). There is Isaiah,
who before the holiness of God, the Wholly Other, cries out:
'Woe is me! For I am lost; for I am a man of unclean lips, and

I dwell in the midst of a people of unclean lips. . . . And He touched my mouth, and said: "Behold this has touched your lips; your guilt is taken away, and your sin forgiven." And I heard the voice of the Lord saying, "Whom shall I send, and who will go for us?" Then I said, "Here am I! Send me" ' (Isa. 6:5, 7, 8). Likewise, Jeremiah said: 'Ah, Lord God! Behold, I do not know how to speak,' and the reply came: 'Whatever I command you you shall speak. . . . Behold, I have put my words in your mouth' (Jer. 1:6, 7, 9). With such endowment of speech, divine speech, things become events, and events are the creative power of God (cf. Gen. 15:1).

JESUS CHRIST, SOURCE OF ALL GOOD

It is against this setting that the writer to the Hebrews declares:

> In many and various ways God spoke of old to our fathers by the prophets; but in these last days He has spoken to us by a Son, whom He appointed the heir of all things, through whom also He created the world. He reflects the glory of God and bears the very stamp of His nature, upholding the universe by His word of power.
>
> (Heb. 1:1–3)

The variety and fullness of the prophetic word was given, says the writer, yet it remained fragmentary. Now the Incarnation has ushered in a new era, that of the revelation of Jesus Christ, the instrumental cause of creation. Through Christ God made the worlds—so that, however our understanding of them may differ with the ages, He is the same God. Moreover, the Creator is also the provident God, for He continues to uphold 'all things by His word of power'.

To link this reality to our world, we remember again the Christmas season when:

> . . . girls in slacks remember Dad,
> And oafish louts remember Mum,
> And sleepless children's hearts are glad,

And Christmas morning bells say 'Come!'
Even to the shining ones who dwell
Safe in the Dorchester Hotel.

And is it true? And is it true,
This most tremendous tale of all,
Seen in a stained-glass window hue,
A Baby in an ox's stall?
The Maker of the stars and sea
Became a Child on earth for me?

Christmas—John Betjeman[11]

We can forget this 'most tremendous tale' in the 'tissued frip-
peries' and 'the sweet and silly Christmas things', 'so kindly
meant'. We can also drown the truth in scholars' ink, and merely
devote our attention to how the early church first conceived of
the christology of Jesus as Co-Creator, and so avoid the issue
of how we ourselves are to face up to this overwhelming assertion. What we cannot avoid is that, if He is the Creator, then
it is only by the exercise of creatureliness—that is, by exercising
our prerogative as image-bearers of God, in stewardship, in
relationship, in dependence upon His Word—that we can know
who He is. That is why the writer to the Hebrews speaks of
acceptance of such belief as being possible only by faith.

To the question, how is the world to be conceived as a
good world in spite of evil within it, the biblical answer is simply,
'in Christ'. The evidence that God loves the world, and cares
for mankind, is the Cross of Christ. There he has shown full
proof of His love, 'For God so loved the world that He gave
His only begotten Son . . .' (John 3:16). So much did He love
that He actually sacrificed His only Son, the Son who is absolute
in His standing before the Father. Unlike Hilary, we are not
merely 'word children'; we are love children, children of God.
That is how much God cares for His creation—much, much
more than any cosmic clockmaker or any Principle of Causality
could conceivably express. Consistent with the agency of creation in the Old Testament, the New Testament speaks of Christ
as the Word of God and the Wisdom of God, in whom, through
whom and by whom all things were made.

Just as we struggle amid the moulding influences of
various world-views, so did Judaism in the intertestamental

period. Even while Israel languished in exile in Babylon, Babylonian culture was still somewhat peripheral to Israelite faith. But after the third century B.C., when Alexander the Great had established his vast empire between Greece and India, the Jews found themselves saturated by Hellenism, both in the diaspora and in Jerusalem. The apocryphal literature of the intertestamental period bears much evidence of Hellenism polluting Hebrew faith with Platonism and Stoicism.[12] Just as there are many polemical slants to creation in the Old Testament, so the New Testament attacks the world-views of the Hellenistic and Hellenised Jewish cultures. It is against such views that the apostles set forth the Good News of Jesus Christ.

As we have seen, man's understanding of the origin of the world will reflect upon his hopes in that world. That is why cosmology reflects upon soteriology, or creation upon salvation. If the cosmological foundations are wrong, then the hopes and solutions offered are also false. Thus Greek abstractions about reality could offer only speculative remedies for man. The Greeks made much of *Sophia*, wisdom, as an absolute, for the mind was the glory of Greek life. The Jews made much of the *Torah*, for its liturgy was also glorified. When therefore the Word was also objectified and absolutised as an abstract principle, there was no defence against Greek culture. The equivalent of those abstract principles in our culture today is perhaps *Nature*, which again is an absolutised way of seeking to know reality. It is therefore the teaching of the New Testament that all the false ontologies of Torah, Sophia and Nature are destroyed by the advent of Jesus Christ.

1. The Word of God

In the New Testament, the agent of both creation and redemption is the Word of God. As we have seen, the consistent description of Scripture concerning the agency of creation is, as the church fathers described it, *creatio per verbum*, creation by the Word. Not only is this seen in the impressive emphasis of Genesis 1, but the Psalmist declares: 'By the Word of the Lord the heavens were made, and all their host by the breath of His mouth' (Ps. 33:6). The writer to the Hebrews speaks of 'upholding the universe by His Word of power' (Heb. 1:3b).

The apostle Peter calls to mind that 'by the Word of God, the heavens existed long ago, and an earth formed out of water' (2 Pet. 3:5b). These writers corroborate what the Psalmist had said:

> For ever, O Lord, Thy Word
>   is firmly fixed in the heavens.
> Thy faithfulness endures to all generations;
>   Thou hast established the earth, and it stands fast.
> By Thy appointment they stand this day;
>   for all things are Thy servants.   (Ps. 119:89–91)

The Jews had long been familiar with the realisation that the word was the mind and will of God. Now, says John in his prologue, 'the Word has become flesh.' That is to say, the divine meaning and purpose behind creation is now revealed in the life and ministry of Jesus Christ: the word is now the Word. Three important aspects of the Word are emphasised by John: the Word reveals a causative agency in reality that transcends any other understanding of creation; the Word indicates a special relationship, for the Word became flesh; and the Word is redemptive as the manifestation of a new covenant.

In Platonism, creation was understood as the analogy of the way in which man creates. The Platonists argued that as creation is still going on with man's creative activities, so God once created. It is typical humanistic distortion that God is such a projection of man. Man has an idea, and with this idea before him, the potter creates a vase. It gets broken, but new vases can be created because he still has the idea before him; so the idea is the power by which there *will* be vases. It is the ideas that are eternal. Whether God precedes the ideas or not, Plato is not clear. Philo, a Hellenised Jew (c. 30 B.C.–A.D. 40), adopted Platonism but argued as a Jew that God was the Creator of the ideas. So before the world began, God created in His own mind the ideal pattern for the world, according to which He later made the world. Like Plato, Philo believed the ideas *caused* the world's creation. This left Philo confused between the idea that God created the ideas, and the idea that the ideas were God and so were not created.[13] Just as some scholars previously thought Genesis 1 borrowed from ancient cosmologies and now we know it was clearly against them, so John's prologue was thought to be influenced by Hellenism and Philo, when careful reading of it clearly shows it is polemically against their views.

First of all, John states that the Word of God is not different from God: 'In the beginning was the Word, and the Word was with God, and the Word was God.' This tells us, first of all, that our geocentric view of life is not the ultimate explanation. There is also a theocentric basis for life, which as *fiat* creation is the ultimate meaning of all things. For 'all things were made through Him, and without Him was not anything made that was made' (John 1:3). This seeks to convey the trinitarian affirmation that the whole counsel of God, uttered by the Father, through the Holy Spirit, was accomplished in creation by the Son. God the Father (God in essence), through the Holy Spirit (God in exercise), has been manifested in God the Son (God in expression), to create (in origin) and to love (in continuance) the world. The Word then reveals a causative will and purpose for creation that transcends any human understanding, for it is the mind, will and essence of God in His creative activity.

Following closely the Genesis passage, where light is the first of God's acts, on the first day of creation, John speaks of the Word as the life that was the light of mankind.[14] As the world is the creation of the Word, it is possible for revelation to take place in the world, so that the Word is both the source of existence as life, and the source of revelation as light. Where there is light there is life. But the light is not all pervasive, for in 'the bent world' of its cosmic fall, there is darkness too, distortion and ignorance. There is the polarity of good and evil, as we have seen. Unlike Plato or Philo, John the Baptist bore witness to the true light of creation in Christ, not in false cosmogonies (John 1:6–8). For the real light was not a Platonic copy, it was God's light in Christ.

The darkness has not overcome the light, any more than chaos could overcome creation in Genesis 1:2. For God's sovereignty over the polarities of reality is very different from our own experience of them. We find that where there is more darkness, there is less light; more evil, less good; more hate, less love; more falsity, less truth. But with God, increasing darkness brings forth more light, as in the Cross. At the same time, the 'true' or 'real' light of God judges man, for it exposes his condition of darkness in the super-abounding light of God. So Paul tells the Romans that 'ever since the creation of the world, His invisible nature, namely, His eternal power and deity, has been clearly perceived in the things that have been made' (Rom. 1:20). Instead, the perversions of Roman society—Paul then goes on to describe them—only illustrate the darkness in which man has preferred to dwell. There is light that follows every man, as the longing of the devout Hindu for *Avatara* or the personal God, or the sense of the supreme god of the Igbo in West Africa, or the desires for Tao in Confucian life all testify. Yet, unaided, man is powerless to respond to the true light, for it is not innate in man to find that light, whether by the Stoics' natural reason or the mystics' strivings. For it is 'not of blood, nor of the will of the flesh, nor of the will of man, but of God' (John 1:13). A new birth, a new creation, is required to overcome such darkness—birth by the Word.[15]

Secondly, says John, the Word is indicative of a special relationship between man and the Creator. For 'the Word became flesh and dwelt among us'. *Fiat* creation has always implied a special relationship, a personal one, not like the Platonic, impersonal emanation of the divine. The ultimate reality is not man's discovery of the laws of nature, but the address of God to man. Man is created to be a being responsive to the commands of God, so that unlike the Greek and Cartesian definition of man, 'I think, therefore I am', the biblical description of man implies, 'I respond, therefore I am.' But because of man's darkness, John speaks of the rejection of the Word: 'He was in the world, and the world was made through Him, yet the world knew Him not. He came to His own, and His own received Him not.' But, adds the apostle, 'to all who received Him, who believed in His name, He gave power to become the children of God' (John 1:10–12).

It is possible for man to respond to the Word, for the Word became flesh. The Creator has entered the finitude of creaturely existence, Christ has become a man. Unlike the impersonal principle of *Maat* for the Egyptians, of *Logos* for the Greeks, of Physical Causation for secularists today, the secret of the universe is 'the Word made flesh', which men have seen, and heard, and handled (1 John 1:1–3). That is to say, the ultimate truth about creation is not discovered by the exercise of the intelligence, but by the submission of the will to God. The Christian faith in the Word is, therefore, not a philosophy but a personal relationship with God in Christ. It is given to those who believe 'in His name' (John 1:12), that is to say, in the attributes He reveals of Himself. As revealed to Moses, He is 'I am that I am', the one who causes to be, the Creator-Redeemer (cf. John 18:5; Rev. 1:17–18).

Thirdly, the Word is redemptive as the manifestation of a new covenant. 'No one has ever seen God,' says John[16] (cp. 1 John 4:12). This is a truth held in tension with what we have just said, but also with the narrative of Exodus 33–34, to which he refers. Moses had requested to see God. Hid in the cleft of the rock, he saw God's 'back parts'. Moses saw God in the incident of the breaking of the two tablets of the law, for he saw the mercy of God. Likewise John could speak of those 'who believed in His name' (John 1:12), that is to say, who trusted in the attributes of God's character. Moses therefore 'saw' God when he proclaimed the name of 'the Lord . . . merciful and gracious, slow to anger, and abounding in steadfast love (*chesed*) and faithfulness (*emeth*)' (Exod. 34:5–6). That is to say, Moses saw God through His attributes. John picks up his theme by showing that while 'the Law came by Moses', expressing its covenant in a temporary fashion, that is, Israel's relationship with God, the new covenant abides for ever in God's eternal loving-kindness and faithfulness in Christ: 'grace and truth came by Jesus Christ.'[17]

Just as creation manifests the character of God, in His mercy as a faithful, loving Creator, so new creation is evidence of the loving-kindness and faithfulness of God. In Scripture, where *chesed*, or grace, is reinforced by *emeth*, or truth (which is essentially faithfulness), the phrase expresses in the strongest possible language the absolute dependability of the Creator,[18] for it is in accordance with His character. This is a dependable world, whose laws men have harnessed successfully, because of the faithfulness of the Creator. Moreover, adds John, 'and of His fulness have we all received, grace upon grace' (John 1:16). Here is the full expression of the providence of God, the Creator-Redeemer, for it is based upon His faithfulness, mercy succeeding mercy, like waves constantly breaking upon the shores of His bounty. For 'His mercies are new every morning' (Lam. 3:23).

Thus what the Prologue of John teaches emphatically is that the whole universe has come into being through the Word. Whatever is good has its source in Christ. The power of God alone brings both intellectual illumination and moral guidance, not some fantasy of man's innate reason or his self-contained will. When John says it is the Word 'that has made Him known' (John 1:18), he is saying literally, Christ has 'exegeted God'! It has also been God's purpose from 'the beginning' to give life, both in creation (Gen. 1) and in redemption (John 1). We now see this clearly, for we see Jesus Christ as the embodiment of God's purpose and character of love and mercy.

2. *The Wisdom of God*

The New Testament, however, also balances the reality of the Word, of revelation, of transcendence, of the grand announcement of the Incarnation, with the reality of Christ as the Wisdom of God. Thus *kerygma*, or proclamation, is complemented by *didache*, or teaching. Divine disclosure is related to the realities of daily life, transcendence is linked to immanence. The living presence of the Word made flesh enables us to be wise in all aspects of reality. The translation of knowledge into wisdom is increasingly difficult in our generation, since it is so readily corrupted into selfish power. We can, therefore, apply some of the struggles of faith during the intertestamental period as the background to the apostle's declaration that Christ is made unto us wisdom.

The apocryphal literature reflects the increasingly marked influence of Hellenistic culture within Jewish faith. Desperate nationalistic efforts to preserve its 'Jewishness' only exacerbated the apostasy that ensued. Symbolic of this nationalism was the exaltation of Wisdom, to be equated with the Torah, the law given to Moses, as seen in the second century B.C. in the *Wisdom of Ben Sirach*. As Alan Richardson has said, 'It became a commonplace of rabbinic Judaism that Wisdom and Torah were one and the same, and therefore Torah was the pre-existent instrument of creation without which nothing was made that was made. . . . By the first century A.D., Judaism had developed a doctrine of wisdom which had much in common with the Stoic conception of *Sophia*, the imminent reason of things.'[19] The metaphor of Wisdom in Proverbs 8 was first hypostatised, then made into an absolute, then divinised. Plato argued that reason could be developed intuitively by men. Aristotle claimed men's intellectual ability could build it empirically. The Stoics believed that from the cosmic order, by some form of natural theology, man could rationally perceive Wisdom. Already in the *Wisdom of Solomon* (7:22–23) it appears that Wisdom's divinity and completeness had been affirmed, having twenty-one qualities that deliberately outlined its virtues as multiples of two sacred numbers, seven and three. In *Ecclesiasticus*, Wisdom is platonised as 'a breath of God, and a pure emanation of the glory of the almighty' (Ecclus. 24:9), getting very close to pantheism. Greek philosophers were themselves viewed as the disciples of Moses, who reached the highest level towards godhead that the mind could attain, through the intellectual grasp of the law.[20] Under Hellenism, therefore, such thinkers assumed that man is educable, and that knowledge is a virtue. How different was the stance of the apostle Paul, who saw that man is incapable by works of the law, or by the innate exercise of reason, of relating to God.

The undue elevation of Wisdom then (as the scientific spirit today) gave it a mediatorial role in creation and history that distracted from the glory of God, while God's withdrawal from His world was exaggerated by His presumed use of Wisdom as mediary, at the same time that He remained remote from life and its processes. Wisdom then was a dominant force in the world, pretty much as Nature is today for secular man. The remoteness of the worldless God deepened the pessimism of Jewish faith, cut off from the biblical knowledge of a personal God, who keeps covenant with His people.[21] So in the *Book of Enoch*, Wisdom now roams the earth, and having no abode has to return to heaven to dwell with the angels (*Enoch* 42:1–2). This is where John's polemic in his Prologue is so distinctive: 'the Word became flesh and dwelt among us, full of grace and truth; we have beheld His glory, glory as of the only Son from the Father' (John 1:14). The nerve centre of Jewish faith had already been destroyed in Hellenistic syncre-

tism. Now Wisdom ontology was shattered by the advent of
Jesus Christ.

W. D. Davies has argued that Paul, familiar with the Jewish equation of Wisdom with Torah, could readily make the
new claim that Christ, the new Torah, was Wisdom.[22] This,
however, understates Christ's own claims to be Wisdom. As the
master sage, Jesus made full use of the literary skills of the wise
men—parables, proverbs and wisdom themes—in His public
ministry. About sixteen wisdom parables are quoted in the Gospels, some of whose purpose was to entrap the hearers to a
moral response. La Selle has recently shown the importance of
the parabolic genre to hook, to cause response, to goad the
hearer to His teaching. In addition to our Lord's use of the
extended metaphor of the parable, He also spoke in proverbs,
such as in the beatitudes in the Sermon on the Mount. And
He often challenged His audience with puzzling questions. In
all these ways He taught wisdom.

However, Jesus not only used the techniques of the wise,
but He claimed to identify Himself with Wisdom. Surely it is
His wisdom that will be justified by her deeds (Matt. 11:19).
He claims later in the same passage to have a depth of understanding of the will and ways of His Father unique to Himself
and those to whom He will reveal it (Matt. 11:25). Jesus also
claims of Himself, 'and behold, something greater than Solomon is here' (Matt. 12:42), alluding to the Queen of Sheba who
visited Solomon to hear his wisdom. It is said that when Jesus
finished speaking in parables 'they were astonished and said,
"Where did this man get this wisdom and these mighty works?" '
(Matt. 13:54).

It is in the light of the Resurrection, however, that Paul
makes explicit what Jesus had claimed implicitly. Wisdom, claims
Paul, is not some mythological *Sophia*, but the person of Jesus
Christ, who has also been made 'our righteousness and sanctification and redemption' (1 Cor. 1:30). It is, however, 'a secret
and hidden wisdom of God' which 'None of the rulers of this
age understood; for if they had, they would not have crucified
the Lord of glory' (1 Cor. 2:7–8). Referring to Psalm 24, where
the elemental powers challenge 'Who is this King of glory?'
because of the uncertainty of His Messiahship, hidden by His
humiliation of manhood, the apostle makes clear that Christ

has more power than they have, for He is 'the Lord of glory', 'the Lord of powers' (1 Cor. 2:8; cp. Ps. 24:8–10). The vindication of Christ's wisdom as the King of all is in His death and Resurrection.

This is the transcendent wisdom that is 'not a wisdom of this age or of the rulers of this age, who are doomed to pass away' (1 Cor. 2:6). The wisdom of Christ is not know-how by which to gain mastery of the world. It is obedience: to do the will of God in justice and the fear of the Lord. It is the moral exercise of relationships with God and man, not the intellectual search for truth. God therefore uses 'what is foolish in the world to shame the wise . . . so that no human being might boast in the presence of God.' 'He is the source of your life in Christ Jesus', Paul claims, 'whom God made our wisdom, our righteousness and sanctification and redemption; therefore, as it is written, "Let him who boasts, boast of the Lord" ' (1 Cor. 1:27, 29, 30). For it is 'in Christ that all the treasures of wisdom are hid' (Col. 2:3).

JESUS CHRIST AS THE PURPOSE OF CREATION

The biblical claim is, therefore, that Jesus Christ Himself is what the creation is all about. He is the centre, the rationale and the clue to all reality. Thus the writer to the Ephesians reminds Christians that they have been chosen 'in Him before the foundation of the world'. 'He has made known to us in all wisdom and insight the mystery of His will, according to His purpose which He set forth in Christ as a plan for the fulness of time, to unite all things in Him, things in heaven and things on earth' (Eph. 1:4, 9–10).

This is profound thought, but it begins to make sense if we start with the assumption that God made the whole universe to reflect His glory. We will then seek to apprehend created things through the clear shining of His uncreated light. Since God is everywhere present, we are imbued in mind and spirit to sense His presence in creation, to wonder and adore. Religion then is the response of human life to the Creator. The light in which we perceive creation is in terms of its intelligibility, its inherent rationality. But because of sin, man has alienated himself from the goodness of God, so that the whole moral structure of the universe is refracted and distorted by the revolt of evil against the order of creation. The opacity of understanding, and the ambiguity of good, fragment and darken man's thinking, as witnessed in the origins and diversifications of so many religions. At best, man can only set up an altar to the unknown God (Acts 17:22–31).

Jesus Christ is the revelation of what 'God' means, who fulfils the hidden desires for good in all religions. This is not to say that other faiths are variations of one general revelation or that Christ is one of many ways to God. For God has only one mediator, one fulfilment, one revelation of His will and purpose. He is the One God. If this makes Christianity inclusive, its inclusiveness is not in cultural interpretations of its faith, but in God. All, therefore, that other religions may seek as good, is only affirmed, fulfilled and sustained in Jesus Christ. Christianity itself needs constant correction, renewal and understanding in the light of Christ, who is the church's one foundation.

This unique claim is evidenced in the New Testament in a threefold manner: Jesus Christ as the image of God; Jesus Christ as the 'Adam' of new humanity; and Jesus Christ as the Son of Man.

1. Jesus Christ, the Image of God

To say that Jesus Christ is co-equal with God is to speak of what God is, a God who communicates in love. To say that Jesus Christ is the meaning of creation, as the centre and rationale of the events within space and time, is to speak of a God who can be known, and of how that knowledge is to be interpreted. Yet is it reasonable, it may be asked, that Christ should have such ultimacy as 'the image of the invisible God' in all the universe? Is it not a much more limited view, like the Ptolemaic world-view, in which everything was so much more anthropocentric and restricted to this planet, around which wheeled all the heavens (Appendix C)? But can we say Christ is the coinherence of the whole universe, now that we know how much vaster it is than was ever conceived before?

With this ambiguous earth
His dealings have been told us. These abide:
The signal to the maid, the human birth,
The lesson, and the young Man crucified.

But not a star of all
The innumerable host of stars has heard
How He administered this terrestrial ball.
Our race have kept their Lord's entrusted Word. . . .

Of His earth-visiting feet
None knows the secret—cherished, perilous;
The terrible, shameful, frightened, whispered, sweet,
Heart-shattering secret of His way with us.

No planet knows that this
Our wayside planet, carrying land and wave,
Love and life multiplied, pain and bliss,
Bears, as chief treasure, one forsaken grave.

Nor, in our little day,
May His devices with the heavens be guessed;
His pilgrimage to thread the Milky Way,
Or His bestowals there be manifest.

But, in the eternities,
Doubtless we shall compare together, hear
A million alien Gospels, in what guise
He trod the Pleiades, the Lyre, the Bear.

Oh be prepared, my soul!
To read the inconceivable, to scan
The infinite forms of God those stars unroll
When, in our time, we show to them a Man.
           Christ in the Universe—Alice Meynell[23]

Is, then, thought of Christ as the image of God, the coinherence of all creation, the revelation of God, simply earth-
talk? Just as we look back to the beginnings of life on this earth,
to a pre-human condition, is there then a post-human state on
other planets, elsewhere in the universe? Certainly, our concept of God must be large enough for Him to be the Creator
of the entire universe, even though light from the most distant
galaxies takes twice the age of our earth and half the probable
age of the universe to reach us. But scale does not affect status,

nor does quantity affect quality. God is love and God's relationship to all creation is love. Man, created in the image of God, was made for the reciprocal relationship of love with his Maker. Jesus Christ is like God and one with God, for He has communicated to us on this earth the love of God (John 3:16). Should science fiction ever be shown right, that there are extraterrestrial creatures elsewhere in the universe which relate with God as man can, then as creatures loved of God, their true being will also be expressed in divine love. The antithesis between Creator and fallen creature is in fact annulled in Jesus Christ, who is both God and man. Likewise, all other antitheses will be annulled in the light of the Cross, where His love has been for ever revealed. What then shall separate us from the love of Christ (Rom. 8:38–39)?

It is striking to see the numerous references in the New Testament to Christ as 'the image of God'. That man has been created in the *imago dei* we have already discussed. What then does it mean in Col. 1:15, 'He is the image of the invisible God, the first-born of all creation'? The previous context is one of exhortation to believers—that they 'may be filled with the knowledge of His will in all spiritual wisdom and understanding, to lead a life worthy of the Lord' (Col. 1:9–10). In Proverbs 8:22, Wisdom was the companion of the Creator in His work of creation. Here Christ is portrayed also as the exemplar of creation, for He knows fully and does fully the will of the Creator.

In 2 Cor. 4:4, Christ, the likeness or image of God, is the light of creation. 'For it is the God who said, "Let light shine out of darkness", who has shone in our hearts to give the light of the knowledge of the glory of God in the face of Christ' (v. 6). Christ is the mirror of God's purposes, both in creation and new creation. Likewise, the writer to the Hebrews says of Christ, 'He reflects the glory of God and bears the very stamp of His nature, upholding the universe by His word of power' (Heb. 1:3). Here the further metaphor of an impress of wax that witnesses the seal of sovereignty is used, to signify that Christ reveals the royal stamp of the Creator's purpose, as well as maintains the providential rule of God in the created world. Although no one has seen the Creator, yet, as John declares, it is the Son who has made him known (John 1:18; cf. John 14:9).

Cosmically, then, Christ has manifested the purposes of the Creator, of all that God intended to come to pass. Christ, then, is the reflection of God. What God intended for creation we do not fully know, because of the cosmic fall. But we are enlightened concerning the intentions of the Creator for man, for whose restoration all creation waits in travail, the adoption of mankind as sons (Rom. 8:23).

2. Jesus Christ, the 'Adam' of the New Humanity

It is in His humanity that Christ is the image of the invisible God. Image implies limitation, as a reflection is not the essence of the light itself, but a reflector of it. The humanity of Jesus belongs to the creaturely realm, to the outer sphere of God's creation. So Christ came as man to show mankind the kind of relationship he should have before the Creator. So also Christ, who knew the whole plan and purpose of creation as an architect who has designed the plans, executes the plan Himself, as the master workman who works alongside and shows the workers how the plan should be completed. Jesus Christ is God's true representative. He did not represent God, however, in stoic fashion, with an abstract entity called 'humanity', but with every single person in his or her unique individuality. For 'we, being many, are one body in Christ' (Rom. 12:5; 1 Cor. 12:12).

Christ as the 'Last Adam' is well illustrated in Hebrews 2, in its application of Psalm 8. As Gen. 1:26–28 had affirmed that man was given dominion over creation, Psalm 8 extols this mandate: 'Thou hast given him dominion over the works of Thy hands; Thou hast put all things under his feet' (Ps. 8:6). Yet, says the writer to the Hebrews, 'we do not yet see everything in subjection to him' (Heb. 2:8). For since man is mortal, death is not yet in subjection. There is incongruity between man's creation status and his actual state. The way of hope is only in the Son of Man who is the 'pioneer of salvation', and whose intention is to bring 'many sons to glory'. So the writer of Hebrews re-interprets Psalm 8 with significant changes.

Mankind was created to be little less than God (*Elohim*,

the heavenly council), says the Psalmist. But the writer of Hebrews translates *Elohim* as 'angels'. Again, while man's permanent state was to be less than God, Christ was made lower than the angels for 'a little while'. Christ substituted for man as vicegerent, for God 'left nothing outside His control' (Heb. 2:8b). In place of man's sin affecting all mankind, we now see Jesus, who is 'crowned with glory and honour because of the suffering of death, so that by the grace of God He might taste death for every one' (Heb. 2:8-9). In this deepened understanding of Psalm 8[24] we have the fundamental difference between Judaism and Christianity. The Messiah has come, to deliver His people and to give them their true purpose and identity in Christ.

Christ alone bears the essential image of God. But in the New Adam, we do bear the moral image. 'For those whom He foreknew He also predestined to be conformed to the image of His Son, in order that He might be the first-born among many brethren' (Rom. 8:29). As He was the witness of Wisdom at Creation (Prov. 8), so He is the first witness of the conquest of death in His Resurrection, 'the first-born from the dead', and thus 'the first-born among many brethren'—the many redeemed in the New Adam (Rom. 8:29). For, says the apostle, 'as we have borne the image of the man of dust, we shall also bear the image of the man of heaven' (1 Cor. 15:49). Therefore the new man must put off this old nature, so that he may 'put on the new nature, which is being renewed in knowledge after the image of its Creator' (Col. 3:10).

3. Jesus Christ, the Son of Man

Thus the Incarnation has restored, is restoring and will restore fully, the *imago dei* in man, as he is identified 'in Christ'. In His earthly ministry Jesus was conscious of this fulfilment, as shown by the one title He ascribed to Himself: 'the Son of Man'. It occurs 82 times in the Gospels, exclusively on the lips of Jesus.[25] Just as the loyal people of God in the heavenly court in Daniel 7 were vindicated, so too Jesus, as God's loyal servant, will be vindicated as God's true Man, obedient, whatever the cost, to the purposes of the Creator. He comes humbly as the servant, *incognito*, to indicate His essential unity with the poor, the weak and the suffering, and also to show that the cause He served will be vindicated, rather than anticipating merely a personal triumph. Thus this further title of Christ is not from the cosmic perspective of the eyewitness of Wisdom at the beginning of Creation but from that of the eyewitness of the sufferings of mankind and of their vindication and redemption.

As Son of Man, then, the Creator is *incognito* in humiliation, as the lowly Jesus of Nazareth, who had nowhere to lay His head, even though foxes have holes and the birds of the air their nests. The one who suffered a shameful death on the cross is yet the Lord enthroned (Ps. 110:1), whom Stephen in his martyrdom saw at the right hand of God (Acts 7:56). He is also the one depicted in the apocalyptic vision of Daniel (Dan. 7:13f.), who will come again with the clouds of heaven (Mark 14:62), in the glory of His Father, with His angels, to render to each man according to his deeds (Matt. 16:27).[26]

Thus it is in the humanity of the Son of Man that Creator and creature are related, and in Him there is no longer alienation and disparity between God and man.[27] In Him the Creator is identified with the whole of suffering humanity— the hungry, thirsty, outcast, naked, sick and imprisoned (Matt. 25:31–46). This service-existence of God reveals the character of God as love. It is the pledge, too, that the creation God affirmed was good, is a word kept in the Incarnation. As T. F. Torrance finely says:

> Without the Incarnation of the Creator Word the fallen world would crumble away finally and irretrievably into nothingness, for then God would simply let go of what He has made and it would suffer from sheer privation of being. But the Incarnation has taken place—once and for all the Creator Word has entered into the existence of what He has made and bound it up for ever with His own eternal being and life, yet the Incarnation had come to mean, in this union of the Creator and the creature, the final negation by God of all that resists His creative will.[28]

Jesus' miracles of healing were concerned, then, with saving creation. The Son of Man is the Creator at work, re-creating what He had made, by sharing in all the creaturely pain and distress, poverty and powerlessness, trouble and futility. By sharing, by suffering, by serving, He healed and blessed anew the groaning creation, 'never to leave us, never to forsake us'. He is for ever pledged to the creation by His character as a good and faithful Creator.

JESUS CHRIST, COSMIC LORD

Jesus Christ, as the 'last Adam', is Man as God intended him to be, dependent and obedient. He is also the visible Image of God's own character: He is the Wisdom and the Word of God. To see Him is to see the mirror in which God has contemplated the plan of the universe.[29] The cosmic or rather supra-cosmic scope of Christ is expressed magnificently in the Hymn to Christ in Colossians 1.

v. 15   He is the image of the invisible God,
        the first-born of all creation.
v. 16   For in Him all things were created,
        in heaven and on earth,
        visible and invisible,
        whether thrones or dominions
        or principalities or authorities—
        all things were created though Him and for
            Him.
v. 17   He is before all things,
        and in Him all things hold together.
v. 18   He is the head of the body.

v. 18b He is the beginning,
        the first-born from the dead,
        that in everything He might be pre-eminent.
v. 19   For in Him all the fulness of God was pleased to
        dwell,
v. 20   and through Him to reconcile to Himself all things,
        whether on earth or in heaven, making peace
        through the blood of His cross.

In these two stanzas on the first-born of all creation and the first-born from the dead, the pre-existence of Christ is reaffirmed. Pre-existent in creation as Wisdom, He is also pre-existent in redemption as Saviour. He is the Beginning of creation as well as the new creation.

The priority that He enjoys as the first-born of all creation is glimpsed in Job 28. Man, argues the passage, may be highly ingenious and skilful, as in mining deep under the earth. There he may explore the 'path no bird of prey knows, and the falcon's eye has not seen it. The proud beasts have not trodden it; the lion has not passed over it' (Job 28:7–8). Nevertheless, man does not know the secret ways of Wisdom in creation. Only 'God understands the way to it, and He knows its place. . . . He saw it and declared it; He established it, and searched it out' (Job 28:23, 27). In His wisdom God knows the ways of creation, even of the most capricious of the cosmic elements such as the wind, the waters, the rain and thunder. Add to that Proverbs 8:22–23, 'The Lord created me at the beginning of His work, the first of His acts of old. Ages ago I was set up, at the first before the beginning of the earth.' The Hebrew is uncertain, but it implies priority in status, as witness of creation, not the first created thing. That which was dimly perceived in the Old Testament, the pre-existence of Christ, the writer of Colossians 1 now declares explicitly.

By three propositions the character of the cosmic Christ is described: 'in Him, through Him and for Him' were all things created (v. 16). 'In Him' creation has its origin, as the Word and Wisdom of God. 'Through Him' creation is integrated, so that in its interdependence it is upheld by Him. 'For Him' all creation exists, having its climax in Christ. Creation, redemption and *eschaton* are thus all summed up in Christ.

The second stanza of this hymn repeats the fact that Christ is the first-born, this time not as witness and agent of creation, but as the agent of re-creation. A new power has entered creation, to permit new creation, or redemption. If one cannot speak of creation without reference to Jesus Christ, neither can one speak of redemption without Jesus Christ. Creation and redemption cannot be isolated. No longer can the church, then, as the redeemed of Christ, be isolated from God's purposes for the rest of the universe. Moreover, what happens in the church is for the sake of the whole universe. For it is in Christ that 'all things hold together'. That is to say, all creatures have their coinherence in Christ, the Creator and Sustainer.

The continued existence of all things is 'in Him'.[30] This is in part why the New Testament speaks of Christ as 'the Lord'. The writer to the Hebrews speaks of Christ as 'upholding the universe by His word of power' (Heb. 1:3). Quoting Ps. 102:25, a passage clearly attributing creation to the Creator, the writer boldly assumes this speaks of Christ (Heb. 1:10). Christ is the Lord of the Universe, by original creation and by sustaining providence.

In India especially, dialogue with Hinduism has led to considerable concern in applying 'cosmic Christology' to other religions. As has been pointed out, the 'all things' over which Christ is Lord are not the result of redemption, but of creation. That is to say, all the good there may be in other religions reflects back upon the goodness of the Creator. But there is still need of the Redeemer in all creation, for all religions need to be redeemed.[31] Like the 'bent world', they reflect inherent ambiguities and fallenness in sin and error. Emil Brunner has summarised this in terms of closed systems. 'None of the religions knows the self-communication of the holy and merciful God. Hence in the last resort they are all religions of self-redemption.'[32] There is the 'grace' religion of India, with its practice of *bhakti* or love of God, but 'it is not the grace that comes to us in the self-acting intervention of God in the history of mankind, but a grace that is discovered upon a mystical "way" of meditative recollection by man. Nor is this "grace" communion with God and through Him with all creatures, but it is union with God, and forgetfulness of all that is creaturely, which is mere illusion.' In eastern Buddhism there is the doctrine of grace of *Amita Buddha*. He is not the Creator, nor is he the Saviour known personally, but nirvana, dissolution into nothingness. Thus Brunner concludes: 'The Eastern religions of grace come no less under the judgment of Christ than the two Semitic monotheistic religions which lay so much stress on the will, and on righteousness through "works".'[32] We do not yet see all things put under Christ, argues the writer to the Philippians; not all principalities, powers, cultures, religious faiths are subject to His redeeming grace, even though He is the Creator of the entire universe. It is still a *fallen* world.

In conclusion, it is important, as J. C. Hindley has remarked, to see that 'in the New Testament, the teaching of the cosmic Christ is a correlative of, and subordinate to the proc-lamation of redemption.'[33] There is always the danger that Christianity will be absorbed in broad and tolerant syntheses of the mind, such as Hinduism or Hellenism, that speak im-personally of God and 'cosmic figures' or 'principles'. It is the historical Jesus, crucified under Pontius Pilate, of whom the apostles speak when they proclaim the cosmic Christ, dead and risen again. It is the historicity of His redeeming triumph that brings me salvation, and enables me to declare with Luther, 'I believe God created me.' Christ's lordship moves, not *from* na-ture, but from redemption *to* nature and *to* us.[34] In His son-ship, I can then sing, 'This is my Father's world,' for He, 'the Maker of the stars and sea, became a Child on earth for me.' As such, I am not only a 'word child' but a 'love child'.

> This is my Father's world,
> O let me ne'er forget
> That though the wrong seems oft so strong,
> God is the Ruler yet.
> This is my Father's world,
> The battle is not done,
> Jesus who died shall be satisfied,
> And earth and heav'n be one.

Maltie B. Babcock

NOTES

1 See the helpful analysis of his films by Arthur Gibson, *The Silence of God*, New York, Harper and Row, 1969.
2 George Steiner, 'The Retreat of the Word', *The Listener*, 1964.
3 Marshall McLuhan, *The Medium is the Message*, New York, Bantam Books, 1967.
4 Dallas High (edit.), *Language, Persons and Beliefs: Studies in Wittgenstein's Philosophical Investigations and Religious Uses of Language*, London, Oxford University Press, 1967, p. 27.
5 Iris Murdoch, *The Word Child*, St. Albans, Herts., Triad Panther Paperbacks, Chatto and Windus Ltd., 1975, p. 21.
6 Ibid., pp. 379, 383–384.
7 Iris Murdoch, *The Sovereignty of Good over Other Concepts*, Cambridge, Cambridge University Press, 1967, p. 3.

8   Jacques Ellul, *Hope in Time of Abandonment*, New York, Seabury Press, 1972, pp. 98–114.

9   E. A. G. Thornton, 'The Hebrew Conception of Speech as a Creative Energy', *Hibbert Journal*, 44, 1945–46, p. 132.

10   André Neher, *L'Exil de la Parole*, Paris, Editions du Seuil, 1970.

11   Helen Gardner (edit.), *The Faber Book of Religious Verse*, London, Faber & Faber, 1972, p. 328.

12   See the excellent survey of the issue in Martin Hengel, *Judaism and Hellenism*, Philadelphia, Fortress, 1974, 2 vols.

13   Burton H. Throckmorton, Jr., *Creation by the Word*, Boston, United Church Press, 1968, p. 82.

14   One writer has actually tried to impose the structure of Genesis 1 on John 1–2, but this is perhaps too exaggerated. See W. F. Hambly, 'Creation and Gospel, a brief comparison of Gen. 1:1–2, 4 and John 1:1–2, 12', *Studia Evangelica*, V, 1965, pp. 69–74.

15   See Ian S. Kemp, ' "The light of men" in the Prologue of John's Gospel,' *Indian Theol. Journal*, 1965, pp. 154–164.

16   This statement seems to challenge the experience of Jacob at Bethel (Gen. 28) and at Penuel (Gen. 32), also of Moses on Mt. Sinai (Exod. 34).

17   John is saying that as Jesus Christ is *chesed* and *emeth*, Moses in fact saw the Word (Exod. 34:6; John 1:14). See A. T. Hanson, *Jesus Christ in the Old Testament*, London, S.P.C.K., 1965, pp. 108–113.

18   Nelson Glueck, *Hesed in the Bible*, trans. by A. Gottschalk, Cincinnati, Hebrew Union College Press, 1967, pp. 30–31, 55, 62, 65, 71, 72, 76, 79, 94, 99, 100.

19   Alan Richardson, *An Introduction to the Theology of the New Testament*, London, S.C.M., 1958.

20   Martin Hengel, *Judaism and Hellenism*, op. cit.

21   David A. Hubbard, 'The Wisdom Movement in Israel's Covenant Faith', *Bulletin of the Tyndale Society*, Cambridge, 1965, p. 26.

22   W. D. Davies, *Paul and Rabbinic Judaism*, London, S.P.C.K., 1948, pp. 147–176.

23   Helen Gardner (edit.), *The Faber Book of Religious Verse*, Faber & Faber, 1972, p. 292.

24   Brevard S. Childs, 'Psalm 8 in the Context of the Christian Canon', in *Biblical Theology in Crisis*, Philadelphia, Westminster Press, 1976, pp. 151–163.

25   M. D. Hooker, *The Son of Man in Mark*, London, S.P.C.K., 1967.

26   I. H. Marshall, *I Believe in the Historical Jesus*, London, Hodder & Stoughton, 1977.

27   C. F. D. Moule, *The Origins of Christology*, Cambridge, Cambridge University Press, 1977.

28   T. F. Torrance, 'Service in Jesus Christ', in *Service in Christ, Essays presented to Karl Barth*, edit. James I. McCord and T. H. L. Parker, Grand Rapids, Eerdmans, 1966, p. 7.

29 A. Feuillet, 'La création de l'univers "dans le Christ" d'après l'épitre aux Colossiens', *N.T.S.*, 12, 1965–66, pp. 1–9.

30 F. B. Craddock, 'All things in Him: a critical note on Col. 1:15–20', *N.T.S.*, 12, 1965–66, pp. 78–80.

31 J. C. Hindley, 'The Christ of Creation in New Testament Theology', *Indian Theol. Journal*, 1965, pp. 89–105.

32 Emil Brunner, *Revelation and Reason*, Philadelphia, Westminster Press, 1946, p. 271.

33 J. C. Hindley, op. cit., p. 105.

34 John G. Gibbs, *Creation and Redemption*, Leiden, E. J. Brill, 1971, p. 158.

CHAPTER SIX

Culture and Civilisation Before the Creator

The reality of Christ as Creator-Redeemer makes little or no sense to our society because the world is no longer seen as creation. Yet the whole structure of Western civilisation has been founded on biblical faith—that man is created in the image of God, to be God's deputy or 'lieu-tenant', to cultivate God's creation. Michelangelo's frescos in the Sistine Chapel, Dürer's and Rembrandt's engravings of Bible stories, Bach's *Passion according to St. Matthew,* Handel's *Messiah,* Milton's *Paradise Lost* and Bunyan's *Pilgrim's Progress* are all unthinkable without the Bible. Likewise our democratic institutions, our hospitals and our universities were founded on the basis of Christian motives and values. Even the beginnings of modern science are unthinkable without the biblical dedivinisation of nature. The rise of secularism has to a great extent brought about the demise of Christendom. Will it also mean the end of Western civilisation as we now know it? Fruits soon rot when the roots are cut. Is this what we are now witnessing in the rapid changes of our society? This should alert Christians today to the need for radical reflection and action, radical in the sense that it penetrates to the roots of contemporary challenge.

We are all aware of the apathy of many who are nominal Christians, living unreflectively, content with 'churchianity' that reflects a sociological phenomenon rather than any transcendental power over or against the drift of contemporary life. But how far is any one of us free from his culture? Is culture not like a man's shadow, which he carries wherever he goes? Does he not project it in infinite ways? Yes, this is so, and like Faust, he may exchange his very soul for it. Yet culture is as man's shadow, not man himself. Nor are the material expressions of culture and civilisation to be confused with the living relationships of human beings. Just as living matter cannot be reduced to the absolutes of physics and chemistry—even complicated physics—so, too, man cannot be reduced to the attributes of culture; their sum total would never create a single human being. Living matter is distinguishable from non-living matter not by its material character but by the relational, collective behaviour it has in the course of time; so, too, man is more than the culture he bears.

When we consider the relationship between faith and culture, the history of Christianity, as H. Richard Niebuhr has shown in his book *Christ and Culture,* reveals at least five approaches.[2] Neatly, Neibuhr has summarised these as Christ against culture; the Christ of culture; Christ above culture; Christ and culture in paradox; and Christ, the transformer of culture. Do we turn our backs to the whole world system, as Tertullian and Tolstoy advocated? Do we accommodate Christ to our culture, as Abelard, John Locke, Thomas Jefferson, Paul Tillich and many others have done? This sweet reasonableness of our culture is what many are advocating today in the so-called 'born again' movement in North America. Or do we create a new synthesis, as men like Clement of Alexandria and supremely Thomas Aquinas sought to do? Do we assume a dualism between Christ and culture as Augustine, Luther, Kierkegaard and Karl Barth have tended to see? Or do we seek to transform culture as a Christian challenge and duty, as Calvin, Jonathan Edwards and Dooyeweerd have attempted to do?

These questions raise big issues today because of the fragmentation of society into numerous subcultures, as well as because of the complexity and professionalisation of the technological society in which we are placed. So Niebuhr's questions tend to be ignored, and instead we focus on special aspects of our culture, speaking rather of 'Christianity and science', 'Christianity and the arts', 'Christianity and politics', etc. For we all have to 'become experts' to penetrate any given territory of our culture today. T. S. Eliot's vision of a Christian culture or society appears now more ancient than modern.

Perhaps, however, this focus on expertise in relating Christian faith to the segments of our culture has its own concealed entrapment of the Christian spirit. For if our expertise is the ultimate authority, then there can be no prophetic voice to protest against the pressures of our culture. It might mean that authentic man always has to be eccentric to his times, so that, like the prophet, the clown and the mystic, he can speak the truth freely. Perhaps that was why the wise men and the peasant shepherds alone witnessed the birth of Jesus, not the professional bureaucrats of Jerusalem. Perhaps, then, the credible Christian has to be eccentric to his culture, standing apart from its values, to appraise it with a critical eye and never to take it too seriously in order to avoid its idolatries. 'The present time is of the highest importance—it is time to wake up to reality', is how J. B. Phillips translates Romans 13:11. For as Walt Whitman has confessed:

> Never was there more hollowness at heart.
> Genuine belief seems to have left us,
> with the atmosphere of hypocrisy throughout.

The gods have failed us. It is time, not for the rehabilitation of a dying culture and a passing civilisation, but for sober re-appraisals and the re-establishment of the basic foundations of our human existence.

THE FOUNDATIONS OF CULTURE BEFORE THE CREATOR

Civilisation is the macro-scale of culture, which reflects geographically and historically the ways and means in which man is rooted in his environment of space and time. Culture is the local scale at which man builds up his social environment, and which reveals his reflective and creative abilities, showing he is not an animal, for his spirit transcends the merely instinctual behaviour of the animal world. Even beyond the material expressions of his cultures and civilisations, there are the deeper powers within man which relate to his understanding of being and reality, of truth and meaning, of time and eternity, of creativity and work, of order and justice.[3] It is in the light of these foundations of his humanity that a culture will be assessed as good or bad, and we can then assess the cultural synthesis we call science, or art, or other congeries of culture. For the real issues lie much deeper than the cultural manifestations. If then we are to assert 'I believe in the Creator', we have much home-work to do before we can speak effectively of such a faith.

1. Being and Reality

Basic to human thought is the question, what is real and what is mere appearance? As we have seen in regard to inter-pretations of evil, the answers of a monist, a dualist, a naturalist or a believer in the Creator will differ fundamentally.

According to the Hindu tradition of the Upanishads, the *advaita*-doctrine would say reality is not what we can sense or grasp. Reality is the One, which we can never touch, nor per-ceive, nor know. It is the furthest removed from the material world, so that the world of the tangible and the sensible, the Many, is the illusory. Science therefore could never have de-veloped in such a culture, for the objective world is not, nor can be, taken seriously.[4] For the truly real in monism is the Brahma, the indivisible, because it is also the indefinable.

Greek thought, with its dualistic tendencies, has been much influenced by such Eastern thought, but it has modified it, since Greek culture was more speculative than mystical. Thus the real-spiritual/unreal-material dichotomy has been me-diated, so that the world is perceived as real, but what is grasped of it is considered not to be reality but only one of its aspects, just as a shadow may fall on a mirror. The Idea, which is the Eternal, the Real, is imprinted on the material world, as the imprint of the *Logos*. The unity of God and the world, mind and spirit, eternity and temporality, animates the whole. Greek views differed as to whether one can, or should, seek to escape from the material to the spiritual, and as to whether therefore their co-existence is good or bad. Today the tendency in such philosophies and religious systems as 'process-thought'[5] is to embrace a variant of neo-platonism as a means of being eco-logically-minded, scientifically reputable and mystically assured. Although it includes influential theologians, it is Platonic—not the biblical stance of faith.

Naturalism, realism, materialism and stoicism, in all their varied forms, test reality by one criterion—that the material is the sensible and the real. The most real is the solid and the material, as the atom was to Democritus, the organic was to Lucretius, or the whole realm of 'Nature' is to contemporary naturalists. All of reality is seen as one continuum, from the lowest particle to the greatest galaxy of the universe. It is, as we have seen, a closed system, in which human values are ultimately reduced to matters of physics and chemistry. The world is merely the unfolding, the coming-to-be and the coming-to-pass, of processes, of the infinitely cyclical. But as Ovid and Tennyson teach us, the meaning of reality lies also in the unreal.

> . . . Nature knows
> No steadfast station, but as ebbs or flows
> Even in motion she destroys her old
> And casts new figures in another mould.
>
> The fact of places and their forms decay;
> And that is solid rock that once was sea;
> Seas, in their turn, retreating from the shore
> Make solid land, what ocean was before.
>
> *Metamorphoses*—Ovid

> There rolls the deep where grew the tree.
> O earth, what changes hast thou seen!
> There where the long street roars, hath been
> The stillness of the central sea.
>
> The hills are shadows, and they flow
> From form to form, and nothing stands;
> They melt like mist, the solid lands,
> Like clouds they shape themselves and go.
>
> *In Memoriam*—Alfred Tennyson

There are no events in nature; only processes. There is no place for the human in nature; only the natural. There is nothing unique in nature; only the general.

How contrasted to Ovid and Tennyson is the faith of the Psalmist.

> Thou didst set the earth on its foundations,
>   so that it should never be shaken. . . .
> The mountains rose, the valleys sank down

> to the place which Thou didst appoint for them.
> Thou didst set a bound which they [the waters] should
>   not pass,
>   so that they might not again cover the earth.
> Thou makest springs gush forth in the valleys;
>   they flow between the hills,
> they give drink to every beast of the field;
>   the wild asses quench their thirst.
> By them the birds of the air have their habitation; . . .
> Thou dost cause the grass to grow for the cattle,
>   and plants for man to cultivate,
> that he may bring forth food from the earth.
>
> (Ps. 104:5, 8–12, 14)

Here the biblical atmosphere exudes the sense of dependence upon the Creator. Everything has its specific fitness and uniqueness, which reinforces its concreteness and particularity. Creation, then, is a realm of specific relationships where every creature has been created 'after its own kind'. Thus the Bible is full of specific affirmations, contexts, illustrations and vignettes: of lilies among thorns, gazelles leaping over rocks, sheep in their pastures, a people in their promised land—all expressing the aesthetic delights of what is specific, appropriate and proper. There is kindliness in creation, that is to say, appreciation and the exercise of what is unique, and therefore of fitting relationships. There is courtesy in creation, the acceptance of a structured, hierarchical realm of coinherence, where rule is by recognition rather than by domination.[6] Creation expresses the appreciation of an ordered world, whose maker is righteous, and who cares truthfully.

This perfect 'is-ness' of all things would be frightening without hope in the creator God. It may not matter to an oak tree that it is, for it does not think. But it matters to man, and it would be frightful if what is, does not matter to God too. This perhaps is one aspect of what it means that 'God so loved the world', that He has created the reality of all that is, and that He constantly upholds the 'is-ness' of all that exists. So at rock bottom, the reality of all created things depends upon the love of God, for God is love. Thus reality itself is upheld by the absolute reality of the Creator. Such an outlook provides the believer in the Creator with a view of reality profoundly contrasted to that of the naturalist, the dualist or the monist. For it is a *personal* view in which God, who loved the world, loves me. Such a view of reality ultimately depends, then, upon the love of God.

2. Truth and Meaning

Clearly, it is impossible to separate an understanding of reality from the question 'what is truth?' Truth has always been of fundamental importance to man, since he is an agent of change in the world. To the Hebrews, truth or *emeth* had the basic meaning of fidelity to what is, to reality. Tomorrow the world's future may literally depend upon man's understanding of reality, as we view the global issues of the environment with apocalyptic concern. Truth, too, has the restrictive authority of teaching man who he is, enlightening him to enjoy freedom and to use power wisely. Truth, then, has the same relevance to modern man as *Sophia* had for the Greeks.

The dilemma, however, of modern man is that the quest for objectivity in the sensible world, now so materialistic in its outlook, is at the same time so deeply undermined by the relativism of modern thought. Empiricism and scepticism share the same bed in our culture, producing the offspring of materialism, totalitarianism and collectivism. Essentially, this is so because if the truth resides in the object itself, then man, too, is merely an individual part of nature.[7] If, on the other hand, the truth lies in the subject, then truth becomes relativised to the vanishing point.[8] Thus the gulf between 'the two cultures', as C. P. Snow called them, the objectivism of science and the subjectivism of art, ultimately will polarise society between collectivism and individualism, materialism and humanism, the general and the particular, until the final alternatives appear to be totalitarianism or social disintegration. That is the intellectual appeal of Marxism today—to accept materialistic objectivism as the truth, within a framework of efficient totalitarianism. This, then, is the fundamental misconception of our times, that we have located and fixed truth within the object-subject relationship. It inhibits any capacity to believe in truth outside of space and time. So the external reference, to truth in God, has vanished in much of our culture.

We can be thankful to the counter-cultural protest, which reflects a hunger for spiritual realities and a growing demand for liberation from too restrictive a way of looking at things. But the counter-culture is fuzzy in its protests. It is only when we know God as the Creator that we recognise that all truth is God's truth, and that He has created both the objective world and the mind of man to think His thoughts after Him. However, the sad history of the Christian church has shown unhappily that Christians, too, have not always distinguished the absolute truth of God from the truths granted to man, by which mankind can exercise his dominion over the earth.

Clearly, God's truth is absolute. As Isaiah declares, God's thoughts are not our thoughts, nor His ways our ways (Isa. 55:8). The transcendent Creator cannot be the object of our investigation, nor is He our knowing subject. He is Lord. So absolute and ultimate truth cannot be our possession. It can only be by the divine disclosure of a loving God, who desires to communicate, to reveal His ways to man, that we can share such knowledge. Without this distinction between God's absolute truth and our own scholarly pursuits, knowledge will tend to be pursued idolatrously, as that which 'puffs up', whereas divine love 'builds up'. So the apostle Paul exhorts us: 'If any one imagines that he knows something, he does not yet know as he ought to know. But if one loves God, one is known by Him' (1 Cor. 8:2–3). This may help us to understand Jesus' claim, 'I am the truth' (John 14:6), a knowledge that is not something, but Someone—God. Being-in-the-truth, then, means being-in-love-with-God, that is, being 'in Christ'. This is not mere knowledge, it is communion—union—love—in God. To convey such truth requires more than rhetoric or logic; it requires that we 'speak the truth in love'.

Truth, however, has also been given to man by the Creator. Because man has been set in a dependable world, by a faithful Creator, he can learn mathematical or logical truth about the world, which he can then develop axiomatically. He can also learn scientific or experimental truth, in which the data of knowing do lie in the objects studied as well as in the exercise of faith on the part of the observer. For the world is not based on chance and randomness, but reflects the faithfulness of the Creator. Thus we have what we call 'the laws of nature'. However, we also have a third kind of knowledge that we call personal, relational or experiential knowledge, where personal encounter is the criterion of knowing. It requires intercourse, communion, presence, self-revelation and ultimately love to experience such knowledge.

These forms of knowledge call for deeper and fuller relationships between the knower and the progressively known. In mathematical knowledge, the knower is isolated from his axioms. In scientific knowledge, the I-it relationships imply some communication with the outside world. In personal knowledge, the I-you relationships are deeper and richer still.[9] But in the absolute knowledge of God, the I-Thou relationship is never one of human enterprise or skill or love, but of divine election, of being called, of obedience to the call and grace of God, who initiates the gracious disclosure of Himself. It is muddled thinking about these differing levels of knowledge that has beclouded such issues as science and faith with false antitheses.

Truth, however, does not stand on its own; it is a function of meaning. Man seeks wholeness, as well as meaning and purpose in life. This is why the Greeks idolised *Logos*, the meaning of life. Indeed, it can be said that culture is the materialisation of meaning. So when life becomes fragmented, as it is becoming now in our culture, men begin to despair of its cohesion and unity, and describe it as meaningless and absurd. Perhaps much of the ecstasy of our age, erupting both from above and from below—in religious movements, the drug culture and the counter-cultural revolution—are all protests of the human spirit, attempts to live more fully in a deadening materialistic, technocratic and totalitarian age.

The Christian faith affirms that meaning in life is not contained, however, within human culture, nor in man as a rational being. It is the gift of God the Creator, who is the Way, the Truth and the Life. Man's own life has no meaning in itself, argues the Preacher in the book of Ecclesiastes, whether it is conceived of in terms of naturalism, historicism, rationalism, hedonism, materialism or any other idolatrous *-ism*.[10] To absolutise any of these is to be condemned to futility and vanity. Rather, truth in Hebrew *(emeth)* is an expression of fidelity to reality, to the character of God, who is the good and righteous

Creator. Loyalty to God is itself response to the character of God, who is faithful and loyal, so that godliness is loving-kindness or loyalty *(chesed)*. This meaning of reality, argues John in his Prologue, has now been fully manifested: 'grace *(chesed)* and truth *(emeth)* came by Jesus Christ' (John 1:17). 'And from His fullness have we all received [in the Incarnation], grace upon grace.'[11] Such reliance on the truth in Christ does not come easily, for it requires repentance, a change of heart, the abdication of autonomy. But once there is this *metanoia* or conversion, the full faculties of man are released to love God with heart, soul, mind and strength.

3. *Time and Eternity*

Human existence also requires that man should know the significance of time. For as the Greeks realised, time is not only quantitative *(chronos)*, measured by the clock or the seasons, it is also qualitative *(kairos)*. Nature, however, knows only of *chronos*, flowing endlessly and cyclically. This way of thinking, however, is not time at all, but timelessness, the infinite present of the uneventful, such as the millions of years geologists demand for the re-shaping of land and sea. We smile at the Spanish tendency to postpone time to *mañana* when it cannot be faced in the present. Perhaps there lies behind this Islamic fatalism, leaving all to the will of Allah, the inscrutable and unnameable. Timelessness, too, is valued in the Orient as the Nirvana of eternal being. But we have inherited, in the so-called 'Puritan Work-Ethic', time with meaning, time to be used. Unfortunately, this time-ethic has degenerated to the equation 'time is money' (of which we never have enough). So we have become a chronometric civilisation, making the temporal the real, doing all sorts of time-and-motion studies, trying to 'save time', without knowing what to do with such time 'saved'. Time, too, is lost, like meaning and reality, when man forgets that God created time, that it too is a gift of the Creator. 'Now is the accepted time, today is the day of salvation,' takes on new meaning when we view it as an appointment with our Creator-Redeemer. For history, like creation, is the realm of God's government.

> Have you not known? Have you not heard?
> Has it not been told you from the beginning?

Have you not understood from the foundations of the
     earth?
It is He who sits above the circle of the earth,
and its inhabitants are like grasshoppers;
who stretches out the heavens like a curtain,
and spreads them like a tent to dwell in;
who brings princes to nought,
and makes the rulers of the earth as nothing.

(Isa. 40:21-23)

In this passage, the prophet proclaims the marvellous
good news that the God who created all things from the beginning, who calls out the host of the heavenly bodies (v. 26)
as the chronometers of the human seasons, is the Lord of time
and Master of all the makers of history. He it is who, 'calling
the generations from the beginning', says, 'I, the Lord, the first
and with the last; I am He' (Isa. 41:4). Thus the Hebrews compared time to the point of an arrow. On the one side this gave
full confidence in what God had done in the past, both in the
creation and in the Exodus. On the other side this gave confidence to hope in the faithfulness of God for the future.[12]
Past and future, like the two sides of an arrow, then reinforced
the power of the present, as that point of time where trust
could be exercised in such a God. How different is the 'now'
of boredom for many in our secular culture. This poverty of
awareness may be attributed to a past blocked by guilt and a
future repressed by anxiety; thus boredom becomes the emotional experience of the present.[13] For the Christian, release
from past guilt through forgiveness, plus future hope and
therefore freedom from anxiety, makes possible the enjoyment
of the 'now'.

In the Christian conception, time is therefore both intense and lasting. On the one hand, there is its utmost intensity,
like that of a runner who competes to win the race, but on the
other hand, there is the relaxation of one who lives in the light
of eternity. The believer agrees with Ecclesiastes that there is
a time for everything, without nostalgia for its passing, for the
Creator 'has made everything beautiful in its time'. He can
afford to enjoy its passing, for he also knows that God 'has put
eternity into man's mind, yet so that he cannot find out what
God has done from the beginning to the end' (Eccl. 3:11). For

him, time is always eventful and meaningful. It is eventful, most of all, because 'in the fulness of time' Christ came to give us the datum line of B.C. and A.D., of promise and fulfilment.

Thus the Christian understanding of history is sharply contrasted with the cyclical view of time in Oriental thought, the uncertainty of fate in Greek thought and modern astrology and the spurious ideas of 'progress' and 'evolution' that were spawned by nineteenth-century materialism. Time is not directed to some Marxist Utopia, that is, 'no place', but to God, who in Christ is Alpha and Omega. Death remains for all mankind the badge of his finitude, but it is the fear of death that is the bondage of man without God. There is no fear of death to those who live in the Risen Christ. Life for the believer is the rehearsal of a thousand deaths while in life, so that 'not I but Christ liveth in me'. To such, eternal life is present enjoyment, and death but the entrance to an abundance of life. It is a view of life that is hopeful now, and full of joyous glory yonder.

4. Creativity and Work

In the presence of death, we can understand the creative desires of man to live on, through the monuments of his culture, whether it be in pyramid, temple or ziggurat. They, at least, will outlive him. He can aspire also to pass on his skills to his children, and to live again in their achievements. Yet the creativity of man is more than his desire to transcend death. It is also the drive to transcend the biological necessities of survival and to transform desire, thought, will and spirit into substantial embodiments of culture.

How does man generate creative powers? A genius is not invented, nor does he always appear to inherit his gifts; he is born. In the Promethean myth, man displays the powers of usurpation by stealing fire. In the story of the Tower of Babel, man is also seen as rivalling God, seeking to build an edifice that reaches heaven. However, behind these similarities there are profound differences in understanding the role and value of human creativity. It is from jealous gods that Prometheus steals his power. But it is from the goodness of the Creator that man is given power to build and to create a culture. In the

Bible creativity is God-given, so that man is obligated to 'do all to the glory of God' (1 Cor. 10:31).

At the same time, creativity has also been seduced by many dark forces: by the lust for power, by the greed for money, by the hunger for personal fame, by the worship of self. Without 'the fear of the Lord' the human spirit can become destructive. It is a most seductive temptation, whereby in the very powers of youth man may forget his Creator (cp. Eccl. 12:1). The high-rise buildings in the centre of our cities symbolise the ease with which modern man finds that the more he lives without God the Creator, the more he has to devise an artificial reality out of his technocracy, so that he is increasingly fantasised by the impression he is his own creator.

Today, as the powers of man are cut off from their source in God, man's creativity becomes increasingly meaningless. This is the conclusion of many of our artists. After his sequence of films, in which Ingmar Bergman first struggled with the existence of God, and then lost all faith, he concluded in 1972:

> On the whole . . . art is shameless, irresponsible . . . the movement is intense, almost feverish, like, it seems to me, a snake-skin full of ants. The snake itself has long been dead, eaten, deprived of its poison, but the skin moves, filled with meddlesome life.[14]

What a symbol this is of modern art! In contrast stands the biblical symbol of creativity that Jesus used when He said: 'I am the true Vine.' What a daring symbol of what might be identifiable with Dionysian man, with bacchanal wildness and evil ecstasy, but which Jesus used to signify the source of real fruit, not wild. John's Gospel emphasises particularly the absolute dependence of Jesus upon His Father for His power, His ministry, His message, His love. He is the embodiment of human creativity in His dependence upon God for all His gifts of wholeness, restoration and fruitfulness.

Without Christ man is tempted to be like Sisyphus, who rejects the principle that to be human is to be dependent and to receive. Instead, he believes in self-reliance, self-involvement, self-imprisonment.[15] He is his own god and his own devil. Today the powers of the technological society encourage man to be modelled more and more upon Sisyphus.

For it is the essence of *techne* to extend the powers available to man, as an axe is to man's hand, or a computer to his brain, or an organisation to his presence. This reinforces his attitude that, given the right tools, 'convivial tools',[16] man can do anything and everything. This in turn tempts man to assume that efficiency is the only requirement, so that technical efficiency eliminates the need for morality, which is then replaced by organisational skill.[17] C. S. Lewis, in his essay 'The Abolition of Man', has thus shown that when the technical reigns supreme, man disappears.

What many Christians do not appear to realise is that *techne* is the trojan horse in the City of God. Innocently, we introduce techniques for counseling, tools for Bible study, organisation for church life, only to find that when they become substitutes for the 'fear of the Lord', technocratic religion usurps the sphere of the Holy Ghost. The Kingdom of God cannot be extended by the technological society, for it is not a kingdom of this world. The pastor was never intended to be an entrepreneur or a corporation manager.

Another threat of technology to the spiritual life is its powers of procurement. Our society demands both instant coffee and instant gratification. However, the very strength of personal commitment is measured by the scarcity or unavailability of personal values. So when a value is made readily available or is artificially substituted, so that what was once scarce is now mass-produced like the sands of the seashore, one is no longer committed to its search. This is the grave threat of the technical, that it appears to make available readily, easily, universally and even instantly what was once scarce and valued. Commitment then ceases to be an exercise of the soul. If, then, the spirit of the technical undermines the need for commitment, is it not likely that faith in *techne* tends to atrophy the spirit of man, so that the exercise of prayer, of personal discipline and of human relationships becomes increasingly difficult? The further threat is that when the state is itself recognised as the ultimate form of technology, man finally abdicates living as a real person. Then non-commitment leads inevitably to totalitarianism in government, and to the abolition of personal responsibility.

Our society therefore needs desperately to return to a

faith in the Creator, to see man as made in the image of God, to act in responsibility and stewardship, for the glory of God and the service of his fellow man. Man is to work in order to eat, and beyond his own needs to feed his hungry neighbour (2 Thess. 3:10; cp. Eph. 4:28). Man's identity does not lie in his work, as *Homo faber* assumes, but in the Creator-Redeemer, who calls him to a vocation of service. The issue is not so much *what* he does, but for whom he does it, that is, 'unto the Lord'. When man loses this intrinsic understanding of work, he loses his freedom, his motive and his true identity.

In the frenetic activism of modern life, man has forgotten that his creativity is contemplative as well as active, expressed in worship as well as labour. The root meaning of 'Sabbath' in Hebrew comes from a word meaning 'to desist'. Sabbath originally meant the time designated for ceasing from all activity, and simply acknowledging and enjoying the goodness of a finished creation.

> Six days you shall labour, and do all your work; but the seventh day is a sabbath to the Lord your God; in it you shall not do any work, you, or your son, or your daughter, your man-servant, or your maid-servant, or your cattle, or the sojourner who is within your gates; for in six days the Lord made heaven and earth, the sea, and all that is in them, and rested the seventh day; wherefore the Lord blessed the sabbath day and hallowed it (Exod. 20:9-11).

Meditation as well as work, contemplation as well as action, being as well as doing, companionship with God as well as service for God—these are the creative mandates of man. More than anything else, the Sabbath rest symbolises man's awareness of living in God's creation. In God's purposes, man commences with leisure, to be aware of God and of a completed creation. Then he assumes his daily tasks, giving work its significance, aware of who he is before God, and of what his responsibilities should be in God's world.

5. *Order and Justice*

The Sabbath reminds us that God ceased to create, yet He has not ceased to govern. We therefore cut the nerve of

biblical creation if we assume God created only at the beginning, as if He were only the Originator of creation, and then
left the world to fend for itself. As we have already seen, the
biblical use of *bara* for God's activity refers as much to salvation
as to what we commonly mean by creation. The central meaning of the biblical word 'to create' is divine activity. So creation
is not principally an account of origins, but of dependence
upon God. What God originates, as in the common biblical
usage of *asah*, is both nature and history. The Creator *is* the
Redeemer, and these two ideas about God are inseparable. God
is the initiator and maintainer of all things in space and time,
whether we conceive of these activities as the realm of nature
or the sphere of history. Thus Psalm 104 is equally as important
as Genesis 1–2 in affirming the goodness of the Creator.

> Thou dost cause the grass to grow for the cattle,
>   and plants for man to cultivate,
> that he may bring forth food from the earth,
>   and wine to gladden the heart of man,
> oil to make his face shine,
>   and bread to strengthen man's heart.
> . . . These all look to Thee,
>   to give them their food in due season.
> When Thou givest to them, they gather it up;
>   When Thou openest Thy hand, they are filled with
>   good things.
> When Thou hidest Thy face, they are dismayed;
>   When Thou takest away their breath, they die
>   and return to their dust.
> When Thou sendest forth Thy Spirit, they are created;
>   and Thou renewest the face of the ground.
>   (Ps. 104:14–15, 27–30)

Calvin clearly saw this bond between creation and providence. 'Herein lies the unfathomable greatness of God,' he
said. 'Not only did He once create heaven and earth but He
also guides the whole process according to His will. Thus he
who confesses God as Creator while supposing He remains
tranquilly in heaven without caring for the world, outrageously
deprives God of all effective power.'[18] Indeed, we can only
truly confess God as Creator of all being, truth, life, time and

all the other constituents of reality when we appreciate His power as effectually at work in the present. This is Calvin's understanding of the providence of God. In Gen. 22:8, *Deus providebit*, he explains, is not so much the foreknowledge of God as His care of His creatures. Because of the general providence of God, there is order and not chaos, both in nature and history.

There is also the particular providence of common grace, which gives all the qualities and virtues necessary for the conduct of the world, great talents, genius, the exercise of intelligence, the development of the arts, etc.[19] Thirdly, there is saving providence, which brings to man a new nature or life, so that the Holy Spirit enables redeemed man to will and to do of His good pleasure. God's ordering of all things, which we call 'providence', is difficult for our age to believe, as we have seen, because it is so much influenced by naturalism.[20] Yet the ordering and regularity of nature is itself a reflection of the righteous rule of the Creator.[21] Thus in the parable of the cultivator and miller in Isaiah 28:23-29, as well as in many other references to the righteousness *(mishpat)* of the Lord, the rule of the Creator is everywhere observable. It is only man who is so perverse as not to recognise this rule.

> Even the stork in the heavens
> knows her times;
> and the turtledove, swallow, and crane
> keep the time of their coming;
> but my people know not
> the *mishpat* of the Lord.   (Jer. 8:7)

Man is challenged to order his ways in the same way that God's other creatures obey the laws of their created natures.

> But ask the beasts, and they will teach you;
> the birds of the air, and they will tell you;
> or the plants of the earth, and they will teach you;
> and the fish of the sea will declare to you.
> Who among these does not know
> that the hand of the Lord has done this?   (Job 12:7-9)

Our response should be 'Let us fear the Lord our God, who

gives rain in its season, the autumn rain and the spring rain, and keeps for us the weeks appointed for the harvest' (Jer. 5:22, 24). On this Paul and Barnabas comment, 'He did not leave Himself without witness, for He did good and gave you rain from heaven and fruitful seasons, satisfying your hearts with food and gladness' (Acts 14:17).

In a world filled with sin and rebellion, God's ordering of creation implies judgment as well as mercy, justice as well as grace.[22] So the biblical understanding of providence implies the absolute demands of God as well as His help. Man's highest self-realisation, therefore, is in obedience to the will of God, which includes both judgment and salvation. Knowing God entails the experience of Him as a 'consuming fire' as well as 'a refuge and strength'. We do not have a choice between a God of judgment and a God of mercy. He is the same God, who preserves the world as much in His justice and judgment as He does in His love. His is therefore a severe mercy, which permits us to suffer, to have pain, to endure loss, and yet to love us when He so chastens. Judgment, then, is implicit in creation, the dark side of His mercy, but nevertheless the manifestation of His mercy. For it reveals that God has never abdicated His rule and maintenance of the world.[23] Man, too, is created 'upright' (Eccl. 7:29), to appreciate God's law and to obey it.

In this view justice is therefore very different from the false assumptions our society has gained, for example, from Roman law. The Roman idea of fixed, inalienable rights, such as the law of property, of *dominium,* is foreign to the Old Testament. Man has no rights, for he is a creature, not the Creator, and therefore only a steward of the earth. It is therefore because of the application of Roman law that our civilisation is now being fragmented by the breakdown of consensus, in which each pressure group demands its 'rights', while our earth is ravaged and raped by the law of *dominium.*[24] The rhythm of sabbath, seventh year and the year of jubilee reminded the Israelite that man is only a tenant on the earth, accountable to the justice and judgment of his Creator. There is no absolutism of rights, nor of property.

Likewise, the creation ordinances, while recognising the uniqueness of each person, were promulgated in the midst of the divisions of mankind. Yet these divisions cannot be absolute, for 'there is neither Jew nor Greek, there is neither slave nor free, there is neither male nor female; for you are all one in Christ Jesus' (Gal. 3:28). The differences of mankind in race, in status and in sex are diminished, not exacerbated, by mercy and justice. According to Emil Brunner, the Christian doctrine of creation 'combines the two principal elements of equality and unlikeness, which everywhere else are in conflict with each other. It is this combination of the transcendental and the psychological, of the personal and the functional aspect, which gives the Christian idea of justice a flexibility, a dialectical subtlety which no other has.'[25]

Yet we have seen in our own lifetime the diabolical way in which the doctrine of creation has been misunderstood by Nazism, to legitimise racism and to bring about the holocaust. For it was theologians like Adolf Stoecker, Paul de Lagarde, Paul Althaus and Friedrich Wienecke who advocated 'a cleansed version of Christianity' that eliminated its 'Jewishness', and who argued that it was anti-creational not to distinguish between Semite and Aryan.[26] So in the name of the Creator Himself, one of the most heinous crimes of all time was perpetrated. At the same time that we deplore such deeds, we are also being judged by the breakdown of our society over the false issues of 'our rights', in a greedy and individualistic libertarianism that may hasten the advent of totalitarianism within our governments. Behind it all we cannot but see the wrath of God, which continues to be revealed against all who refuse to see in the things that have been made the eternal power and deity of the Creator (Rom. 1:20).

THE EDIFICE OF CONTEMPORARY CULTURE

In T. S. Eliot's 'Choruses from *The Rock*' he says, 'it seems that something has happened that has never happened before; though we know not just when, or why, or how, or where. Men have left God not for other gods, they say, but for no gods; and this has never happened before.' Is this why, in *Waiting for Godot* and other contemporary plays, the feeling is that Western civilisation has spent its creative energies and imagination, so that it is just 'waiting around' for new spiritual power and direction that it does not yet possess? How shall we then live?

With more technology? In counter-cultural consciousness? Or just waiting for something new to turn up? For the state of two aspects of our culture—science and art—reveals much that is foreboding.

1. Science

We think predominantly of our age as a scientific one, where science and technology have combined to build a complex and massive edifice of power. It is also one profoundly oriented to weapons of destruction, since over half of our scientists are engaged in weaponry research. Since about 1945, science therefore has lost its innocence: no longer is it an enterprise of knowledge for knowledge's sake, but it is increasingly geared towards science for power's sake. It is now, in its secularisation, a far cry from the Reformation, when science was first promoted for the Creator's sake. The early postulates of Christian thinkers like Palissey, Gerardius, Galileo and Boyle, that the scientist was the priest of creation, placed in the world to articulate the praise of all created things, has been totally lost.[27] They viewed the world from the biblical perspective that in seeing the world, man could see the power and wisdom of the Creator exhibited there. Men like Francis Bacon first began to distort this biblical perspective when they assumed that man could himself re-dress the Fall by exercising the human mandate of dominion over the earth by the promotion of science.[28] It was a humanistic optimism which very quickly cut science adrift from its biblical moorings.

Today the secularisation of science has gone so far that even the philosophical and metaphysical interests of scientists in the 1920s and 1930s have been replaced by the 'freezing' attitude of a 'common sense' approach that inhibits deep thought about mysteries. It replaces deep enquiries with a clever problem-solving style of mind that is hard-boiled and hostile to profound questioning. After all, research grants tend to go only to what is deemed practicable and useful. When this is compounded by the selfish nature of the intellect, there is little hope for the kind of marriage of science and theology that men like T. F. Torrance would seek to bring about.

What needs to be recognised is that theology itself prepared the way for the secularisation of science. Briefly, three major steps may be summarised, represented by Augustine, Thomas Aquinas and René Descartes. These men reflect the high points of the Church Fathers, the later Middle Ages and the beginning of modern science.

Augustine energetically sought to defend the church against the dangers of Greek thought. He therefore excluded philosophy, that is, Greek thought, from Christian theology. But the dualism of philosophy and theology was in fact Aristotelian, not biblical, for it was Aristotle who first spoke of theology as the queen of the sciences, the ultimate good, in his *Metaphysics*. In Augustine's *Soliloquies* he argues, 'God and soul, that is what I desire to know. Nothing more.'[29] In consequence, Augustine saw creation as separated from the Fall, which he ignored, to dwell almost entirely upon redemption and the future hope of another creation, the new creation. His focus was man–redemption, rather than Creator–Redeemer–creation–man. The natural world could only be seen and studied theologically, and this Augustinian position dominated Scholasticism until the revival of Aristotle in the age of Albertus Magnus and Thomas Aquinas.

In the twelfth century there was a return to a serious interest in nature as viewed by Aristotle, and this led Aquinas to renew the concepts of 'nature' and 'grace'. These terms were already well known in the church, but the result of this dualism was that the created world was seen under two aspects, the natural and the supernatural. Aquinas assumed that as the Fall affected only man and not nature, the natural sphere had its own autonomous reality, which should be studied separately from the supernatural realm of grace. Thus arose the idea that the objective realm of nature, or 'science', should be studied independently and separately of the subjective experience of grace, or 'theology'.[30] While Aquinas attempted a synthesis of nature and grace, the nominalists, such as William of Ockham, gave primacy to grace, deprecated the sphere of the natural world and denied the autonomy of natural reason.

At the Reformation, the opportunity to reform the processes of thought concerning creation was missed. It took up again the dualistic maxim: 'For faith one must go to Jerusalem; for wisdom one must go to Athens.' Luther, in his 'doctrine of twofold truth', argued that the truth is not the same in different disciplines, opening the way for the liberalism that has so dominated German theology in modern times. René Descartes was unchallenged, therefore, when he set nature apart from grace, assuming the autonomy of the natural realm, the objective realm of science being studied completely separately from the subjective realm of theology. Descartes proposed the compartmentalisation of reality into *res extensa* (nature) and *res cogitans* (grace). This opened the way for the complete secularisation of science, with his proud statement later repeated by Kant, 'Give us material and we shall construct a world for you', or the similar boast of Hume that theoretical thought could create just like God Himself.[31] Later it was assumed that the sphere of science or nature was largely neutral, with no ethic of man and nature, and no realm of creation continually dependent on the Creator. Out of this split between the realms of science and theology, the secularism of science has sentenced the Creator to be exiled from His creation, and has left the world without God. That, too, is why today we have theology that is largely a-cosmic, soteriology without creation.

Today the conflict between science and faith is not over a territory of knowledge. There can be no conflict if the creation mandate to rule, to name the animals and to subdue the earth is taken seriously, as man must do in scientific and environmental responsibility today. The conflict arises when science is not seen as the gift of God, when science serves man's greed and fears, and when it is not recognised that absolute trust rests only in the Creator of all things. Science is truth, but it is only secondary truth about reality, not the all-inclusive Truth, who is God in Christ, the Creator of all things.

Lacking an adequate biblical synthesis that takes Creator–Redeemer–creation–man seriously, the church has been very vulnerable in the last hundred years to alternative syntheses. Evolution and evolutionary philosophies have therefore become formidable rivals to biblical faith, as synthesised in views such as those of Teilhard de Chardin and now of the process-theologians. Today their views have become the most acceptable alternatives to classical theism, stimulated by the writings of Bergson and Whitehead, and of Spinoza before them. A basic assumption is that God and created reality inhere in one another, belonging to one whole which is in process of evolution. Evolution or process is therefore the key to its synthesis of science and theology. Its science assumes the reality of panpsychism, that is, that all things, including matter, possess psychic energy and contain a measure of consciousness—a latent consciousness in matter, and full consciousness in man. Its theology assumes that God is 'panentheistic', a God who is created as well as creating, and who is as much dependent upon the world as the world is dependent upon Him. Thus the dualism between the natural and the supernatural is really dissolved, not resolved, since the natural merely swallows up the supernatural. The sovereignty and the holiness of God, the biblical Creator, is implicitly denied. Clearly, there are internal differences of view. Teilhard de Chardin makes much of the cosmic Christ, but has little to say of the incarnate Christ. His four steps of 'genesis'—from matter to life (morphogenesis to biogenesis), life to man (biogenesis to anthropogenesis), man to Christ (anthropogenesis to Christogenesis), and then all 'Christified' in the Omega point—is too explicit a hypothesis for most process thinkers to swallow.[32]

The weakness of this attempted synthesis of science and faith is that it is neither science nor biblical faith. As W. H. Thorpe, the biologist, has said:

> My trouble with panpsychism, as advanced by Whitehead and, for instance, his disciple Hartshorne, is that I see no conceivable scientific possibility of investigating its significance. It is easy enough to assume some sort of psychic element in the ultimate physical particles; indeed, Eddington himself toyed with that idea. It may be, as Carl von Weizsäcker (1968) has boldly suggested, that since the concept of a particle itself is just the description of a connexion which exists between phenomena, there may be, if we are prepared to jump into strict, metaphysical language, no reason why what we call 'matter' should not in fact be 'spirit'. This, I think, amounts to saying that not only physical theories but biological theories portray, not nature itself, but our knowledge of nature. Again the trouble here is that I see no conceivable scientific possibility of confirmation. Nor does the combination of physical units, in so far as modern physics reveals them, suggest to us how, or by what laws, psychic units could similarly

combine and so produce what we recognise as the mental. We can indeed say that if reductionism were right, in the sense that the mental, spiritual, artistic and ethical values, which we experience, really are in any sense 'in' the electrons, and other primary components of which the world is made, then they don't *appear* to be there. It follows that a great and unjustifiable leap of faith is required to believe it—a leap without, so it seems to me, any scientific evidence. Thus in fact reductionism requires at least as great a faith, if not much greater faith, than does any form of syncretism or organicism.[33]

Exactly so. In fact, we are required to believe what we can in no way detect, as a scientific postulate. This is mysticism, not science.

Likewise, process-theology is not Christian theology, in spite of its appearance. It is a reaction against classical theism and an Aristotelian god, the immoveable, static, absolute, necessary Being, not against the dynamic, merciful Yahweh who is the God and Father of our Lord Jesus Christ. The Incarnation is not a particular event but a universal event for process-theology. The Bible is viewed as theologies of human faith, not the revelation of the living, personal God. The love of God is interpreted (for example, by Daniel Day Williams in *The Spirit and the Forms of Love*) as the Creator proving himself in the creation, as a necessary act of greater self-reality. Is this not a semi-selfish and compulsive love in the end, which lacks the quality of gratuitous and free love the Bible reveals in the Cross of Christ? The 'theology of process' sacrifices the vertical dimension of the Godness of God, imprisoning God the Creator-Redeemer within the space-time *continuum*.

It is here that the study of T. F. Torrance's *Space, Time and Incarnation* (1969) is so helpful in showing the absolute priority of God over space and time, which God produced as orderly functions of contingent events within the creaturely world. Clearly, creation would be unintelligible to us without space and time, since there would be neither sequence nor pattern, nor any continuous coherent structure of reality. In the Incarnation, Christ assumed created truth and rationality, space and truth, making them His own. Nevertheless, He is distinct from them. So while this creation is the only possible world there could be, from God's perspective this is the form of creation, of all the forms He chose in His sovereign will. The spatio-temporal freedom Christ exhibited, even as a man, is described, for example, when He entered a boat in the midst of a storm-tossed sea and 'immediately the ship was at the land to which they were going' (John 6:21). The causal freedom of Christ is witnessed in His turning water into wine at Cana of Galilee (John 2:1–11) or the feeding of the five thousand with five loaves and two fish (Matt. 14:13ff.; Mark 6:30ff.; Luke 9:10ff.). We see, too, the loving freedom of the Creator-Redeemer, who came not to be ministered unto but to minister, and to give His life a ransom for many (Mark 10:45). Process-theology gives no such freedom to the transcendence of God. In projecting creatureliness, it makes God the Creator creaturely.

Thus, without biblical faith in the Creator, modern man finds it easier to accept some form of reductionism than to have a valid synthesis of science and faith.

2. Art

While science is concerned with the interconnectedness of the world in its causal relationships, art sees the world in its specific traits, as objects to delight the senses. Poetry sees from within; art more obviously revels in the external world. But both take aesthetic delight in the 'is-ness' of what is. However, unlike science, whose foundations are Christian, art has been more extensive as the human ability to enjoy the world whether man was aware of the Creator or not. Nevertheless, each culture has reflected its view of reality in its art.

Thus Oriental art has differed very significantly from Western art. Since everything that is not the Absolute is illusion in Eastern thought, the first duty of an Oriental artist is to forget himself, to loathe realism and instead to mirror a universe of myth, of universals and of timelessness. Thus the wise man looks for pure aloofness, with no spiritualisation of visible things, which is of course the antithesis of biblical teaching.

In Greek art there was a shift towards the intelligibility of things, with the connivance of Reason. There was thus the Greek discovery of self-awareness in beauty, which was a discovery unknown to the Oriental world. Man's body was thus perceived to be the most beautiful object in nature. But the idolatrous worship of beauty as such, and therefore of the human body as its symbol, still hid the possibility of discovering the inner mystery of man as a person. Moreover, man was seen in conflict, between Reason and his Dionysian passions, and between his dignity and freedom in the fatefulness of life.[34]

It is the unique achievement of Christian art that there the notions of person and personality were first realised, or rather revealed by the Incarnation. Hebrew faith was perhaps inhibited in some artistic expressions, such as making any graven image, though the quality of music and the dance were great artistic expressions of joy before the Creator. But Christian art became free to transform Greek sculpture and art into the full meaning of human personality, of friendship, of man as a relational being as well as a rational being. For there was the unveiling to man's heart and mind, to receive his identity 'in Christ', so that to know Christ was to be 'a new creation'. To Paul, the apostle to the Gentiles, there was this unfolding of the mystery of God—the union of the triune God and the union of God and man in Christ, through the Holy Spirit. This mystery of fellowship was revealed in God the Son, purposed in election by God the Father, and worked out by the fellowship of the Holy Spirit in the corporate life of the believing community.

The theological influence of this on Western art has been profound. A sense of the human self as object and as agent, and of Christ's divine-human self as exemplar, led to man's grasp of the self as subject and as artist. Thus the immense reality of the human soul is made possible by the divinity of Christ, which soars over everything—Gothic cathedrals, Cistercian monasteries and all the great hymns and paintings of the medieval world. Christ's humanity is also the influence to realise the human self. However, by the Renaissance, the human self is beginning to be exaggerated, and human *hubris* all too apparent. Art, too, becomes less occupied with the objective world of God's creation, and more obsessed with human abilities, techniques and modes of artistic performance. Man, not God, begins to occupy centre stage.[35] Preoccupation with means in art leads to loss of sight of ends.

The beginning of modern art in the middle of the last century now begins to internalise human consciousness, to exaggerate the subjective over against the objective, to seek to penetrate the inner meaning of things in themselves. Eventually, in our century, in schools such as surrealism and its successors, neither God nor human reason is seen as holding things together. Instead, there is the eruption of emotions, of fears, of fantasies, which the Russian novelists Dostoyevsky and Tolstoy explored in the unconscious, and Freud and behavioural science have so fully exploited ever since. Modern art is now faced with chaos and nihilism, which sweeps the modern spirit like a flood. So there is the strong element of madness in modern society, which William Blake anticipated when he said:

> All pictures that's painted with Sense and Thought
> Are Painted by Madmen, as sure as a Groat;
> For the Greatest the Fool is the Pencil most blest,
> And when they are drunk they always paint best.

Modern art—which Erich Kahler describes as suffering from 'the loss of form'—clearly reveals the loss of structure, of order, of meaning, of truth, when man the creature loses sight of God the Creator.[36] Instead of obeisance to 'the Lord of Hosts', the moral Governor of the universe who orders and sustains all harmony, all structures, all rule, man ultimately loses all sense in the darkness of his own licentious subjectivism. Speaking of the *Poetics of Music,* Stravinsky thus admits: 'What delivers me from the anguish into which an unrestricted freedom plunges me is the fact that I am always able to turn immediately to the concrete things. . . . in art as in everything else, one can build only upon a resisting foundation: whatever constantly gives way to pressure, constantly renders movement impossible. My freedom thus consists in my moving about within the narrow frame that I have assigned myself for each one of my undertakings.'[37] There must be discipline in every worthwhile task, and the ultimate framework of life is the recognition that man is the steward and cultivator of God's good gifts.

It is our bloated subjectivism, then, that has obscured from view the reality of the Creator-Redeemer. Lionel Trilling has shown us how our artists have descended from sincerity to insanity by making an absolute of humanistic values.[38] At first we see in Shakespeare a form of Christian humanism that seems innocent enough. Let man only be sincere. So, as Polonius speeds Laertes on his way in *Hamlet,* he advises him paternally:

> This above all: to thine own self be true,
> And it doth follow, as the night the day,
> Thou can'st not then be false to any man.

What a concord is proposed; the marriage of my idealised self and my real self. Were the two ever suited in such a union! Me, as I think I am and as I really am! However, by the time of Matthew Arnold, men began to realise that such a union was impossible. For—

> Below the surface-stream, shallow and light
> Of what we *say* we feel—below the stream
> As light of what we *think* we feel—there flows
> With noiseless current strong, obscure and deep
> The central stream of what we are indeed.

Following the awareness of the torrid and tumultuous experience of human subconsciousness, Yeats, who was a great lover of *personae,* further unmasked mankind.

> Those masterful images because complete
> Grew in pure mind, but out of what began?
> A mound of refuse or the sweepings of a street,
> Old kettles, old bottles, and a broken can,
> Old iron, old bones, old rags, that raving slut
> Who keeps the till. Now that my ladder's gone
> I must lie down where all the ladders start
> In the foul rag-and-bone shop of the heart.

Unlike Jacob, modern man has no ladder up to heaven. So today, in the writings of Norman O. Brown, R. D. Laing and others, madness is advocated as the one retreat left for human authenticity. It is an extraordinary regress from the Dutch art of still life in God's world, or the confident certitude of Calvinist portraits of men and women of faith.

Today we need a new moral realism, as the imagination of man opens more profoundly into the abyss of nothingness. This difficult summary of our civilisation before the Creator, difficult because of the scope to which our culture has broken down and lost the heart of things, is intended only to challenge us to see how vast and how complicated our task is today to see again the reality of God as Creator, and of man as creature. Our little games of churchmanship, of pietism, of much activity, are as nothing compared with the cultural and personal task yet before us, to see God once more as the Creator-Redeemer. Our world is to be seen then, not as the area of rejection, but the arena of task, where God may be affirmed in everything.

NOTES

1   H. H. Pattee, 'Can life explain quantum mechanics?', in *Quantum Theory and Beyond*, edit. Ted Bastin, Cambridge, Cambridge University Press, 1971, p. 308.

2   H. Richard Niebuhr, *Christ and Culture*, New York, Harper & Brothers, 1951.

3   Emil Brunner, *Christianity and Civilisation*, 2 vols., New York, Charles Scribner's Sons, 1948 and 1949.

4   Stanley L. Jaki, *Science and Creation: From eternal cycles to an oscillating universe*, Edinburgh, Edinburgh University Press, 1974.

5   Among contemporary theologians who are involved in process-thought are John Cobb, Norman Pittenger, John Macquarrie, Charles Birch, Ian Barbour, Daniel Day Williams, and to some extent Germans like Pannenberg and Karl Rahner.

6   The great contemporary exponents of these realities of creation are Charles Williams, C. S. Lewis and J. R. R. Tolkien.

7   Madeleine L'Engle, *A Circle of Quiet*, New York, Farrar, Straus & Giroux, 1972, p. 8.

8   Brunner, op. cit., vol. 1, p. 35.

9   Robert L. F. Boyd, *Can God be Known?*, London, Inter-Varsity Press, 1967, p. 6.

10   David A. Hubbard, *Beyond Futility*, Grand Rapids, Eerdmans, 1977.

11   A. T. Hanson, *Grace and Truth*, London, S.P.C.K., 1975, pp. 5–20.

12   Simon John DeVries, *Yesterday, Today and Tomorrow*, Grand Rapids, Eerdmans, 1975.

13   Thomas C. Oden, *The Structure of Awareness*, Nashville, Abingdon Press, 1969.

14   Ingmar Bergman, 'The Snakeskin', *Film Comment*, Summer 1970, p. 15.

15   George Gloege, *The Day of His Coming: the Man in the Gospels*, trans. Stanley Rudman, Philadelphia, Fortress Press, 1963, p. 292.

16   Ivan Illich, *Tools for Conviviality*, New York, Harper & Row, Perennial Library, 1973.

17   Jacques Ellul, *The Technological Society*, New York, Random House, Vintage Books, 1964.

18   Quoted by Wm. Niesel, *The Theology of Calvin*, trans. Harold Knight, Philadelphia, Westminster Press, 1956, p. 70.

19   Etienne de Peyer, 'Calvin's doctrine of divine providence', *Evangelical Quarterly*, X, 1938, pp. 30–44.

20   Jaroslav Pelikan, 'Creation and Causality in the History of Western Thought', *Pastoral Psychology*, Jan. 1960, pp. 11–20.

21   A writer who has seen this most forcibly is Gustaf Wingren, *Creation and Law*, Edinburgh, Oliver & Boyd, 1961, especially chapter two.

22   See W. Eichrodt, *Theology of the Old Testament*, vol. II, especially chapter 16, 'The Maintenance of the World', Philadelphia, Westminster Press, 1967, pp. 151–185.

23   D. J. Wiseman, 'Law and Order in Old Testament Times', *Vox Evangelica*, VIII, 1973, p. 15.

24   Klaus Bockmühl, *Conservation and Lifestyle*, Grove Books on Ethics, no. 20, trans. Bruce N. Kaye, Bramcote, Notts., Grove Books, 1977, p. 12.

25   Emil Brunner, op. cit., vol. 1.

26   Richard Gutteridge, *Open thy Mouth for the Dumb!*, Oxford, Basil Blackwell, 1976, pp. 19, 48.

27   R. Hooykaas, *Religion and the Rise of Modern Science*, Toronto, Scottish Academic Press, 1972.

28   William Leiss, *The Domination of Nature*, New York, George Braziller, 1972.

29   Herman Dooyeweerd, 'The Secularisation of Science', *International Reformed Bulletin*, July 1977, p. 7.

30   Gerhard Siegwelt, 'Cosmologie et Theologie', *Etudes Theol. et Relig.*, 51, 1976, pp. 313–331.

31   Dooyeweerd, op. cit., p. 14.

32   Teilhard de Chardin, *The Divine Milieu*, London, Fontana, 1964.

33   W. H. Thorpe, *Animal Nature and Human Nature*, New York, Doubleday, 1974, pp. 349–350.

34   Jacques Maritain, *Creative Intuition in Art and Poetry*, New York, Pantheon Books Inc., 1953, p. 21.

35   H. Rookmaaker, *Modern Art and the Death of a Culture*, London, Inter-Varsity Press, 1970; also *Art Needs No Justification*, London Inter-Varsity Press, 1978.

36   Erich Kahler, *The Disintegration of Form in the Arts*, New York, George Braziller, 1968.

37   I. Stravinsky, *Poetics of Music*, Cambridge, Mass., Harvard paperback, 1970, pp. 64–65.

38   Lionel Trilling, *Sincerity and Authenticity*, London, Oxford University Press, 1972.

CHAPTER SEVEN

Living Wisely Before
the Creator

The spirit of technocracy today that would inhibit the enjoyment of life in all its fullness is also causing the break-up of the notion and the exercise of wisdom. Our technological society values technicians, not sages, even in our church life, for the power utilisable by *techne* is more appealing to our pragmatic age. Science has become the quest not for truth as truth, but as knowledge for power. Even the aesthetic exercise of the arts that had previously been viewed as the art of enjoyment rather than the exercise of utility, has been largely seduced by the same spirit. The technical efficiency of the hi-fi set, for example, so that the very breathing of the conductor can be picked up, ends up by dominating the original motive of simply enjoying good music. Behind this trend towards *techne* is the characteristic of all idolatry, that when a creaturely thing is made absolute in itself, such as knowledge for knowledge's sake, or art for art's sake, in what we assume to be an objective stance to reality, sooner or later it is corrupted and seduced by power for power's sake. For fallen man is intrinsically a rebel against God when he is left to his own devices.

The rise of the analytical spirit, so successful in splitting the atom or in de-coding the cell's information, has given man awesome powers of utility. Our machine-oriented society pours out endlessly a flood of information on 'how to do' everything imaginable. But we stop reflectively in the chaos of it all, to ask again in the questioning of T. S. Eliot:

Where is the wisdom we have lost in knowledge?
Where is the knowledge we have lost in information?

179

> The cycles of twenty centuries
> Take us further from God, and nearer to the dust.
>
> Chorus from The Rock

Analysis for its own sake, rather than synthesis of all around us, takes us into futility and despair. The essence of created things is to be intermediaries that connect, that heal, that lead us back to God. Data and criteria are of themselves never adequate. They need to be turned from a finite to an infinite direction as signposts to the Creator. Wisdom, then, is not just world-thought, but thought and action towards God.

THE DECLINE OF WISDOM

When man no longer believes in the Creator, there is the breakup of the notion of wisdom. The French philosopher Gabriel Marcel has examined this decline of wisdom.[1] He sees its decline leaving untenanted a central zone of life, a *milieu* or 'middle', which leaves the human being threatened by impersonal forces. If 'nature abhors a vacuum', then the vacancy is filled by the prevailing principalities, such as the spirits of utility and power.

Wisdom is the awareness of mystery in a structured world, not the exercise of self-will by free spirits. The novel *Jonathan Livingstone Sea-Gull* has been popular because it expresses the spirit of modernity, to 'do your own thing'.[2] This, however, is the antithesis of wisdom, which sees we have no rights of our own, so that we have to be nothing in order to have everything. 'All things are yours; and you are Christ's, and Christ is God's', says the apostle (1 Cor. 3:21). To the measure we are living in our Father's world, absolutely dependent upon God in the spirit of Christ's dependence upon His Father, to that measure we can enjoy the whole richness of creation, as we have seen. Simone Weil, the young French thinker, struggled fiercely to pass from critical intelligence into the beginning of wisdom. She acknowledged, 'We have to be nothing in order to be in our right place in the whole.'[3] Perhaps that is what Jesus meant when He said, 'Foxes have holes, and birds of the air nests; but the Son of man has nowhere to lay His head (Matt. 8:20). Self-assertion and self-actualisation, which so dominate the modern world, are the antithesis of the notion of wisdom.

Wisdom matures slowly like vintage wine. That is why our own and other cultures have always assumed that wisdom lies with the elders of society. But today we lock away our old people in institutions that displace them from having any significant role in society. The family, too, has been the nursery of wisdom, where slowly one learned one's station in life. When home and workshop were one, the discipline of personhood and the crafts of livelihood were learned together. The factory and the office have divorced workplace from home, so that today we all live too many lives, play too many roles, enjoy sensately too many experiences and expand into too many complexities, to settle into the contentment of simple pleasures, ordinary living and an integrated, plain-spun world. Perhaps that is why there is such nostalgia for Gandhi's spinning wheel or 'ye olde world' of the pioneering days in America. Instead, we are distended in spirit to live horizontally, unreflectively and superficially.

Our culture is too impatient for the maturity of wisdom. We drink instant coffee, we demand instant technical results, and we seek instant gratifications. That is why immediate sex is confused with the maturing of life-long love, and why the drug culture seeks the ability to 'switch on and tune in'. We also seek instant success in our religious life, with popular lectures on 'how to live the victorious life' or 'how to be born again', as if faith in the living God were a utilitarian enterprise that we could turn on at a whim, provided we had the right 'know-how'.

This temper of impatience, reinforced by the morality of the efficient, is hostile to the 'waiting upon the Lord' that is essential for the maturity of Christian character. Patience is much more than the brake to the impatient spirit. It is also the exercise of docility, accepting the will of God in all areas of life, waiting upon the grace of God, the conviction that literally 'all things work together for good to those who love God'

(Rom. 8:28). Humility is acceptance of waiting, partaking of God's patience, to gain His wisdom.

Wisdom, too, needs the sanctions of what we call 'common sense', which is unfortunately no longer common in our culture. For common sense cannot exist without consensus; without a common life and the common notions of a people, about a people. When, however, we live with the pluralism of cultures, with the fragmentation of individualism or with the mobility of Protean man changing life-styles like clothes each year, then there can be no popular wisdom. When, moreover, the machine takes over the regimentation of 'Organisation Man', then the spirit of abstraction removes both the relevance and the possibility of wisdom. Wisdom can only be experienced by real people, not bureaucrats, not robots. When the morality of the efficient takes the place of wisdom, there can be no escape for wisdom.

For wisdom to exist, there must be the challenge of choice. For the attitude of determinism, the herd instinct, or the impersonal stance allows no room for the growth and nurture of wisdom. Evil has to be purified, redeemed, or life is not possible. But only God can do this, so that wisdom without the appeal to God is impossible. To underestimate the fearsomeness of evil or the intensity of ambiguity is to be foolish. Thus the exercise of wisdom requires the milieu of freedom, to choose freely and therefore responsibly.

Man's life is set within a framework of options that relate to his culture, his temperament, his circumstances and his motives. Nothing is absolutely inevitable other than the consequences of his own choices. So wisdom cannot live under legalism; it cannot be prescribed. If a Christian's life can only be defined and articulated in terms of do's and don't's, then he has no possibility of being a wise Christian. In such taboos, others will see nothing of reality, only a system of repression and sterility. Today the obsession with legal rights in the Western world is too cold, too selfish, too formal to promote genuine human existence. 'Whenever the tissue of life,' says Alexander Solzhenitsyn, 'is woven of legalistic relations, there is an atmosphere of moral mediocrity, paralysing man's noblest impulses.'[4]

In choosing freedom, however, man is not granted boundless space. The abyss of endless experimentation or of lawlessness is both destructive and decadent. A barrel that has no bottom is useless for anything. So a fundamental requisite for wisdom is to live in the exercise of contingency, coping within limits set by a bounded and a structured world. Guidelines are necessary for coping with life. Love needs reality. It is expressed by concrete relationships between real people. Friendship cannot be dreamed; it can only be exercised. It is a miracle, not because we fantasise about it, but because it can actually exist. Wisdom is likewise actualised only in a real world, coping with actual situations and real people. It cannot exist in a vacuum, nor can it be abstracted like mathematics. That is why some timid souls may prefer to excel in mathematics, because they cannot cope with real people.

Another folly of our society is to assume that happiness is the supreme virtue. Unrestrained enjoyment is folly, however, because, as Solzhenitsyn has also said: 'If humanism were right in declaring that man is born to be happy, he could not be born to die. Since his body is doomed to die, his task on earth evidently must be of a more spiritual nature. It cannot be unrestrained enjoyment of everyday life. It cannot be the search for the best ways to obtain material goods and then cheerfully get the most out of them. It has to be the fulfilment of a permanent, earnest duty so that one's life journey may become an experience of moral growth, in that one may leave life a better human being than one started it'.[5]

Along with choice and contingency, the exercise of wisdom is also awareness that there exists a hierarchy of values. Sublimation and transvaluation are exercises of the soul of man to discover higher values than the material existence of the merely animal. Giving up cigarettes may help us to avoid lung cancer. Giving up 'weights' of many sorts may help us to run the race of life more effectively (Heb. 12:1). Wisdom, then, comes to us like the dietician who gives instructions on how to avoid obesity so that we can exercise disciplined lives. The sage is one who seeks mastery over himself. This requires distance, perspective, reflection, so that the hierarchy of values is not crowded out in the jostle of pressures too close for us to exercise discernment. It requires supremely the detachment of the presence of God, seeing life within the orbit of eternity. Sometimes it helps us to gain perspective, as when we see the comedy of God rather than the tragedy of man. Then we can laugh with God at all the antics of our idolatries in the light of His transcendence, which we must take absolutely seriously. When we know God to be the compassionate God, then His laughter both heals and reveals the sinfulness of our hearts before Him. Wisdom thus requires us to take sin very seriously, and to view ambiguity as intrinsic to our lives.

BIBLICAL WISDOM

There are, however, many styles of wisdom. At the age of nineteen, in A.D. 373, Augustine of Hippo was attracted by Cicero's book *Hortensius,* to seek 'Wisdom'. There he read, 'if the souls which we have are eternal and divine, we must conclude that the more we let them have their head in their natural activity, that is in reasoning and in the quest for knowledge, and the less you are caught up in the vices and errors of mankind, the easier it will be for them to ascend and return to Heaven.'[6]

This exhortation to love wisdom is as old as civilisation, and as diffused as every traditional culture in the world today. The Sumerians, in the earliest Near Eastern civilisation, had a word for the overall concept of wisdom, *namlulu,* that implied the collectivity of the destiny of mankind, that is, the idea of *humanitas.*[7] The Egyptian *Maat* and the Greek *Logos* are also collective concepts of wisdom, order, reason, self-sacrifice, moral adjustment, personal discipline to the highest ideals of a culture, such as the quality of life the Romans called *Romanitas.* These distinguish the wise man in every culture.

But Augustine as a youth, before he became a Christian, was misled into the 'wisdom' of the Manichees just as we can all be seduced today by worldly wisdom. What, then, are the characteristics of biblical wisdom?

1. Wisdom Is Godliness

When Augustine first turned to his Bible he was disappointed. Instead of a book cultivated and polished, scrupulous in style and lucid in the classical excellence of the Greeks, it was homespun, with earthy stories of immoral men, who were no heroes of idealised wisdom. The Latin translation was full of slang and jargon. Considering the 'unspiritual' and uncouth character of Old Testament morality, it is no wonder some wanted to slough off the 'new Christianity' in a classical, sophisticated society, in order to idealise Christ as the principle of Wisdom par excellence;[8] a cosmic Christ who was no carpenter's son in Nazareth, but the enlightener of the Greek intellect. Such were the Manichees. Only later in life did Augustine realise that Manichean wisdom is 'food in dreams'. Then he confessed: 'Food in dreams is exactly like real food, yet it does not sustain us, for we are only dreaming.'[9] How many of us still so dream!

Augustine learned, as so many of us have consistently to relearn, that no wisdom, no truth, no ideals, no principles, no vision—even of service for God—can be absolutised as an end in itself, without becoming an idol we worship. Only as all of life is kept constantly under the sovereignty of our Creator God can we avoid idol-making. No value can be regarded as independent of God, not even wisdom. 'Good in this and good in that', said Augustine; 'Take away this and that and see, if you can, the good itself, so you will see God, good not through any other good thing, but the good of every good.'[10] All values are dependent and derived from the Creator. As the Psalmist declares, 'for all things are thy servants' (Ps. 119:91).

The biblical revelation of wisdom is not then an abstract, self-contained principle, but the reflection of the character of God. Creation is good because He created it good. Wisdom is possible, but He is 'the only wise God' (Rom. 16:27). 'If any of you lacks wisdom', says the apostle James, 'let him ask God, who gives to all men generously and without reproaching, and it will be given him. But let him ask in faith, with no doubting' (James 1:5, 6). To seek wisdom is truly to seek God. That is why the Old Testament is so insistent that 'the fear of the Lord is the beginning of wisdom'.[11]

The Bible also denies the abstraction of a commodity or ideal called 'wisdom', even though we persist in talking about such values as 'scholarship' or other values esteemed in our society. The Hebrew word for wisdom (chokma) is not one single, invariable term. It is used for wisdom alongside other terms for understanding: knowledge, plan and thought, correction and discipline.[12] Clearly, all these are interconnected:

> For the Lord gives wisdom;
> from His mouth comes knowledge and understanding.
> (Prov. 2:6)

> The fear of the Lord is the beginning of wisdom
> and the knowledge of the Holy One is understanding.
> (Prov. 9:10)

This use of synonyms is not simply to stylise nuances of words, but to point to the fact that God alone is the source of wisdom. Wisdom is not attainable by self-improvement. It is a gift of God. Solomon rightly understood this when he prayed: 'O Lord, my God, Thou hast made Thy servant king in place of David my father, although I am but a little child; I do not know how to go out or come in. . . . Give Thy servant therefore an understanding mind to govern Thy people, that I may discern between good and evil' (1 Kings 3:7).

Life is too complicated to live without the Creator's guidance. So the biblical writers pull out the entire range of instruments, as in a full orchestra—'knowledge', 'understanding', 'correction', 'right discernment', 'discipline'—in order to express the need to live wisely. To do so, however, means unwavering trust (James 1:6), opening our hearts honestly and humbly, and depending on the will of God in everything. This clearly goes against the grain of professional scholarship or powerful business acumen, or the strong, mature personality that does not know and therefore does not seem to need the Creator. 'For he who doubts is like a wave of the sea that is driven and tossed by the wind. For that person must not suppose that a double-minded man, unstable in all his ways, will receive anything from the Lord' (James 1:6–8). Real wisdom comes only to those who accept the right conditions. God is patient with blunderers, but He rejects the proud, for pride is the heart of folly.

The Bible, then, is full of references on the conflict between real wisdom and secular or humanist wisdom:[13]

Thus says the Lord, your Redeemer,
who formed you from the womb:
'I am the Lord, who made all things,
who stretched out the heavens alone,
who spread out the earth—Who was with me?—
who frustrates the omens of liars,
and makes fools of diviners;
who turns wise men back,
and makes their knowledge foolish'.   (Isa. 44:24–25)

Even the book of Proverbs, with all its appreciation of the role of wisdom in society, has to admit: 'No wisdom, no understanding, no counsel, can avail against the Lord' (Prov. 21:30). For 'my thoughts are not your thoughts', says Isaiah, speaking of the sovereignty of God (Isa. 55:8, 9). Just as enjoyment of creation is based fundamentally upon monotheism, belief in One God, the Holy God, so wisdom has this same foundation. Apart from God there can only be idolatrous fantasy. God has created all things, so that apart from the Creator nothing has power or existence.

Who has directed the Spirit of the Lord,
or as His counsellor has directed Him?
Whom did He consult for His enlightenment,
and who taught Him the path of justice,
and taught Him knowledge,
and showed Him the way of understanding?
(Isa. 40:13–14)

There is a great gulf between a humanistic and a biblical understanding of wisdom. It is the contrast not of two different cultural contexts, but of the Creator and the creature, the living God and an image or idol in the mind of man. This distinction alone saves biblical wisdom from capitulating to moral relativism, to the fashions and processes of culture in each age. The reality of the transcendent God provides the fundamental criterion for distinguishing between true and false wisdom. A man may have all kinds of knowledge about this world, its physical, social and psychological phenomena, but still be wide of the mark because his basic presuppositions are wrong.

His is a wisdom centred on this world, 'under the sun', whose earth-bound existence has no awareness of the Creator of all things.

2. The Fear of the Lord

Biblical wisdom begins with the 'fear of the Lord'. It is a wisdom based not on our own devising, but on our relationship to the sovereign, covenant God. Yet this 'fear' is not one of terror, of craven fearfulness, but it is like the filial fear of a child who does not desire to lose a paternal relationship.[14]

> As a father pities his children,
> so the Lord pities those who fear Him.   (Ps. 103:13)

It is wisdom, not based upon an innate rationality as the Greeks and Western humanism have assumed, but dependent entirely on God. Biblical wisdom can never be absolute knowledge functioning independently of faith in God. Folly is this lack of realism that lives in the deception of self-endowment, self-achievement, self-boasting. The mind of the fool is not sound (Prov. 15:7), for it has a false sense of security. Folly is practical atheism: 'The fool has said in his heart, "There is no God"' (Ps. 14:1).

The Old Testament frequently affirms that 'the fear of the Lord' leads to wisdom (Prov. 15:33). It does so because such a man is wholly committed to God, not in compliance but in deepest obedience and dependence. 'Fear of the Lord' expresses the knowledge of the will of God in that it entails both awareness of it and whole-hearted response to it. For wisdom and law are very closely associated in the Hebrew faith, the one being impossible without the other. To 'fear the Lord' is thus closely akin to 'knowing the Lord', an affective covenant knowledge of God that puts a man into a right relationship with the world. For the godly Israelite, the experience of God was also experience of God's world, and the experiences of the world were always divine experiences as well.

All human knowledge starts and ends with personal commitment to God, who made all things. Affective knowledge of

God is the only thing that puts a man in a right relationship with all the objects of his perception. If we really believed and practised that today, it would have shattering implications for science and the arts in our society. True wisdom, says the Bible, stands or falls according to our attitude to the Creator. No wonder the Preacher could urge youth, 'Remember also your Creator in the days of your youth' (Eccl. 12:1). For that 're-membrance' affects the whole of one's life.

'The fear of the Lord is a fountain of life' (Prov. 14:27). Wisdom is universal and affects every area of personal and social life—the home, the schoolroom, the marketplace, the palace and the church. Its concern is with *humanitas*, man as he should be. There is a catholicity about wisdom that enables the book of Proverbs, for example, to contain not only the sayings of Solomon, but also those of a foreign king Lemuel and a prophet like Agur. Today, to see Christ as the Wisdom of God, we need to see Him filtered through the values of all cultures, as 'the other Spanish Christ' described by John MacKay,[15] or the primal vision of Christ found in African cultures, as John V. Taylor[16] has so sensitively recognised. For if the acceptance of the will of God for my life is the most authentic choice I can make in order to have what Bishop Stephen Neill has called *a genuine human existence*,[17] then this is wisdom indeed.

Fear, or reverence for God, is also associated with both distance as awe, even a holy terror, and with proximity and communion. 'The friendship of the Lord is for those who fear Him' (Ps. 25:14), for His eye is upon them (Ps. 32:18); there is no want to them (Ps. 34:9); the Lord pities them (Ps. 103:13); and His mercy (Ps. 103:17) and His salvation are with them (Ps. 85:9). Concern, favour, grace, intimacy, gratitude and praise are all included in this exercise of fear. It also promotes ethical conduct that is wise by obeying God's voice (Deut. 13:4), walking in His ways (Deut. 8:6) and keeping His commandments (Deut. 6:2; 8:6; 10:12f.).[18] Such fear brings blessing in every sphere of life. Wisdom and law are thus bound together as one, so that it is impossible to exercise one without the other. To know Yahweh is to exercise mastery over the whole of one's life, and this is wisdom.

3. Knowing God

In the last resort, one will never become wise without knowing God. For life is not determined ultimately by rules, but by God. This is the tragedy of so many socially compliant Christians. They have little knowledge of God, so they can only invent taboos and prohibitions to give them identity as Christians. The mysteries of life have no independent existence, so in them man is directly confronted by the mystery of God. No intellectual powers, no religious activities, no moralism can therefore be a substitute for the personal experience of the reality of God. To know the Creator is to be dependent upon him for everything; however, our self-sufficient technological society and our crass materialism insulate us from needing, and therefore from knowing, God. We have to live maimed lives, broken and poor, before we are ready to seek and to know God deeply. There can be no intellectual independence of the Creator, no righteousness apart from Him. As Jeremiah asks:

> How can you say, 'We are wise,
> and the law of the Lord is with us'?
> But, behold, the false pen of the scribes
> has made it into a lie.   (Jer. 8:8)

> No wisdom, no understanding, no counsel
> can avail against the Lord.
> The horse is made ready for the day of battle,
> but the victory belongs to the Lord.   (Prov. 21:30, 31)

To be truly wise, it is thus essential to know God. This knowledge is no mere theoretical knowledge of God's nature and will, like the theological chatter of so much seminary scholarship, but the practical application of a covenant relationship of love and obedience. Hosea the prophet compares such knowledge to the love relationship of a true wife and her husband, as responsive love and trusting surrender, awakened by the unmerited mercy of God.[19] Where God is not known in this sense of total trust and submission, there the character of God—His trustworthiness, His covenant kindness and His revelation of reality—is not experienced. The effect is a crisis

(Greek *krisis*, a judgment) upon the world too, so that the actual state of society and the earth is one of chaos, as we are sensing in the impending ecological crisis: 'There is no faithfulness or kindness, and no knowledge of God in the land . . . therefore the land mourns, and all who dwell in it languish' (Hosea 4:1–3).

Without the knowledge of the Creator there can be no authentic covenant with the earth. The consequences are the anti-creational activities of chaos. Jeremiah describes what seems to be a complete reversal of all that God did in Genesis one.[20]

> I looked on the earth, and lo, it was waste and void;
>   and to the heavens, and they had no light.
> I looked on the mountains, and lo, they were quaking,
>   and all the hills moved to and fro.
> I looked, and lo, there was no man,
>   and all the birds of the air had fled.
> I looked, and lo, the fruitful land was a desert,
>   and all its cities were laid in ruins
>   before the Lord, before His fierce anger.
> For thus says the Lord,
> 'The whole land shall be a desolation;
>   yet I will not make a full end.
> For this the earth shall mourn,
>   and the heavens above be black;
> For I have spoken, I have purposed;
>   I have not relented nor will I turn back.'   (Jer. 4:23–28)

Yet the common principle of both Genesis one and the above passage is that God has spoken; His will is revealed whether in the blessings of creation or in the judgment curses of chaos. For He is still sovereign as the moral governor of the universe. Indeed, as we have seen (p. 16), He is providential in judgment as much as He is providential in blessing. He needs to be known in obedience as the covenant God, or as the judge of covenant severance, which is what exile really means. Folly, then, is not the antithesis of wisdom; it is simply the lack of wisdom, in disobedience and ignorance of the will of God.

WISDOM IN COPING WITH LIFE

What we have described as the traits of biblical wisdom are

resented by many people today, not because they are indifferent to the merits of wisdom, but because they see values in society as merely utilitarian. They want it that way because in essence they wish the Creator would just mind His own business. There is inconsistency in this attitude, for either God is God, or He is not God. He cannot be just a fussy, well-meaning but inquisitive neighbour. In her biographical book *A World I Never Made* the agnostic Barbara Wootton takes this attitude,[21] quoting approvingly from A. E. Housman:

> The laws of God, the laws of man,
> He may keep that will and can;
> Not I: let God and man decree
> Laws for themselves and not for me;
> And if my ways are not as theirs
> Let them mind their own affairs.
> Their deeds I judge and much condemn,
> Yet when did I make laws for them?
> Please yourselves, say I, and they
> Need only look the other way.
> But no, they will not; they must still
> Wrest their neighbour to their will,
> And make me dance as they desire
> With jail and gallows and hell-fire.
> And how am I to face the odds
> Of man's bedevilment and God's?
> I, a stranger and afraid
> In a world I never made.
> They will be master, right or wrong;
> Though both are foolish, both are strong.
> And since, my soul, we cannot fly
> To Saturn or to Mercury,
> Keep we must, if keep we can,
> These foreign laws of God and man.

Last Poems

Are the laws of God and man really foreign? Or are they what make us most authentic, simply because, as the ordinances of creation, they are the most genuine thing we can be and do? The story is told of Sir John Laing, the successful building contractor, that his firm once installed new machinery which did not seem to run effectively. After a telephoned complaint, the manufacturer simply retorted: 'Had they read the manufacturer's instructions?' They hadn't. Often the moral mess we get into is just that simple. We have not been wise enough to read and obey the Creator's injunctions. It is as foolish to ask the Creator to mind His own business as it would be to take this attitude with the manufacturer's manual of instructions.

Often, however, the very people who resent the Creator doing His business are the very ones who see Nature as the teacher of man. But as C. S. Lewis has argued:

> If you take nature as a teacher she will teach you exactly the lesson you had already decided to learn; this is only another way of saying that nature does not teach. The tendency to take her as a teacher is obviously very easily grafted on to the experience we call 'the love of nature'. But it is only a graft. While we are actually subjected to the 'moods' and 'spirits' of nature, it points to no morals. Overwhelming gaiety, insupportable grandeur, sombre desolation are flung at you. Make what you can of them, if you must make it at all. The only imperative that nature utters is 'Look. Listen. Attend.'[22]

All that nature does is to illustrate words and ideas. As Lewis adds: 'Nature never taught me that there exists a God of glory and of infinite majesty. I had to learn that in other ways. But nature gave the word "glory" meaning for me. . . . I do not see how the word "fear" of God could have ever meant to me anything but the lowest prudential efforts to be safe, if I had never seen certain ominous ravines and unapproachable crags.' The world, says Hopkins, is 'charged with the glory of God', as icons pointing towards the Creator and illustrating His powers. But we must first see and hear Him before this is evident.

The biblical insights of those who live wisely before the Creator are vast, but we can perhaps summarise three major aspects: living in a structured world, living in a suffering world and living without the immediate presence of the Creator. These three aspects are illustrated respectively in the books of Proverbs, Job and Ecclesiastes.

1. Living in a Structured World

Implicit in ancient thought on creation is the recognition of a primeval ordering of life. The Sumerians conceived of an inner ordering of each element of reality as *me*. This was the active principle of the world, its *modus operandi*. It provided the narrative pattern of everything. Thus, to approach the norm, what was fitting was *me-te*.[23] The Egyptians likewise had this principle of world ordering in their concept of *Maat*. The *Hymn to Amen-ope* has often been likened to the famous song of wisdom in Proverbs 8.[24]

But wisdom has no divine status in Proverbs 8, nor is it a hypostatised attribute of Yahweh;[25] rather, it is something created by Yahweh and assigned its proper function. 'For the Lord gives wisdom; from His mouth come knowledge and understanding' (Prov. 2:6). 'The Lord by wisdom founded the earth; by understanding He established the heavens' (Prov. 3:19). These statements are preparatory to the admission of personified Wisdom that 'the Lord created me at the beginning of His work, the first of His acts of old' (Prov. 8:22). This is consistent with the first act of creation in Genesis 1:3. The creation of light, of revelation and illumination, is the first consequence of the speech of God. To create is to reveal the will of God. Wisdom then, as the illumination of God's will, is 'the first of His acts of old'. Thus the speech of Wisdom in Proverbs 8:1-5 is a guide for everyone in the marketplace of life, in all ordinary circumstances: 'from my lips will come what is right' (Prov. 8:6). This wisdom is not just prudent living, however, but moral integrity (Prov. 8:6-13); it is godliness. This may have material benefits, but moral benefits such as the thought of 'righteousness and justice', 'better than gold', prevail (Prov. 8:14-21). Thus two of the motifs of God's speech in creation—revelation and promise—are also emphasised in this song. Here creation reveals itself, for the revelation of the Creator is basic to the biblical emphasis of *creatio per verbum*. This is totally foreign to the idea of the Egyptian *Maat*, which never could address man on anything.[26]

Wisdom's prime credential is that the Lord created it. But Wisdom is older than 'the first of the dust of the world' (Prov. 8:26), and prior to the bounds of the sea or the ordering of the foundations of the earth (Prov. 8:28). Here the third element of the speech of the Creator is illustrated, creation as command and obedience to the will of the Creator. The folly of what happens when the command of the Creator is broken in disobedience is seen in the story of the Fall in Genesis 3. So Wisdom admonishes: 'listen to me: happy are those who keep my ways. Hear instruction and be wise, and do not neglect it. . . . For he who finds me finds life and obtains favour from the Lord' (Prov. 8:32, 33, 35). So then, just as God's creative Word in Genesis 1 is revelation, promise and command (see pp. 61– 66), so Wisdom is here described as illumination, covenant blessing and commanding obedience.

Instead, then, of being like Housman, '. . . a stranger and afraid/In a world I never made', the godly are at home in the world. Since everything comes from Yahweh, the covenant God, who is mentioned over eight times in the book of Proverbs, man lives in a reliable and good world, provided he lives wisely. He faces recognisable orders and structures in life, which he has the prerogative to name, and he is the beneficiary of all things, which are his to enjoy! Thus Solomon, in his knowledge of the onomastica of creation, spoke of 'trees, from the cedar that is in Lebanon to the hyssop that grows out of the wall; he spoke also of beasts, and of birds, and of reptiles, and of fish' (1 Kings 4:33).

Solomon also 'uttered three thousand proverbs, and his songs were a thousand and five'. He saw that creation discharges truth. The trapped gazelle is a warning against easy-going carelessness; the leech the symbol of insatiable greed; the industry of the ant or the locust is an example to us; the proudly stepping lion, the he-goat and the cock have the mien of a king. The world is filled with symbolic realities that are pointers to deeper mysteries beyond themselves, teaching man the immanence of the Creator in His world.

Thus the whole book of Proverbs is the judicial exercise of practical wisdom that leads to prudent living. It focuses on human relationships in the court, in the marketplace, in the home and in the classroom. For all the affairs of ordinary life, the appropriate attitude is 'the fear of the Lord', which is the basis for living in a dependable world. But lest we begin to think we have a Dale Carnegie approach to pragmatic living, some manual on 'How to Cope with the Creator', we now turn to the book of Job.

2. Living in a Suffering World

To see the linkage between the rational clarification and ordering of the world and the goodness of its Creator, however, can lead one to base his faith upon a simplistic observation and understanding of life. We can readily generalise from regularities. This was the fallacy of Job's friends. They relied too much on what the eye saw, the ear heard and the intuitions of mind might be, in an inadequate understanding of the Creator (compare 1 Cor. 2:9). It was too much of an intellectual adventure, rather than a venture of relationship with God. For unjust suffering does exist in the world God has called 'good'. There exist in His creation natural catastrophes, pain, disease and death. There are runaway powers that create disorder and disharmony for other forms of life, as in drought, famine, storm, earthquake and disease. This happened to a just man like Job, and it is a perennial problem of mankind. Why do the just suffer? asked the Akkadian poet-king Shushi-Meshri-Nergal about the year 2000 B.C. *The Plaint of the Poor Peasant* in the Middle Empire of Egypt asks likewise. Oedipus Rex, Prometheus and Heracles of the Greek tragedies asked the same question. Each recognises his weaknesses, but he cannot coordinate suffering evil with doing evil. Evil is often undeserved.

Unlike Proverbs, which teaches that there are ordinances that are useful in gaining wisdom, the book of Job teaches that to live in a meaningful world one needs to cultivate proper attitudes rather than depend upon simple answers. Relating to God is more profound than knowing about God. For many of the sufferer's questions remain within the sphere of the 'secret things' that 'belong to the Lord' (Deut. 29:29). The mystery of the meaning of creation is God's, and man can never fully explore it. This is eloquently described in the didactic poem of Job 28. Man as *Homo faber* can accomplish incredible feats, like digging into the heart of a mountain for gold, silver and precious stones. But the most precious reality of all is the mystery of creation, which he will never discover by his own unaided skills. Only God knows its place and purpose. It is beyond the reach of man. Thus to say the creation is ordered and meaningful, that is, can be grasped by the awareness of its regularities, as the book of Proverbs suggests, is not to say it is fully

understandable. Its truth, says the book of Job, is still elusive
and beyond us.

> Where were you when I laid the foundation of the
>   earth?
> Tell me, if you have understanding.
> Who determined its measurements—surely you know!
>   Or who stretched the line upon it?
> On what were its bases sunk,
>   or who laid its cornerstone,
> when the morning stars sang together,
>   and all the sons of God shouted for joy?
>
> (Job 38:4–7)

The mistake made by Job's three friends, Eliphaz, Bildad
and Zophar, is to reduce God to workable definitions, so that
they depend on systems of knowledge and belief, not the living
Creator. They build upon idealistic systems, so that their God
is of their making. Thus Elihu's God is so remote that he has
forgotten that He is the God of the covenant. Significantly, he
refers to El the transcendent God, but only in Job's own speeches
is He sought as the giver and maintainer of life. So Job rejects
all systematised explanations of God, reduced within the com-
pass of man's own thoughts. For Job is aware of the transcendent power of God over mountains, the earth and the sun (9:5–
7). He cannot argue with such a God, who has sovereignty
even over the monsters of chaos (26:13). But he knows of God's
past care for man (29:4), and he senses that somehow God will
vindicate trust in Him (13:18; 14:15, 17; 16:17, 20; 17:3, 9;
19:25, 26; 23:6; 31:4, 35). After his suffering, he anticipates,
'I shall come forth as gold' (23:10). For he rejects the moralistic,
mechanistic view his friends have of the Creator.

God first vindicates Himself by speaking out of the whirl-
wind. No created thing is so powerful that the Creator cannot
transcend it. And while His speeches make Job feel so insig-
nificant, yet they reveal that God does care for His creature,
man. Man, however, can never challenge the Creator, either in
power or in knowledge. Man was not a witness of the creation
of the earth (38:4, 21), nor does he know how it was created
(38:5–7), nor how the seas were formed (38:8–11). Man cannot

cause rain (38:26–28) nor freeze the water (38:29–30). Nor can man know the secrets of even the animals, whether it be the mountain goat (39:1–4), the wild donkey (39:5–8), the ox (39:9–12), the ostrich (39:13–18), the horse (39:19–25) or the hawk (39:26–30). What does he know of the hippopotamus (40:15–24) or the crocodile (41:1–34)?

The fact is, Job is not the cosmic housekeeper. God is. So Job's repentance lies in accepting once again that he is only a creature, who can trust the Creator when he cannot know His ways. Job had made the mistake of thinking he was God's equal, while his friends had overlooked the special position of man in creation. As Cortensen has said,

> God may slap the rump of Leviathan, and make a plaything of Behemoth, but He talks to man, He holds him responsible. Job must be something of an alien in the universe to be a companion of God. To sink back into natural law and resume his creaturely role, living even by the sublimely rationalized instinct of justice, is really to lose self, to lose God.

Life is not self-perpetuation. Knowledge of God is not a human enterprise. True wisdom is to know that in God's hand 'is the life of every living thing and the breath of all mankind' (12:10). It is to realise, in spite of insoluble suffering, that God is to be trusted, and to be praised and worshipped.[27]

In *The Hound of Heaven,* the poet concludes the chase of the fugitive from God with God's arresting voice,

> All things I took from thee
> Not for thy harm,
> But that thou might'st find them in my arms.
> Francis Thompson

Job, too, had first said, 'The Lord gave, and the Lord has taken away; blessed be the name of the Lord' (1:21). But he learned through all his bitterness to be content with seeing the Creator God, even when there were no solutions to the issue of theodicy.

> I know that Thou canst do all things,
> and that no purpose of Thine can be thwarted.   (42:2)

3. Living with Understanding but Not Comprehension

If the book of Proverbs speaks of the regularities of life as created by God, and Job reminds us God cannot be systematised, the writer of Ecclesiastes, Qoheleth, points out that the created world cannot be an end in itself. This is the 'vanity of vanities'—as a puff of air or dust without life—to assume that man can absolutise any created thing as if it were God the Creator, or as if it were a compensation for His absence. Job was concerned about his own life and his personal suffering, but Qoheleth is much more ambitious in seeking to generalise about the enigma of life. He concludes that a thorough naturalistic understanding of life is impossible, for it is God who determines every event. Man is incapable of discerning the meaning of all those events. Thus life is vanity. Toil bears no relationship to what is gained from it, and honesty does not always pay, since the wicked often prosper more than the righteous. So even thinking deeply to attain wisdom about such puzzles in life can be as striving after wind. Yet life is not random and haphazard. Everything has a time and a way set for it by God (Eccl. 3:1-8, 17; 8:6). But this should not depress man into accepting it deterministically, but rather lead to faith in the wisdom of God.

> I know that whatever God does endures for ever; nothing can be added to it, nor anything taken from it; God has made it so, in order that men should fear before Him.
> (Eccl. 3:14)

However, instead of comforting the Preacher, this awareness only sharpens the poignancy of his futility. God complicates his life the more intensely. Sometimes life would be much simpler without God. But since it is God who has put 'eternity into man's mind' (Eccl. 3:11), man has an infinite longing and an insatiable curiosity of desire that nothing creaturely can satisfy. As J. Stafford Wright has said:

> The book is the record of a search for the key to life. It is an endeavour to give a meaning to life, to see it as a whole. And there is no key under the sun. Life has lost the key to itself. 'Vanity of vanities, all is vanity.' If you

> want the key, you must go to the locksmith who made the
> lock. God holds the key of all unknown. *And He will not
> give it to you.* Since then you cannot get the key, you must
> trust the locksmith to open the doors.[28]

Without the Creator, life is a riddle of the Sphinx. It is unknow-
able without Him. Death sets the limit to human existence.
There is much despair and hatred of life, in disillusionment,
because of death. Man's efforts to master life are therefore
misdirected and futile.

Live, then, within the limits of such creatureliness, says
the Preacher. Man's active participation in the world should be
neither manipulative nor assertive, but seeing and rejoicing in
all that is good. The present moment is the gift of God, to be
enjoyed now (3:22). It should be lived in community (4:9–12;
9:9). This enjoyment of creaturely existence is set within the
framework of a theology of creation. Qoheleth recognises, as
does the Genesis account, that man is made of the dust and
will return to it (Eccl. 3:20; 12:7; Gen. 2:7, 21–25). Human
knowledge has God-given limits (Eccl. 8:7; Gen. 2:17). Life is
tiring in its toil (Eccl. 1:3; 2:22; Gen. 3:17–19). Nevertheless,
Qoheleth believes that man is set in an ordered world; for, says
the Preacher, 'He has made everything beautiful in its time.
. . . I know that there is nothing better for them than to be
happy and enjoy themselves as long as they live' (Eccl. 3:11–
12). Life is good if man lives as a creature before God, who
calls creation 'good' seven times in the opening chapter of Genesis. God ordains that we enter into life and live in it joyfully
(Eccl. 9:7).

The heresy of the '-ism' is to assume that its explanation
is the absolute reality. Marxism, materialism, evolutionism, romanticism—all parade through the history of philosophy as
idols of the mind and spirit of man that cannot take the place
of the Creator. It is futile to try. If therefore any part of creation
is made an end in itself, whether it be nature (Eccl. 1:5–7),
history (Eccl. 1:8–11), knowledge (Eccl. 1:12–18), pleasure
(Eccl. 2:1–3), wealth (Eccl. 2:4–11) or work (Eccl. 2:18), it becomes a source of futility.[29] In God's world the maxims of work
for work's sake, knowledge for knowledge's sake, even nature
for nature's sake, are false and idolatrous. Nor is man called of

God to master life as a landlord, for his tenancy on earth is short, and he is limited in both understanding and possession. Rather, he is to enjoy God's gifts and accept the givenness of life.

Perhaps Ecclesiastes dates late in Jewish history, when the temptation was to drink deeply of Hellenistic culture, to comprehend reality absolutely. Likewise, the book is very relevant to our age, which seeks to absolutise science and technology as two gods that would exclude the Creator from His created realm. For the Ptolemaic world was like the Newtonian world through which we are now passing, a self-sufficient world that was foolish and vain in its desire to comprehend life without knowing the appropriate levels of understanding reality. The created world is so 'good' that throughout the history of man there is traceable the littered trail of idolatry, of man worshipping the creature instead of the Creator, whether it be Baal, Nature or the laws of science. The regularity of the seasons, the interconnections of life and the dependability of the laws of the universe are the works of the Good and Wise Creator. But if man confuses the creature with the Creator, he is doomed to the futility spoken of by Qoheleth and other wise men of the Old Testament. Living in God's world, within the mysteries of our life, all we can appropriately know is the confusion of Agur:

> I am too stupid to be a man; I have not the understanding of a man. I have not learned wisdom, nor have I knowledge of the Holy One. Who has ascended to heaven and come down? Who has gathered the wind in his fists? Who has wrapped up the waters in a garment? Who has established all the ends of the earth? What is his name, and what is his son's name? Surely you know! (Prov. 30:2–4)

The search for such wisdom creates within man a chasm that is God-shaped, and which only God's Son, in whom all things have their coherence (Col. 1:17), can fulfil. For as the New Testament unfolds, Christ is in fact the wisdom of God, 'whom God made our wisdom, our righteousness and sanctification and redemption; therefore, as it is written, "Let him who boasts, boast of the Lord" ' (1 Cor. 1:30–31). These three books are

not contradictory, but provide checks and balances to keep
wisdom from being rationalised or reduced to other narrow
bigotries.[30] Above all, they prepare the way for the realisation
that true wisdom is embodied in Jesus Christ, 'in whom are hid
all the treasures of wisdom and knowledge'. The epistle of
James is a commentary on Christian wisdom, grounded in the
teaching of Jesus and centred in His redemptive work.

NOTES

1   Gabriel Marcel, *The Decline of Wisdom*, London, Harvill Press,
     1954, p. 37.
2   Richard Bach, *Jonathan Livingstone Sea-Gull*, New York, Mac-
     millan, 1970.
3   George A. Panichas (edit.), *The Simone Weil Reader*, New York,
     David MacKay, 1977, p. 345.
4   Alexander Solzhenitsyn, 'The West's Decline in Courage', *The
     Wall Street Journal*, June 13, 1978.
5   Ibid.
6   Quoted by Peter Brown, *Augustine of Hippo*, London, Faber &
     Faber, 1967, p. 40.
7   John Burnaby, *Amor Dei*, London, Hodder & Stoughton, 1947,
     p. 46.
8   Peter Brown, op. cit., p. 42.
9   Ibid., p. 45.
10   John Burnaby, op. cit., p. 107.
11   Gerhard von Rad, *Wisdom in Israel*, London, S.C.M., 1972,
     pp. 53–73.
12   Ibid., p. 53.
13   A. Drubbel, 'Le Conflict entre la Sagesse Profane et la Sagesse
     Religieuse', *Biblica* 17, 1936, pp. 45–70, 407–428.
14   R. N.Whybray, *Wisdom in Proverbs*, Naperville, Ill., Alec R. Al-
     lenson, 1965, pp. 95–98.
15   John A. MacKay, *The Other Spanish Christ*, London, S.C.M., 1932.
16   John V. Taylor, *The Primal Vision*, London, S.C.M., 1963.
17   Stephen Neill, *A Genuine Human Existence*, Garden City, N.Y.,
     Doubleday, 1959.
18   R. N. Whybray, op. cit., p. 47.
19   Delbert R. Hillers, *Covenant: the History of the Biblical Idea*, Balti-
     more, Johns Hopkins Press, 1969, p. 123.

20   Bruce K. Waltke, *Creation and Chaos,* Portland, Western Conservative Baptist Seminary, 1974, pp. 22–23.

21   Barbara Wootton, *A World I Never Made,* London, Allen & Unwin, 1967.

22   C. S. Lewis, *The Four Loves,* ch. 2, New York, Harcourt, Brace, 1960.

23   Thorkild Jacobsen, *Towards the Image of Tammuz,* Cambridge, Mass., Harvard University Press, 1970, pp. 11, 359–360.

24   James L. Crenshaw (edit.), *Studies in Ancient Israelite Wisdom,* New York, Ktav Publishing House, 1976, pp. 113–133, 390–400.

25   Derek Kidner, *Proverbs,* London, Tyndale Press, 1964, p. 78.

26   R. N. Whybray, *Wisdom in Proverbs,* op. cit., pp. 62–63.

27   L. Derousseaux, *La Crainte de Dieu dans l'Ancien Testament,* Paris, Cerf., 1970, pp. 328–337.

28   J. Stafford Wright, 'The Interpretation of Ecclesiastes', *Evangelical Quarterly,* XVIII, 1946, pp. 11–34.

29   D. A. Hubbard, *Beyond Futility,* Grand Rapids, Eerdmans, 1976.

30   D. A. Hubbard, 'The Wisdom Movement and Israel's Covenant Faith', Tyndale Old Testament Lecture, London, Tyndale Press, 1965.

CHAPTER EIGHT

The Enjoyment of God's World

Perhaps one of the greatest spiritual events in the modern world has been the reversal in the priority of the values of contemplation and action. Prior to the Copernican revolution, the contemplative life was supreme. Mary chose the 'better part'; Martha was rebuked for her over-busyness. As Thomas Aquinas could say, 'The life of contemplation is simply better than the life of action.'[1] The reversal of this in the modern age exalts *Homo faber,* giving man the fabricator the prerogative to acquire useful knowledge that provides power. Such knowledge is no longer concerned with the question 'why' but 'how'. Productivity and creativity have become the highest ideals. In an age when man no longer trusts in the reliability of any truth that is not pragmatic, means and ends are reversed. Truth must now 'work' towards making a living.

The terrifying danger to the Christian faith today is that the same spirit is at work among so many 'successful' Christian enterprises, with their obsession with tools, techniques and utilitarian objectives. Apart from the monastic life of the Roman Church, the Protestant world is signally without shelter for the contemplative life. Our seminaries are theological workshops, and our churches are also geared to the assembly-line mentality. No wonder much contemporary religion is like picking the blackberries that Elizabeth Browning talked about.

> Earth's crammed with heaven,
> And every common bush afire with God;
> But only he who sees takes off his shoes;
> The rest sit round it and pluck blackberries.
>
> Elizabeth Barrett Browning

The world has forgotten its Creator, and man has fallen in love with his introspective powers instead. We need once more to see the vision of the sanctity of creation, where common things are sacramental. We need to enjoy the creation as well as to know how to live in it wisely.

Many in our generation feel increasingly trapped, like the wasp in the half-filled jam jar, caught between the sticky syrup of contingency and the unscaleable glass walls of transcendence. In such a plight they are asking, is the enjoyment of life really possible? The eighteenth-century composers J. S. Bach, Handel, Glück and, above all, Mozart,[2] clearly answered 'yes'. For as the later composer Haydn was reported to say, 'When I think of God, my heart is so full of joy that notes leap and dance as they leave my pen; and since God has given me a cheerful spirit, I serve Him with a cheerful spirit.' They celebrated the reality of creation far better than any scientific argument of the deists. For they drew their inspiration for celebration from a real world of relationships, which transcended the rational mind through its childlike spirit of serenity.

THE SERENITY OF CHILD-LIKE ACCEPTANCE

Joy is the capacity to accept, to say 'yes' to a good world. Its willingness to accept is no uncritical or blind affirmation of the world as it is. Yet it is not a luxury but a necessity of creation, what C. S. Lewis called 'the serious business of heaven'. Like Beethoven's Ninth Symphony, it tells us that joy lies at the heart of the universe, for in creating man, God has an agent of enjoyment. This is the purpose of man, says the *Shorter Catechism,* 'to glorify God and to enjoy Him for ever.' He does so in receiving all good things as from the hand of a bountiful Creator. Man is intended to be neither Apollonian in self-achievement, nor Dionysian in enslavement to sensual passions. He is made in the image of God, to relate authentically both to the creation as a responsible steward, and to the Creator as a dependent being.

The real meaning of enjoyment is not happiness, which can be selfish, but the act of going outside of one's self, as a small child does, to be involved with other objects for their own sake.[3] It is therefore the antithesis of introspection, of being imprisoned within one's self. Such joy is a desire, yet it is not entrapped in self-seeking. It is a response, even an intellectual response, such as a mathematician may have to the beauty of numbers, yet it is not self-congratulatory. It is love, but not self-love; rather it is love of everything for its own sake. Joy is akin to humility, to unconscious self-forgetfulness and to kindness in respecting the uniqueness of the other. When, therefore, it is joy in God, it is joy indeed, for then it is the response of being in contact with the source and sustenance of all reality. It is the joy of seeing all things as God meant them to be recognised, not for our selfish, utilitarian purposes, but for their own sake. Such joy, then, is deeper than reason, for it binds our lives to the coinherence of all things under the Creator.

1. The Recognition of Identity

Every created thing has its own proper existence and its own law, which has to be recognised in its uniqueness. One writer has described the mystery of being, of the independent reality of each object, as follows:

It is a summer day in Burgundy, where the light has a vibrant clarity quite unlike that of English summers. Sitting at the long white table in the shaded room with its slatted shutters, we seem to be enclosed within that mysterious and complicated world in which, by eating and talk, man transforms what comes to him by way of his senses into his own distinctive life. But, as those who are waiting at table come and go with the dishes, there is revealed through the long doors, in bursts of limpid sunshine, another world of *things*, clear and triumphant in their independent existence, stones and plants and trees, insistent upon being seen in the exactness of their contours, defining themselves in colour and form and movement, simply, gloriously, and beyond all argument *being*. In such a setting only the most insensitive eye could fail to note the challenge of all in the world that *is*, that carries in it a truth and rightness that determines it to be this and not that.   Aelred Squire[4]

If there is this appreciation of the fitness of everything to *be*, other poets and writers have sensed the same need to recognise the reality of the animals.

> I ask sometimes why those small animals
> With bitter eyes, why we should care for them.
>
> I question the sky, the serene blue water,
> But it cannot say. It gives no answer.
>
> And no answer releases in my head.
> A procession of grey shades patched and whimpering;
>
> Dogs with clipped ears, wheezing cart horses,
> A fly without shadow and without thought.
>
> Is it with these menaces to our vision,
> With this procession led by a man carrying wood
>
> We must be concerned? The holy land, the rearing
> Green island should be kindlier than this.
>
> Yet the animals, our ghosts, need tending to.
> Take in the whipped cat and the blinded owl;
>
> Take up the man-trapped squirrel upon your shoulder.
> Attend to the unnecessary beasts.
>
> From growing mercy and a moderate love
> Great love for the human animal occurs.
>
> And your love grows. Your great love grows and grows.
> > Jon Silkin, *Caring for Animals*

But the sense of reverence for other human beings does not necessarily grow from such incipient concern and responsibility for dumb creatures. Why should we accept the uniqueness of each animal, or indeed each mote of dust dancing in a sunbeam? We are driven back to the Word that spoke all creation into being where

> Issuing from the Word
> The seven days came,
> Each in its own place,
> Its own name.
>
> > Edwin Muir—*The Days*

For 'By faith we understand that the world was created by the word of God, so that what is seen was made out of things which do not appear' (Heb. 11:3). God also upholds 'the universe by His word of power' (Heb. 1:3). If our attitude to God is wrong, then our attitude to the least of all His creatures is also wrong. But in the right hands, even 'a little of the common earth, upon which men walk without reflection, can open the eyes of the blind'.[5]

We have already emphasised (p. 153) that the provident God looks after the interests of the least of His creatures, sustaining the 'is-ness' of all that is. It is His love that does so, even playing with His creatures as the objects of His love. Perhaps it is in His joyfulness that the secret of what Paul means when he says that in Christ 'all things hold together' (Col. 1:17) lies. Christ 'did not count equality with God a thing to be grasped, but emptied Himself, taking the form of a servant' (Phil. 2:6–7). Asserting no rights, is it possible that He has created all things? Is this the coherence that really upholds the whole of creation, so that He sustains all things, each in its own place, with its own name?

Certainly it is our experience that when we no longer grasp fearfully after life, fearful of what we imagine we should lose—when it is only possessiveness we would lose—we can recognise the rights of other created beings. When I know that I am held by God with a stronger grasp of me than ever I can grasp, I have an open hand to life, able to enjoy richly all good things. The servant's admonition, 'let each of you look not only to his own interests, but also to the interests of others', has then a cosmic significance that is the secret of the coinherence of the universe. Then we begin to understand the claim that 'all things are yours', as the apostle says, for 'you are Christ's; and Christ is God's' (1 Cor. 3:22–23).

2. The Serenity of Trust

Enjoyment of the world, notes the poet Wordsworth, quickly disappears from childhood as the boy grows to manhood. In the poem 'Recollections of Early Childhood', the child's world of wonder is quickly profaned by the over-seriousness of the adult world.

> Heaven lies about us in our infancy!
> Shades of the prison-house begin to close
> Upon the growing Boy . . .
>
> At length the Man perceives it die away,
> And fade into the light of common day.

It does so because the child who stares wonderingly, in open
acceptance of all that is, becomes the man who creates an intellectual understanding of the order and meaning of things,
so that the playful, carefree world of childish delight soon disappears. In an essay on the stages of development, the psy-
choanalyst Ferenzia speaks of the child's reluctance to
distinguish between himself and the world, in his slow development of objectivity which differentiates the self from external things.[6] In *The Prelude*, Wordsworth described this first
stage of the infant's perception of the world:

> Blest the infant Babe,
> For with my best conjecture (would trace
> Our Being's earthly progress), blest the Babe,
> Nursed on his Mother's breast; who with his soul
> Drinks in the feelings of his Mother's eye!
> For him, in one dear Presence, there exists
> A virtue which irradiates and exalts
> Objects through widest intercourse of sense.

But as David Hartley the philosopher had taught Wordsworth,
the heavenly presence the child brought into this Platonic world
faded, and left the adult with 'vanishings' of such transcendence.[7] Thus 'the Child is father of the Man.'

Very different is the biblical understanding of child-like
enjoyment. This is not childish, unable to objectify, nor is it
innate to childhood. Rather, it is the spirit of absolute trust and
deep faith in God, humbled by His sufficiency. As the Psalmist
acknowledges:

> O Lord, my heart is not lifted up,
> my eyes are not raised too high;
> I do not occupy myself with things
> too great and too marvellous for me.

> But I have calmed and quieted my soul,
> like a child quieted at its mother's breast;
> like a child that is quieted is my soul.
> O Israel, hope in the Lord
> from this time forth and for evermore.   (Ps. 131:1–3)

This quality of trust and dependence is seen in the most child-like Man the world has ever witnessed, Jesus Christ. He came in His Father's name to do the works His Father had given him to accomplish (John 5:43, 36). For 'the Son can do nothing of His own accord, but only what He sees the Father doing' (John 5:19). 'I can do nothing on my own authority' (John 5:30). So identified was He with His Father's will—His meat and drink—that He could say to Philip, 'He who has seen me has seen the Father' (John 14:9). Even His love was not His own, for He could command, 'As the Father has loved me, so have I loved you; abide in my love' (John 15:9). Truly, says the apostle, we 'live by faith in the Son of God,' living unconditionally in the grace of Christ's relationship of dependence, trust, obedience and identity with the Father. Here is no place for Platonic innateness of being, only the merits of Christ's dependence upon His Father.

God is not determined by His creation, as an emanation of His being. That is why He can joyfully play with creation. He plays with His possibilities of love, which are infinite in variety and scope. Yet it is not a capricious world, as we have seen, for He upholds the uniqueness of every created thing. The Hebrew language is rich in the words used—at least ten different words—to express delight in the good world God has made. And if creation is joyous, then living in the presence of the Creator is unmitigated joy.

> Thou dost show me the path of life;
> in Thy presence there is fulness of joy,
> at Thy right hand are pleasures for evermore.
>
> (Ps. 16:11)

Likewise the believer in the New Testament is exhorted to 'Rejoice in the Lord always; again I will say, Rejoice' (Phil. 4:4). With Mozart, the believer answers 'yes' and 'amen' to creation, in total dependence upon God. 'Except you become as little children, you cannot enter into the kingdom of heaven,' Jesus said. He taught His disciples, therefore, to look at the lilies, which 'neither toil nor spin', for God clothes even them. The birds are cared for in the same manner, for they 'neither sow nor reap nor gather into barns, and yet your heavenly Father feeds them' (Matt. 6:26, 28). This indeed is—

> faith serene as a star,
> hope that seeth afar,
> And Christ's own peace.

One of the most child-like celebrants of creation was Thomas Traherne, the metaphysical poet (?1632–1674), who lived at a critical period of Western thought when the rise of science and the resurgence in the sentiment of nature were to intensify the dualism between nature and grace, science and theology, activity and contemplation. He lamented that in spite of his Oxford education—

> There was never a tutor that did profusely teach Felicity, though that be the mistress of all other sciences. Nor did any of us study these things but as *Aliena,* which we ought to have studied to inform our knowledge, but knew not for what end we studied. And for the lack of aiming at a certain end we erred in the manner.[8]

Yet Traherne expressed in his prose masterpiece *Centuries* a marvellous, child-like celebration of the joys of all creation.

> Your enjoyment of the world is never right [he says] till every morning you awake in Heaven; see yourself in your Father's palace; and look upon the skies, the earth, and the air as Celestial Joys: having such a reverend esteem of all, as if you were among the Angels. ... You never enjoy the world aright ... till your spirit filleth the whole world, and the stars are your jewels; till you are as familiar with the ways of God in all Ages as with your walk and table: till you are intimately acquainted with that shady nothing out of which the world was made: till you love men so as to desire their happiness, with a thirst equal to

the zeal of your own; till you delight in God for being good at all: you never enjoy the world.[9]

At first sight, Traherne appears at times to be a romantic, even a pantheist, for he says:

You never enjoy the world aright till the Sea itself floweth in your veins, till you are clothed with the heavens and crowned with the stars.[10]

Is this any different from the argument of the novelist D. H. Lawrence, that to enjoy the world aright we must be part of the living universe, in 'a vivid and nourishing relation'?

We ought to dance with rapture that we should be alive and in the flesh, and part of the living, incarnate cosmos. I am part of the earth my feet know perfectly, and my blood is part of the sea.[11]

Lawrence, we know, was a thoroughgoing pantheist. 'It is no use asking for a Word to fulfil such a need. No Word, no Logos, no literature will ever do it ... it is the *Deed* of life we now have to learn.' In contrast, Traherne's enjoyment of the world was revelatory and biblical, springing from man's inability to understand the deep mysteries of the universe, and yet having confidence in God despite the fragmentariness of life and history. His serenity came from an openness to all of life, knowing that 'all things work together for good to those who love God'.

3. The Source of Joy

But joy is not an entity in itself; there is no joy for joy's sake. It is the possession of some good that is the cause of rejoicing. Traherne had two great sources of joy: that God alone is God, and that God is love. As a practical truth of life, he saw simply that 'God is', and that all else is but His creation. Enjoyment of creation means, then, renouncing 'the leaven of this world ... disentangled from men's conceits and customs ... ambitions, trades, luxuries, inordinate affections, casual and accidental riches, invented since the Fall.' He goes on:

Above all trades, above all occupations, this is most sub-
lime. This is the greatest of affairs. Whatever else we do
it is only in order that we may live conveniently and to
enjoy the world and God within it; which is the sovereign
employment including and crowning all the celestial life
of a glorious creature, without which all other estates are
servile and impertinent.[12]

In contrast to this sentiment, how imprisoned Traherne would
view modern man, caught up in the idolatries of tyrannical
professionalism and such pragmatism of spirit that, instead of
seeing creation with a child-like and overwhelming delight, he
sees it only as data for the intellect and as resources for
consumption.

The purity of this joy did not come to Traherne all at
once. He had first the child's experience of Paradise. This was
the felicity of ignorance, without pain or sickness, evil or death.
Then he learned of apostasy, which like the Fall was the loss
of the sense of the goodness of the Creator. This came through
the corrupting influences of 'the dirty devices of this world',
'by the customs and manners of men', 'by the impetuous tor-
rent of wrong desires', which eclipsed the light of creation. For
like Augustine, in childhood he had been 'swept up to Thee
in Thine beauty', but later, in becoming centred upon himself,
'torn away from Thee by my own weight'.[13]

Then, in his realisation of self-centredness and sin, he
had a conversion experience, when he became aware of his
own sinfulness and of the forgiveness of God. He experienced
purification and acceptance, and from his own personal recognition of the manifestation of the Cross of Christ he saw
again, deeper and with richer hues, the love of God. Like all
other believers, he learned that to the 'poor in spirit' there is
the blessing of the rule of God, to the pure in heart there is
the vision of God, and to the meek there is the inheritance of
the earth. For the beatific life is the enjoyment of God and His
will.

The immediacy of God that follows from such a blessed
existence enabled Traherne to see time and eternity lived not
as extensions of each other, but simultaneously, God's presence
side by side with daily, ordinary living. Intensely, he saw the

interconnectedness of life, 'so piercing this life with the life of Heaven and seeing it as one with all Eternity'. For eternity is the presence of God. From this perspective, Traherne saw that 'every spire of grass is the work of His hands'. There is no separation between this world and the next, earth and heaven, time and eternity, so that there can be no categorical separation between the realms of vision and of reason, of faith and fact, of nature and grace, of theology and science.

> It ought to be a firm principle rooted within us, that this life is the most precious season in all Eternity because all Eternity dependeth on it. Now we may do those actions which hereafter we shall never have occasion to do.[14]

Traherne also realised that 'love is the true means by which the world is enjoyed'. Love is what binds the universe together, far more profoundly than Newton's law of gravity. For God is the guarantor of the care of the universe, as expressed in His love. And love is the most profound manifestation of the triune God, that is, of God the Father (God in essence), God the Son (God in expression) and God the Holy Spirit (God in exercise).

> In all love there is a love begetting, and a love begotten, and a love proceeding, which though they are one in essence, subsist nevertheless in their several manners. For love is benevolent affection to another, which is of itself and by itself related to its object. It floweth from itself and resteth on its object. Love proceedeth of necessity from itself, for unless it be of itself, it is not love . . . so that in all love the Trinity is clear.

> In all love there is some Producer, some Means and some End; all these being internal in the thing itself. Love loving is the Producer, and that is the Father. Love produced is the Means, and that is the Son. For Love is the means by which a lover loveth. The end of this means is Love, for it is love in loving, and that is the Holy Ghost. The End and the Producer being both the same, by the Means attained.[15]

It is in such a frame of mind that we take seriously the statement of the apostle John: 'For God so loved the world that He gave His only begotten Son, that whoever believes in Him should not perish but have eternal life' (John 3:16). 'What a world would this be,' argued Traherne, 'were everything beloved as it ought to be! For who can love anything that God made too much?' We can only love too much when we forget that it is the gift of the love of God.

THE EXPERIENCE OF AWARENESS

Moreover, Traherne argues that 'infinite love cannot be expressed in finite room: but must have infinite places wherein to utter and show itself'.

> It must therefore fill all Eternity and the Omnipresence of God with joys and treasures for my fruition. And yet it must be expressed in a private room by making me able in a centre to enjoy them. It must be infinitely exprest in the smallest moment by making me in every moment to see them all.[16]

Only the man who senses his impoverishment before God is filled with grace. Only when I am weak am I made strong (2 Cor. 12:10). Only when I am lonely do I experience most intensely the presence of God. Only when I am emptied do I recognise that 'God is at work . . . both to will and to work for His good pleasure' (Phil. 2:13). It is no accident that poverty of spirit is the condition for the first of the beatitudes. The grace of God does not erase our poverty, but transforms it into the wealth of true humanity. For as Meister Eckhart said, 'Any flea as it is in God is nobler than the highest of angels in himself.'

1. Boredom

A significant phenomenon of our times is the spirit of boredom that fills so many hearts with a passive, uncommitted attitude to life and its choices. Perhaps many are blocked by a sense of guilt over the past as well as by a sense of anxiety for the future.[17] Between guilt and anxiety, the present is emptied of actualisation or of potentiality. The present is thus perceived as valueless and meaningless. It is the experience of boring a hole and looking into the abyss. If we analyse in order to look through everything, instead of looking at something, we see nothing. So much boredom is the consequence of the analytical spirit that forgets that there is vision as well as reason, faith as well as pragmatism.

Guilt is the awareness of the loss of good, of values negated. Guilt remembers it has failed to respond to disclosures of values. It is failure to respond to reality—the good world God has made. It is therefore a retrospective stance to lost opportunities, rejected values and wrong choices. Anxiety is guilt's consequence, for the prospective fear of being discovered in guilt and judged is the basis of anxiety. This guilt is memory directed towards the past, as anxiety is imagination directed to the future, yet the one intensifies the other. The more guilt I have, the deeper is the abyss of nothingness for the future. Indeed, the future does not exist; there is no future. For if I have irretrievably lost values, I have none to anticipate. This is when guilt and anxiety are intensified by idolatry, that is, the substitution of false values for real values, of created things for the Creator. Only by trust in the trustworthiness of God, which is what biblical faith means, can our hearts be enlarged to celebrate the real world.

To the Hebrews, 'boredom' was an alien experience. Instead of seeing time as divided into past, present and future, their view was more two-dimensional. There is the present, but words for past and future are often essentially the same.[18] Time diverges from two points, from past through present to future, as the points of an arrow converge on one tip. Thus the past and future both reinforce the immediacy, the power and the reality of 'right now', 'this very day'. Life situations are focused upon the present, giving 'this day' its significance. Memorable events have happened, which will have decisive effects on the future, but they have central significance right now. Time therefore has a qualitative rather than a quantitative value. It is this which heightens awareness of God the Creator, so that with the Psalmist we can respond fully to the invitation,

> This is the day that the Lord has made;
> let us rejoice and be glad in it.   (Ps. 118:24)

How then can we experience that infinite joy of the Creator within the finite recesses of our hearts of which Traherne sang?

2. Rest

Simone Weil, the sensitive young philosopher, has answered beautifully this question when she says, 'grace fills empty spaces but it can only enter where there is a void to receive it, and it is grace itself which makes the void.'[19] As we have seen in the summary of the book of Ecclesiastes (pp. 199–202), we need again and again to face the void in our lives, in order to have more room for joy, 'rejoicing in the Lord always'. Alas, our imaginations are constantly at work, filling the fissures of our hearts, through which grace might otherwise pass. Such imagination is false, however, and fills our being with fantasies that we know are idols. Nature, we are told, abhors a vacuum, so either the universe is full of the glory of God, or else it is full of falsity. There is a secular attitude to joy today, a how-to-do-it manual in which joy is expanding human awareness through yoga, breathing exercises and much else; this only gives man a greater capacity to absorb more fantasies in his life.[20] It claims to realise potentials, but potentials for what? we may ask.

God gives man rest from his labours, so that his attention is re-directed to God's rest. 'Come to me, all who labour and are heavy laden, and I will give you rest,' Jesus invites; here is rest even from expanding self-consciousness. The institution of the Sabbath was on the seventh day of creation. Created on the sixth day, man's first consciousness was of entrance into a *completed world,* where God's approval first met man with the verdict, it was all *good.* God did not create man to be Sisyphus, always caught up in the futility of toil. Rather, rest has been available for man since creation; that is to say, all things are in order in their potential. By faith in the Creator man can now live in the light of that reality.

Alas, much legalism has developed over the misunderstanding of the Sabbath rest. Abraham Heschel, the Jewish scholar, recites a delightful tale of one pious rabbi who walked in his apple orchard one Sabbath, making a mental note that one of his trees seriously required much pruning. But it was the Sabbath, so action had to be postponed. Some days later, when he went to prune the tree, he found it had withered and died. He learned from that incident that God destroyed the tree—as He had cursed the fig-tree—to teach the rabbi that even the thought of imperfection on the Sabbath, and so the thought of human work to make good a deficiency, was wrong. It is a matter of consciousness—the use or misuse of our imagination—to be filled by grace or preoccupied with self-endeavour. When we prune a tree we manipulate it, instead of accepting it or 'letting be', as the root meaning of 'Sabbath' conveys.

The Sabbath, then, is not a day for doing nothing. Rather, it is a particular kind of consciousness, mindful of the bounty of God. The poet George Herbert, a contemporary of Traherne, saw, however, that God's provision of rest for man was a cosmic risk, for man might rest in a wrong relationship, 'in Nature, not the God of Nature', as science has so largely done.

> When God at first made man,
> Having a glasse of blessings stand by,
> Let us (said he) poure on him all we can.
> Let the world's riches, which dispersed lie,
> Contract into a span.
>
> So strength first made a way,
> The beautie flowed, then wisdom, honour, pleasure.
> When almost all was out, God made a stay,
> Perceiving that alone of all his treasure
> Rest in the bottome lay.
>
> For if I should (said he)
> Bestow this jewell also on my creature,
> He would adore my gifts instead of me,
> And rest in Nature, not the God of Nature.
> So both should losers be.
>
> Yet let him keep the rest,
> But keep them with repining restlessness.
> Let him be rich and wearie, that at least,
> If goodnesse leade him not, yet wearinesse
> May tosse him to my breast.
>
> George Herbert—*The Pulley*

The dialectic of man's condition, tossed about between the Sabbath and the workaday world, from rest to restlessness, is the same tension that exists in the imagination between mystery and cognition, contemplation and action, vision and facts. It is a split in man, deeper than the dualism deplored in Western civilisation, which only the Son of Man can heal, who having nowhere to lay his head, yet rested always in the Father's will.

3. Holy Humour

Our dilemma, however, is that if we are to take God absolutely seriously, we fall constantly into the trap of taking ourselves too seriously. Arrogance is a temptation of God's servants. Perhaps then we need to take comedy as our ally; it deflates pretensions. Comedy is a good instrument whereby we see the false idols of our world, and knock them down. As finite beings, with infinite desires, we live comical lives, full of incongruities. Perhaps God, too, is the cosmic and compassionate comedian, because if He is God, He will have the last laugh. So indeed the Bible describes Him:

> He who sits in the heavens laughs;
> the Lord has them in derision.   (Ps. 2:4)

This is one of three instances in the Scriptures in which laughter is attributed to the Almighty. Humour, then, is both an attribute of our humanity and the rhetoric of God's grace. Underlying both of these realities is the ordering of the world in creation—not in chaos—and the rule of God as its moral governor.

Righteousness and justice are the foundations of creation, reflecting the character of their Creator. Isaiah, living with a people who had broken covenant with God, says:

> For thus says the Lord,
> who created the heavens (He is God!),
> who formed the earth and made it,
> (He established it;
> He did not create it a chaos,
> He formed it to be inhabited!):

> ... I the Lord speak *sedeq* (righteousness),
> I declare what is right.   (Isa. 45:18–19)

God is not to be sought in the neurotic conditions of modern art, with its loss of form, but in the ordered life. Likewise the Psalmist declares:

> By dread deeds Thou dost answer us with *sedeq*
>   (righteousness),
> O God of our salvation;
> who art the hope of all the ends of the earth,
> and of the farthest seas;
> who by Thy strength hast established the mountains,
> being girded with might;
> who dost still the roaring of the seas,
> the roaring of their waves,
> the tumult of the peoples.   (Ps. 65:6–7)

This God, who measures and divides the realities of life, is also just (*mishpat*). Who else, exclaims the prophet, has done all this?

> Who has measured the waters in the hollow of his hand
> and marked off the heavens with a span,
> enclosed the dust of the earth in a measure
> and weighed the mountains in scales
> and the hills in a balance?
> Who has directed the Spirit of the Lord,
> or as His counselor has instructed Him?
> Whom did He consult for His enlightenment,
> and who taught Him the path of justice *(mishpat)*,
> and taught Him knowledge,
> and showed Him the way of understanding?
>   (Isa. 40:12–14)

This cosmic principle of God's justice extends into every area of human experience. Nothing is too small or too ordinary to exhibit the need of God's justice. Why, even the peasant, says the prophet, can cultivate his land only according to *mishpat*:

> Give ear, and hear my voice;
> hearken, and hear my speech.
> Does he who plows for sowing plow continually?

Does he continually open and harrow his ground?
. . . Does he not scatter dill, sow cummin,
and put the wheat in rows and barley in its proper
    place,
and spelt as the border?
For He instructs him in justice *(mishpat)*;
His God teaches him.   (Isa. 28:23–26)

Even the miller's procedures that yield flour on the threshing
floor are a recognition of God's justice (Isa. 28:27–29).

It is against the background of this dynamic of right doing
that we can exercise humour in the incongruities that fill the
foregound of our lives. Humour is a rightful exercise in this
world, for in heaven it will no longer be proper, and in hell
there will be no ability to laugh. At the same time there is a
broad spectrum of the ludicrous, from humour that gives sym-
pathetic insight into human nature to cynicism that seeks self-
justification in midst of the bankruptcy of personal relations.
Satire, invective and sarcasm will have their victims, but true
humour sees humanity bound together in its incongruities.

Humour is a serious matter, as Søren Kierkegaard realised. He said:

> The more thoroughly and substantially a human being
> exists, the more he will discover the comical. Even one
> who has merely conceived a great plan toward accom-
> plishing something in the world, will discover it. . . . But
> the resolution of the religious individual is the highest of
> all resolves, infinitely higher than all plans to transform
> the world and to create systems and works of art: there-
> fore the religious man, most of all men, discovers the
> comical.[21]

Since technological society takes itself and its abilities deadly
seriously, there is an increasing need for the Christian to exercise more humour than ever before. For there are no gargoyles on the downtown skyscrapers, as there used to be on
our cathedral roofs. The comic provides that detachment from
idolatry which is so deeply needed today. The believer, too,
needs to avoid that deadly seriousness which is not faith but
bigotry, and seeking personal power in the name of the Lord.

The sacred and the comic need each other to check against both tendencies of spirit.

Since the essence of comedy is discrepancy, holy comedy points to the constant need of redemption: of motives, of deeds and of character. There is also the awareness of discrepancy when man sees himself only as an animal, whereas God has given him dominion over the world. And there is discrepancy when man sees himself as his own master and creator, while in reality the Creator is King of the universe. Cosmic cartharsis gives man the fleeting awareness of his finitude, so while in tragedy there is suffering and struggle, in comedy there is ultimate hope and transcendence. The comic, too, is the refusal to accept the *status quo*, unmasking human pretensions and refusing to see human beings as incarnations—as well as incarcerations—of social systems and principles. The Christian goes about the world, tongue in cheek, as God's clown, knowing that the mask he wears on earth will one day become a real face in heaven.

We have emphasised the need for a child-like spirit to enjoy the earth. Humour also prepares us to be child-like, to learn to enjoy heaven. The normal child laughs a lot, so that Kierkegaard had to say, 'the humorous effect is produced by letting the child-like trait reflect itself in the consciousness of totality.' Christ, so child-like, was the great humorist, a theme beautifully developed in Elton Trueblood's *The Humor of Christ*.[22] In His parables, in His encounters with individuals, the wit and humour of Jesus shine out, against Pharisees, priests and the religious establishment with all its self-interest. Humour is needed to enjoy grace, because it is the realm where grace wholly reigns, while the religious bureaucracy operates on the basis of self-endeavour and self-interest.

To enjoy God, to worship Him, to appreciate deeply the bounties of His world, we need humour. That is to say, we need to be liberated from ourselves so that we can be free to enjoy the ultimate presence of God.[23] In laughter we acknowledge the human condition, and seek the transcendent power of God. This, too, we find in incongruities such as the Red Sea, Bethlehem and Calvary. We see it, too, in a shepherd lad, David, facing the giant Goliath with only a sling and five small stones. We see it today in you and me facing the threats of an atomic holocaust. Today men and women without God speak of living beyond tragedy because there is no place left for man to be tragic, dwarfed as he is before the atomic cloud, and beyond comedy because there is no place left for comedy if there is no hope. In both cases man is reduced to a whimper, with no high seriousness left about anything, only absurdity. Only the Cross of Christ, where tears and laughter are reconciled, can save us from such a state.

THE WORSHIP OF GOD

The enjoyment of God is in all its forms the worship of God. For worship is the acknowledgement of the reality and absolute worth of God. He is worthy of all our praise. Thus the exercise of a child-like spirit, trust, joy, a deepening awareness of life, rest and humour, are all acts of worship. For worship points to the end of human existence, not to the means of life. Any satisfaction, solution or joyful spirit we experience in worship is an indirect blessing, rather than the reason for our worship. Too often our church services are for the sake of the congregation, for whose benefit the minister and choir perform, and God is the absentee playwright or producer. Instead, God is more truly the audience, and we are the stage cast.

A people's worship is the acid test of their inner convictions about reality. What people think of their gods will prescribe how they worship them. Consistent, then, with the Egyptian view of evil in the universe (see pp. 88–89)—that is, that it is not a serious issue—is the way Egyptian psalms speak with self-confident assurance. They contemplate the goodness of life using pictorial narration, in a spirit of jubilation. Praise is essentially descriptive, as the obvious response of man. Lament is rarely heard. In contrast, the Babylonian psalms are concomitant with their lack of confidence because of the presence of much evil among their gods. They merely praise the existence of their gods, without much reference to their attributes. Their dealings are only with their fellow gods. In sharp contrast, Israel's praise from beginning to end has as its theme the history of God with His people.

1. The Command to Worship

A sharp contrast that makes Israel's worship unique in this world is that praise is imperative, not indicative. In the Psalms we are almost always called to worship. It is a demand, not a choice as elsewhere in the ancient world. It is not something given to God at will, but something owed to God. For in Israel praise is the ever-new call to remember the deeds of God. Thus God is more the subject than the mere object of worship.[24]

> O give thanks to the Lord, for He is good,
> for His steadfast love endures for ever.
> O give thanks to the God of gods,
> for His steadfast love endures for ever.
> O give thanks to the Lord of lords,
> for His steadfast love endures for ever;
>
> to Him who alone does great wonders,
> for His steadfast love endures for ever;
> to Him who by understanding made the heavens,
> for His steadfast love endures for ever;
> to Him who spread out the earth upon the waters,
> for His steadfast love endures for ever;
> to Him who made the great lights,
> for His steadfast love endures for ever;
> the sun to rule over the day,
> for His steadfast love endures for ever;
> the moon and stars to rule over the night,
> for His steadfast love endures for ever.   (Ps. 136:1–9)

While the deeds of creation elicit praise, central to Israel's worship is the summons to recall the deeds of God in history and therefore in her salvation. The deeds of God are a constant call to worship. For in biblical faith they are always deeds on behalf of His people, while in the ancient pagan faiths they were always the gods' concerns for themselves. Three features therefore are typical of the psalms of Israel:

1. God has acted; let His deeds be praised!
2. Praise is therefore a direct response to the act just enacted.

3. Praise is expressed joyfully.

Theologians like Von Rad[25] and Westermann[26] have shown that creation is a secondary theme of worship. For the Creator is not praised for the sake of creation, but for His own sake. Moreover, the majority of psalms that dwell on creation, such as Psalm 136 quoted above, go on to recite in more detail God's activity in the history of the nations. Behind this emphasis is the exultation of the worshipper, who himself has been heard and saved. Likewise in Isaiah, creation *per se* is never the main theme, but it is always in the context of a saved people. It is only when we come to the intertestamental period, with its strong Hellenistic influences, that attention begins to turn away from the Creator to the praise of creation for its own sake. Such is typical, for example, of Ecclesiasticus. It is not dissimilar to what the Romantic poets have done in modern literature.

We need to emphasise this imperative trait of worship—to give thanks and respond in gratitude—because man so readily forgets God. The parable of the ten lepers reminds us that man's ingratitude is common. Since modern man likes to think of himself as self-sufficient and not in need of God's direct help except in times of extreme emergency, this need to praise God constantly is vital to His spirit. There is also the common view that since God is not very concerned with the details of ordinary existence—God helping those who help themselves—there is not really much purpose in giving God thanks in church on Sunday. If a man's work really is the source of his significance and security, Sunday morning worship may be a yawning bore.

How different is the worship of angels! They, too, are creatures, but creatures in the immediate presence of God. They are not subject to the human conditions of space and time, with all its bentness and obliqueness. In them God's glory shines directly and is reflected directly. Their praise suffers no interruption (Rev. 4:8), for their whole nature is praise, their beings designed for nothing other than the worship of God.[27] Their whole being is one uninterrupted song, rendered in perfect spontaneity, as Isaiah heard, saying, 'Holy, holy, holy, is the Lord of hosts' (Isa. 6:3).

Worship on earth is a dim reflection of what is done in heaven. Nevertheless, it has a cosmic perspective, as if we are rehearsing, even though badly, what we shall one day do perfectly, as the angels do. It is in such anticipation of earth and heaven being eventually united in praise that the Psalmist can say:

> Praise Him, you highest heavens,
> and you waters above the heavens!
> Let them praise the name of the Lord!
> For He commanded, and they were created.
> (Ps. 148:4, 5)

In this psalm, the command to worship is reminiscent of God's command at the beginning of creation itself. For the command of creation and the command of worship are based on the same Word of God. In Psalm 148, all the elements of the universe are called upon to praise the Lord: the sun, moon and all shining stars, fire, hail, snow and fog, mountains and all hills, fruit trees and all cedars, wild and tame animals, creeping things and winged birds, as well as men of all social conditions. This suggests that all God's creatures are now and have always been since their beginning translucent with the glory of God. For they are all evidence of the Word of God in creation. They are what they are by the command of God.

The Psalmist also says:

> There is no speech, nor are there words;
> their voice is not heard;
> yet their voice goes out through all the earth,
> and their words to the end of the world.   (Ps. 19:3–4)

What this difficult passage seems to mean is that while our physical ears may pick up no human language from the creation—'no words, no speech'—nevertheless it speaks in all the languages of mankind the cosmic language of the Creator. In this sense, says the prophet Isaiah, 'the whole earth is full of His glory' (Isa. 6:3). That is to say, all creaturely existence is evidence of the word of command, of the will and sovereign purpose of the Creator. Every creature, from the sparrow in the street and the mayfly in the meadow to the great whales of the sea, owes its being to the word of God. There is a word-relatedness implanted in the being of every creature. That is why the universe is intelligible, because the mind of man is suited to the secret structure of creation itself.

While we hear the music of the stars, however, which the medieval world heard so sweetly, we also hear the groaning of creation, groaning as in travail, because of the curse of man (Rom. 8:19–23). The presence of such groaning implies the need for a Redeemer. The heavenly liturgy is sweetest, clearest and most unalloyed when all creatures surround the throne of the Lamb, the crucified, risen and exalted Christ, as John the Seer heard in the clear doxology of eternity (Rev. 5:13).

But we must add that while the doxology of the whole of creation is still unclear to us, since God's ways of grace with them are unknown to us, yet we do know what God demands of man. He demands a clean heart and a contrite spirit. Humility is the essence of man's worship of God. Whatever may be the forms of dependence all other creatures have on God, for man it takes the form of gratitude, for God has made man in His own image. Thus man is free to respond personally, not instinctually, to his Creator and Redeemer, and God is free to love in all the fullness of His grace. In short, man's gratitude is the relational complement of God's grace.

2. Worship as Confession

Confession and contrition are essential elements of worship. When Isaiah saw the sudden disclosure of God's glory, and even the seraphs dare not look on the mysterious, glorious beauty of God's holiness, he could see only his own imperfection. 'Woe is me! for I am a man of unclean lips!' (Isa. 6:3). Shame and penitence are the traits of the true worshipper. Most of the psalms are laments. They express man's unworthiness as the basis for his need of God, and praise that God takes up the unworthy and hears his petitions. This in turn gives the worshipper a deeper sense of gratitude which is reflected in his worship. Perhaps, then, the preponderance of petitionary psalms in the psalter, as well as of petitions in our own lives, reflects upon the neediness of man—fallen, sinful and frail in heart. Nevertheless, many such psalms of lament quickly revert to praise, as witness to the grace of God who has heard prayer from the depths.

It is faith in the sovereign rule of the Creator that enables Jonah in the belly of the fish, in the depth of the sea, to compose such a hymn.

> I called to the Lord, out of my distress,
> and He answered me;
> out of the belly of Sheol I cried,
> and Thou didst hear my voice.
> For Thou didst cast me into the deep,
> into the heart of the sea,
> and the flood was round about me;
> all Thy waves and Thy billows
> passed over me.
> Then I said, 'I am cast out from Thy presence;
> how shall I again look
> upon Thy holy temple?'   (Jon. 2:2–4)

Yet even in the twilight zone of Sheol, the weakest form of existence, there is still the possibility of faith in the Creator as the source of life. Moreover, even from this extreme position of destitution, in a fish's belly, in the depth of the Mediterranean sea, his prayer is heard. What a transcendence of geography!

> When my soul fainted within me,
> I remembered the Lord;
> and my prayer came to Thee,
> into Thy holy temple. (vs. 7)

Again, in Psalm 139, the intensely personal experience of God is shown from the foetus in the womb (which for ever sanctifies the foetus as a living person), revealing that the whole of life is related to, and utterly dependent upon, the Creator. Nowhere does the worshipper speculate about ideas of God, but instead he explores intimately the omniscience of the living God (vss. 1–6), His ever-relevant omnipresence (vss. 7–12) and His personal omnificence (vss. 13–16). The Psalmist can only confess his inability to comprehend God, considering how great He is (vss. 17–18). The Creator God is present in every reality of life, and in every conceivable situation of existence the worshipper and God are related. For God goes down into bathyscaphic depths as well as up into telescopic heights, and the worshipper can only follow with a sense of wonder.

3. Christ Our Worshipper

The command to worship is clearly stated in Deut. 6:13: 'Thou shalt worship the Lord thy God, and Him only shalt thou serve.' It is a worship that characterises all of life, wholly so. But our confession is that we do not so serve, for we are rebels. We begin to realise the woeful inadequacy of our worship, however, when we find that there is no independent and abstract concept of 'thanks' in Hebrew. Praise and thanksgiving are a way of living and of being, not a disconnected act such as when we say 'thank you' for some gift and then promptly and absent-mindedly leave it behind us to be preoccupied with other tasks. That is totally foreign to the Bible.[28] There praise is collective, not the individualism of a thankful demeanour. There also praise is obedience of heart—not a momentary attitude, but a permanent activity directed towards God for His character and His deeds. There, too, praise is forensic, for it confesses publicly for the benefit of others what God has done for the worshipper in the privacy of his life. It is the double motion of acknowledging the lordship of God, 'believing in the heart' and 'confessing with the lips' (Rom. 10:9–10). The apostle further appeals to us to 'present your bodies as a living sacrifice, holy and acceptable to God, which is your spiritual worship' (Rom. 12:1).

This holistic view of worship forces us to contrition, repentance and the need of a substitute, who is wholly the worshipper. That is why the early church directed their worship to the Father, through Christ, in the Holy Spirit, a trinitarian understanding of worship. We have a woefully limited understanding of worship if we overlook the reality of Christ as the perfect worshipper, whom the epistle to the Hebrews calls our 'Great High Priest', divinely qualified as God, yet sensitive to all our temptations and fallenness (Heb. 5:5–10). Wondrously, Christ 'emptied himself' in the amazing self-abasement of God, to be one with us in our lack of worth and our nothingness

(Phil. 2:5–11), in order to sanctify us, to enrich us by the poverty of His incarnation (2 Cor. 8:9). For God to become man means that God acts, lives, thinks, serves, worships, within all the limits, principles and measures of what it means to be human. It means that as man Christ is both the judge and the judged.

> Sending His own Son in the likeness of sinful flesh and for sin, He [God] condemned sin in the flesh, in order that the just requirement of the law might be fulfilled in us.   (Rom. 8:3–4)

That is why the apostle could claim, as we too can claim, 'I, yet not I, but Christ in me.' I therefore pray in Christ, rejoice in Christ and worship in Christ as my Great High Priest. We are turned away from our praying, our rejoicing, our worship. That is what the request, 'Lord, teach us to pray', means. It is the 'Abba, Father' of Christ which He shares with us—His relationship as Son. In His prayer we pray also, and in His worship we worship.[29] That is why we can experience and know Him as our High Priest. But as man He also brings to the Father all the enjoyment possible for us to give to the Father.

However, the priesthood of Christ involves not only our offering of the sacrifice of praise as He perfectly praised and offered Himself. He also receives our worship, for He is God. Priest and Sacrifice, He is also the One who receives worship. So we pray *to* Christ as well as *through* Christ. For in Him 'all things hold together'. God in Christ has done for us, in a human way, what we were unable to do. Moreover, God in Christ reveals the secret of creation, that its purpose, coherence and fulfilment is the love of God. Thus all our life, in all its many activities, takes place authentically only within the circle of Jesus Christ. God then is properly recognised as the subject of the entire drama of creation and salvation, not merely as the object of religious endeavour. Worship, enjoyment, yes, all the attributes of man, are not then forms of man's self-expression, but of Christ's vicarious worship, offered on behalf of all mankind, in all ages, through all cultures.

For us there is one God, the Father,
from whom are all things
and for whom we exist,
and one Lord, Jesus Christ,
through whom are all things
and through whom we exist.   (1 Cor. 8:6)

NOTES

1   Thomas Aquinas, quoted by John Burnaby, *Amor Dei*, London, Hodder & Stoughton, 1947, p. 47.

2   Jacques Colette, 'Pleasure and Anguish in the thoughts of Barth and Mozart', in *The Theology of Joy* (edit. Johann B. Metz and Jean Pierre Jossua), New York, Herder & Herder, 1974, pp. 96–106.

3   S. Alexander, *Space, Time and Deity*, London, Macmillan, 1920, vol. 1, pp. 12–13.

4   Quoted by Elizabeth Goudge, *A Book of Faith*, Hodder & Stoughton, London, 1976, p. 47.

5   Ibid., p. 48.

6   Quoted by Lionel Trilling, *The Liberal Imagination*, New York, Charles Scribner's Sons, 1950, p. 144.

7   Ibid., pp. 146–153.

8   Anne Ridley (edit.), *Traherne, Poems, Centuries*, London, Oxford University Press, 1966, Centuries III, 37, p. 238.

9   Ibid.

10 Ibid., I, 29, p. 177.

11 D. H. Lawrence, *Apocalypse*, London, Martin Secker, 1932, p. 233.

12 Traherne, *Centuries*, op. cit., IV, 50, p. 339.

13 Augustine, *Confessions*, VII, ch. XVII, trans. E. B. Pusey, London, Dent, 1962.

14 Traherne, *Centuries*, op. cit., IV, 93, p. 363.

15 Ibid., II, 40, p. 234; II, 46, p. 236.

16 Ibid., II, 80, p. 250.

17 Thomas C. Oden, *The Structure of Awareness*, Nashville, Abingdon, 1969.

18 Simon John DeVries, *Yesterday, Today and Tomorrow*, Grand Rapids, Eerdmans, 1975, pp. 31, 39–40.

19 Quoted by George A. Panichas, *The Simone Weil Reader*, New York, David MacKay Co., 1977.

20 See, for example, William C. Schutz, *Joy, expanding human awareness*, Harmondsworth, England, Pelican, Penguin Books, 1973.

21   Søren Kierkegaard, *Concluding Unscientific Postscript,* Princeton, Princeton University Press, 1941, pp. 413–414.
22   Elton Trueblood, *The Humor of Christ,* London, Longman & Todd, Libra Books, 1965.
23   Reinhold Niebuhr, 'Humor and Faith', in *Holy Laughter* (edit. M. Conrad Myers), New York, Seabury Press, 1969, pp. 134–149.
24   Claus Westermann, *The Praise of God in the Psalms,* London, Epworth Press, 1966, p. 50.
25   Gerhard von Rad, *Old Testament Theology,* London, S.C.M., 1975, vol. 1, pp. 136–138.
26   Westermann, op. cit., p. 127.
27   Peter Brunner, *Worship in the Name of Jesus,* St. Louis, Concordia, 1968, pp. 94–97.
28   Westermann, op. cit., p. 25.
29   T. F. Torrance, *Theology in Reconciliation,* Grand Rapids, Eerdmans, 1975, pp. 139–214.

CHAPTER NINE

Living Hopefully Before the Creator

To wait upon the world of 'Nature' is the death of hope, but to wait upon the Creator is to live authentically and full of hope. Nature—we have seen—is a closed world, for eternity cannot penetrate the density of its cyclical processes and impersonal realities when man cannot or will not see beyond its materiality. 'Earth of earth', says the poet Robert Thornton, has 'a foul stink'. It is a 'sick rose', says William Blake, for already in its 'bed of crimson joy' 'the invisible worm . . . does thy life destroy'. From impersonal Nature no word can reach man to give him hope, no promise of fulfilment of being, no life in community. Its basis of power is energy—the sun's energy—not the love of the Creator. Nature's communities are plants and animals, not man and God. No wonder, then, that philosophers and writers like Heidegger, Sartre and Camus see the horizon of human existence as destiny and fate, leading to non-being and ultimate Nothingness. Yet his greying hairs, her creased countenance and their shortness of breath remind us all of our temporality. This radical uncertainty of continuity undermines man's commitment to life, since the measure of our confidence is the measure of our hopes. Between continuation and annihilation, man asks the questions of the 'whence?' and 'wither?' of life, which bring up the matter of the meaning of time and eternity, and of their interaction.

We saw in the first chapter that in Beckett's play *Waiting for Godot* there is a breakdown of language linked with the lack of friendship or true relationships. If man's language is nonsensical, what is left of man's humanity? This goes further into despair than even Iris Murdoch's novel *The Word Child,* where the hero still has his word, if not love. Words judge us, however, said Jesus. 'For by your words you will be justified, and by your words you will be condemned' (Matt. 12:37). For nonsensical words betray the loss of contact with other people. If then there is a famine of hearing the word of the Lord (Amos 8:11–12), man is cut off profoundly from reality. The Exile of the Word is the state of the desert, the empty, drained desiccation of reality, which T. S. Eliot has described as the world of the London Underground, the sphere of daily indifference, where the faces of the passengers are 'filled with fancies and empty of meaning'.

> The desert is squeezed in the tube-train next to you.
> The desert is in the heart of your brother.
> T. S. Eliot—Choruses from the Rock

Thus without the Word of creation there is no community. Now we also need to realise that without the Word of creation there is no time.

TIME AND ETERNITY

In *Waiting for Godot,* Beckett also depicts destructively the meaninglessness of time. Man has long lived with the ambiguity of time, which the Greeks recognised as *chronos,* measured time, time by the seasons, time by the clock, and *kairos,* quality time, the time for opportunities to be seized. The world of *chronos* is 'before-and-afterness', while that of *kairos* is 'nowness'. The one implies duration and succession, the other instrumentation and purpose. Theologians have exaggerated the antinomies of *chronos* and *kairos,* as if these two worlds were set over against each other. In fact each gives reality and meaning to the other, just as longitude and latitude are both needed to map spatial realities. Set one against the other and you smash any possibility of finding your way. Yet this is what Beckett does deliberately with *chronos* and *kairos.* He sets these two understandings of time on collision course.

In the play, Pozzo lives only by chronometric time, seeing it only in terms of minutes and hours in which he performs as

Homo faber. When he loses his watch, he therefore reacts, 'What have I done with my watch?' as a cry of declaration, for he is meaningless if he is not doing something. The two tramps look for the watch, listen for its tick, and then Estragon says, 'I hear something.' Vladimir suggests in turn, 'It is the heart.' But Pozzo, disappointed, rejects this opportunity to live by *kairos,* personal, eventful time, and shouts, 'damnation.' Later he admits, 'I don't seem able to depart.' In the second scene he is re-introduced blind, 'blind as Fortune'. He cries out, 'Have you done tormenting me with your accursed time!' Pozzo illustrates the parable of Jesus about those who were invited to a special occasion, a great feast, but he is too busy with chronometry to live eventfully, and he misses his chance (Luke 14:15–24). He now rages, 'The blind have no notion of time.'

On the other hand, the two tramps appear to be looking for *kairos,* the decisive and accepted time. That is why they are 'waiting for Godot'—the time he will come, with its commanding reality. Yet their anticipation is a basic contradiction of such eventfulness. For Vladimir, 'how time flies when one has fun!' But for Estragon, who is 'not a historian', everything 'oozes'. He admits, 'Yesterday evening we spent blathering about nothing in particular. That's been going on now for half a century'— their whole life. Challenged by Vladimir about the meaningfulness of time in terms of 'the sun. The moon. Do you not remember?', Estragon admits, 'They must have been there, as usual.' At the end of the play, the only eventfulness of 'tomorrow' will be the day of their suicide.

In the play it is this collision between time measured and time evaluated that is so destructive of reality. For man needs to see himself as significant in the light of events, or *kairos,* seeing himself hopefully in the context of a greater reality than his own temporality, or *chronos.* Man is nurtured by *kairos,* or rather by the Creator who has created time and given it its role in His creation. But man is also set in the temporality and contingency of *chronos,* the threescore years and ten of human expectancy, within which he has accountability and responsibility. Beckett deliberately destroys reality, for none of his characters is set within this graticule of life, of eternity and temporality. Man lives in both: he lives by bread, he also lives by every word that proceeds out of the mouth of God.

Western man sees time simplistically as a straight line, divided neatly into past, present and future. Often this view has been associated with progress, so that the future is always better than the past. Time, too, is abstracted into a concept. But biblical time is different.[1] First of all, biblical time is set in the context of each relationship, with 'a time for every matter under heaven' (Eccl. 3:1–12). This therefore is not fateful time, but the Creator's timing, for 'He has made everything beautiful in its time'. God has created time, as the creation narrative of Genesis one implies. However, Qoheleth adds: 'Also He has put eternity into man's mind, yet so that he cannot find out what God has done from the beginning to the end.' There is a beginning, for God has created time. There is also an end, because God the transcendent Creator has set man in the contingency of time. This is not just a barrier hampering his finitude; it is also a protection. For as creatures of flesh and blood, we could not endure the sustained joy or the unbroken vacuity to which full release from temporal limits would commit us. Yet within man's temporality, man experiences God and His ways, so that he relates both to *chronos* and to *kairos*. He needs them both, for he is a man, not an angel.

The Second Law of Thermodynamics, according to which all things 'run down', belongs to the realm of *chronos*. In every process in which exchange of energy is involved, the quality of energy is lower at the end than it was at the beginning. We know this through our senses. In *chronos* we experience the principle of entropy as successiveness, irreversibility and transience or impermanence. Yet we are also aware of realities exempt from this downward trend: the drive for organisms to fulfil needs and to be alive, and for human beings to have faith, hope and love. The instinctual drive for life, for teleonomy, in creation is a mystery. But in our own experiences as human beings, we know how memory breaks the irreversibility of time, so that we can look back and recollect what would otherwise be lost.[2] Memory thus defies *chronos,* and faith's memory builds a whole realm of the indissoluble, as we shall see. Hope is faith on tiptoe, anticipating the future, beyond the reach of *chronos* also. Love is the bridge between faith and hope, and in the possession of the *now.* Entropy therefore is not the ultimate rule of the universe, even in man's own limited sphere of reality.

As we have seen, however, the destiny of fate in tragedy might seem to represent human entropy (see pp. 90–92). This is where biblical time is incompatible with pagan time, for it is founded upon the reality of the Creator of all things. It is not the stars that influence the fatefulness of life, as the ancient Babylonians and modern astrologers believe. It is not the cyclicity of endless time as the ancient Greeks and modern Hindus believe.[3] It is the Creator, who is the Lord of time. 'Thou art my God,' said the Psalmist, 'My times are in Thy hands' (Ps. 31:14–15). Augustine saw that this biblical view of time was the antithesis of the pagan mind:

> They have . . . asserted that these cycles will ceaselessly rear, one passing away and another coming . . . the things which have been, and those which are to be, coinciding. And from the fantastic vicissitude they exempt not even the immortal soul that has attained wisdom, consigning it to a ceaseless transmigration between delusive blessedness and real mystery.[4]

Moreover, eternity is viewed quite differently by biblical faith. Eternity is not changelessness, like the Platonic 'Ideas'. Nor is eternity endless time, as the cyclical view might suggest. Eternity is the mode of being that includes time by transcending it, giving us awareness of that which is available, reliable and inexhaustible, regardless of time's perspectives. Eternal truth is truth 'no matter what', ever timely, as eternal life is ever efficacious and valid. There is also the biblical understanding that the temporal can be taken up into the eternal, although the temporal can never become eternal. For eternity is the presence of God. Thus the significance of *kairos* is that it is like a window or a door opening opportunely for the visitation of the eternal. This makes time real, decisions vital, opportunities not to be missed. As Roger Hazelton has finely summarised it: 'Without real time there can be no real history; and apart from real history there is no real incarnation, revelation or redemption. But what makes time real? Precisely that it is anchored in the being of eternal God.'[5] Time, then, has a vertical dimension of eventfulness as well as a horizontal flow. History therefore is linked with the eternal, making it truly historic, because it is God who controls, continues and completes it.

Time, then, is real because history is real. History is real because eternity, which includes and saves it, is real. Eternity is real because time, which illuminates, experiences and imitates it in fragmentary ways, is real. However, we hasten to add that the Bible knows nothing of them as abstractions, since its language is always concrete, specific and related. There time is God's servant, and eternity is God's presence. It is impossible to divorce creation from the Creator, although it is always distinguished from Him in His holiness.

CHRIST, THE LORD OF TIME

The Christian faith is a historic faith, because God has entered into time, to give time its meaning. This is incompatible with the closed worlds of naturalism and other faiths. Augustine saw this very clearly when he asserted three basic truths of Christian conviction:

1. Christ died for our sins; and rising from the dead, He dieth no more. Death has no more dominion over Him, and we ourselves after the resurrection shall be for ever with the Lord.
2. How can that (soul) be truly called blessed which has no assurance of being so eternally, and is either in ignorance of the truth, or blind to the misery that is approaching, or, knowing it, is in misery and fear? Or if it passes to bliss and leaves miseries for ever, then there happens in time a new thing which time shall not end.
3. For though Himself eternal and without beginning, yet He caused time to have a beginning; and man whom He had not previously made, He made in time. ... God, without change of will, created man, who had never been, and gave him an existence in time.[6]

These Christian affirmations are in direct conflict with the conception of endless cycles, of fate as the inscrutable master of destiny, of man living in a closed world of cause and effect. For the Resurrection of Christ has brought into this world of space and time a new reality. Men are really saved from non-being, and can be born again unto a lively hope of eternal life. For God is the Creator of time and the Redeemer of men.

1. *Resurrection of Christ*

In the Old Testament, the Exodus was one event that changed the whole character of a people. Instead of being slaves under the tyranny of Egypt, the Israelites were now freed to be a people, the people of God, whom God had delivered miraculously from nonbeing.[7] Ever after, all revolved around their remembrance of the Passover, as the event that identified them as the people of God, now identified by their covenant with Yahweh. Likewise in the New Testament, the event of the Resurrection established a new covenant for a new people of God, the church. The apostles were witnesses of the Resurrection, eyewitnesses of the fact that Christ had risen from the dead. And who was Jesus?—raised like Lazarus from the dead to die later? No, with one voice the disciples witnessed that He was the 'Sovereign Lord, who didst make the heaven and the earth and the sea and everything in them', now risen from the dead (Acts 4:2, 24).

On Mars Hill, the apostle Paul likewise spoke to the Athenians: 'The God who made the world and everything in it, being Lord of heaven and earth . . . since He Himself gives to all men life and breath and everything . . . He made from one [that is, Adam] every nation of men to live on the face of the earth . . . that they should seek God' (Acts 17:24–27). In short, Paul gives a summary of God as Creator, His providence, His dual purpose for mankind—to be stewards of the earth, and to serve God—and His lordship over history and the nations. Then he challenges his audience by declaring God 'will judge the world in righteousness by a man whom He has appointed, and of this He has given assurance to all men by raising Him from the dead' (Acts 17:31). He calls all men to repent, to change their whole outlook on reality because of the Resurrection.[8]

The staggering fact is that the Creator entered this creaturely realm of space and time by the Virgin Birth to become a Man among men. He has broken the continuity of frustration and estrangement by evil, to begin a new creation. In the midst of death, He has destroyed the power of death and corruption, to save mankind from being always wholly subject to its bondage and futility. God has done this, not by snatching away man's spirit from material existence, but by actually rising *bodily* from the tomb. Jesus maintains the personal identification familiar to the disciples so that in His resurrection appearances He was recognisable to them, as was His voice when years later He spoke to John the Seer at Patmos (Rev. 1:10). Henceforth, the New Man in creation, who is the Creator, lives in the midst of the old creation, with temporality, and yet eternally so. The bodily resurrection, in contrast then to dualism, is world-affirming. It really has happened within space and time. So the whole range of creation is now liberated from futility, and the promise of its full emancipation is now fulfilled. The fulfilment of the purpose of the Creator is thus focused on the Resurrection.

This means that something wholly new, uniquely so, has intersected with the orders of creation. The intersection of *chronos* and *kairos* is but a fragmentary analogy of what has happened with the temporal reality of the Resurrection event. In Christ, God is not only Lord over time, He is also Lord within time. God does not merely rule over our heads, but also within the the contingencies of creation. This moves the apostle to exclaim: 'Great indeed, we confess, is the mystery of our religion: He was manifested in the flesh, vindicated in the spirit, seen by angels, preached among the nations, believed on in the world, taken up in glory' (1 Tim. 3:16). Now a fundamentally new change has taken place, giving new boldness to the witness of the disciples, who can now sing:

> If we live, we live to the Lord, and if we die, we die to the Lord; so then, whether we live or whether we die, we are the Lord's. For to this end Christ died and lived again, that He might be Lord both of the dead and of the living.
> (Rom. 14:8–9)

There are now opened up an infinite range of possibilities for all those who are 'in Christ'. Resurrection as understood in the Bible is without parallel in other religions. Yet it is consistent with the Old Testament understanding of creation and providence. As God bound Himself to creation, and then to His people Israel, one by implicit covenant, the other by explicit covenant, so in the Resurrection of Christ He has established a new covenant for mankind and all creation. For in Jèsus Christ there is now the hypostatic union of Creator and creature. Jesus Christ is none other than the almighty Creator-Word who spoke and brought all creation into existence, so that now in the Word made flesh, there might be made possible the restoration of creation in re-creation.[9] The Word of the Cross is the Word of the Creator, now operative within as well as over creation. Forgiveness, redemption of the whole man, justification—all flow from the event of the resurrection as specific and real actualities in this world, not just as moral and logical necessities required for man.

2. Living Eventfully

Now that man need no longer be dominated by fears of uncertain destiny, since he is 'in Christ, a new creation', he should have neither anxiety about the future nor guilt about the past (see pp. 215–216). The contrast between man under fate and man in the risen Christ may be illustrated by the difference between Hölderlin's dirge[10] and the apostle's triumphant hymn.

> . . . to us poor men
> Is given no place to rest.
> Harried by pain,
> We grope and fall
> Blindly from hour to hour,
> Like water dashed—
> From cliff to cliff,
> In lifelong insecurity.
>
>   Friedrich Hölderlin—*Son of Fate*

Blessed be the God and Father of our Lord Jesus Christ! By His great mercy we have been born anew to a living hope through the resurrection of Jesus Christ from the dead, and to an inheritance which is imperishable, undefiled, and unfading, kept in heaven for you, who by God's power are guarded through faith for a salvation

ready to be revealed in the last time. In this you rejoice,
though now for a little while you have to suffer various
trials. . . .   (1 Pet. 1:3–6)

Man alone in the world is, as Hölderlin depicts him, alienated
from creation and from eternity. Man 'in Christ' is man with
all the resources available to him, in the *I am* that Moses heard
declare Himself, and whom John saw on Patmos: the *I am*
'which was, which is, which is to come'. That is why, with T. S.
Eliot, we realise we ought not to cease from 'endless exploration'—not in the optimism of humanism, but in the realism of
the Cross and the Resurrection:

> What we call the beginning is often the end,
> And to make an end is to make a beginning.
> The end is where we start from.
>   T. S. Eliot—*Little Gidding*

To get to know the beginning of creation and of new creation
is to end with ourselves, and to begin anew, so that 'we are
born with the dead' and that the end of all our exploring

> Will be to arrive where we started
> And to know the place for the first time.

However, attachment to self, to things and to other people is
such that the potentialities of being 'in Christ' are only glimpsed
by most of us, in fragmentary, momentary ways. We have experiences of Christ, but often miss their meanings, for we fail
to appropriate them *now*, which the apostle said was 'the accepted time', 'the day of salvation'. Instead, says T. S. Eliot:

> Men's curiosity searches past and future
> And clings to that dimension. But to apprehend
> The point of intersection of the timeless
> With time, is an occupation for the saint—
> No occupation either, but something given
> And taken, in a lifetime's death in love,
> Ardour and selflessness and self-surrender.
> For most of us, there is only the unattended
> Moment, the moment in and out of time,

The distraction fit, lost in a shaft of sunlight.

T. S. Eliot—*The Dry Salvages*

It is this unity between time and eternity which Beckett destroyed in the play *Waiting for Godot*. For it is this intersection that gives life true quality, eventfulness, indeed salvation, hope and therefore a future. Lucidly, the Christian poet sees that while man has momentary glimpses and intermittent experiences of the 'intersection of the timeless with time', it is 'a lifetime's death in love, ardour and selflessness and self-surrender', and 'an occupation for the saint'.[11] But the New Testament epistles call us to be saints, in the light of the Resurrection. Likewise, the early Fathers, in words reminiscent of Paul, called upon Christians to live in weakness, self-surrender and death to one's self.

> Now when we die we no longer do as men condemned to death [said Athanasius], but as those who are even now in the process of rising, we await the general resurrection of all, which in its own time He shall show, even God who wrought it and bestowed it on us.[12]

The victory of Easter does not negate suffering, but redeems and transforms it. God is the suffering God. So the Christian rejoices in his tribulations, recognizing that the excellency of the power is of God and not of himself. There is a *but*, a notwithstanding in the Christian experience that gives practical realism to the victory of the Resurrection.

> We are afflicted in every way, but not crushed; perplexed, but not driven to despair; persecuted, but not forsaken; struck down, but not destroyed; always carrying in the body the death of Jesus, so that the life of Jesus may also be manifested in our bodies.   (2 Cor. 4:8–10)

Indeed, we discover how Paul was accused of 'turning the world upside down', which he did. He learned that when he was weak he was made strong. From him we learn, too, that in emptiness we are filled with the Spirit of God; in loneliness we experience the presence of God; all our deficiencies are but the doorway to the life of grace. Thus time's temporality and

contingency are twice needed: as the framework for needy man
to sense his need for eternity, and as the realism that makes
spiritual truths practically applicable. It is a simple truism that
if, like the Laodiceans, I am 'increased with goods'—of personality, of money, of status, of intellect, of many other sources
of self-enhancement—I do not need God! It is indeed the
occupation of a saint, then, to explore and to utilise the potentials of the intersection of *chronos* and *kairos*, of time and eternity, of death and Resurrection, of creation and new creation.

T. S. Eliot therefore concludes this part of his poem with
the need for personal discipline before God.

> . . . These are only hints and guesses,
> Hints followed by guesses; and the rest
> Is prayer, observance, discipline, thought and action.
> The hint half guessed, the gift half understood, is
>   Incarnation.
>
> T. S. Eliot—*The Dry Salvages*[13]

What unifies life, historically and personally, is 'Incarnation',
the life-death-resurrection of the Word made flesh. The mystery that lies behind our temporal framework is the Creator,
mediated to us in the traditional practices of prayer, worship,
Bible study and congruous behaviour. Indeed, in contrast to
Beckett's *Waiting for Godot*, a fantasy of unreal people in an
unreal environment of unreal expectation, the Bible portrays
authentic man in a real world—for God created it—of real
expectations, as the command decrees: 'Wait on the Lord'.

As one writer has indicated, there are at least eight meanings to this oft-repeated word 'wait' in Scripture.[14] First, there
must be *silence* before God—creative silence, as the Psalmist
declares: 'For God alone my soul waits in silence, for my hope
is from Him' (Ps. 62:5). Actually the imperative mood is used:
'be silent'. *Homo faber* in or out of the church has no conception
of what this means.

Secondly, there is *intensity* in waiting on the Lord, often
because of obscurity of understanding and the need of much
patient endurance. For 'To Thee, O Lord, I lift up my soul. O
my God, in Thee I trust, let me not be put to shame. . . . Yea,
let none that wait for Thee be put to shame' (Ps. 25:1–3; cf.

Ps. 69:6; Isa. 26:8–9). It is the mark of our Lord's prayer in earnest agony in Gethsemane (Luke 22:44), as it is of the church (Acts 12:5).

This waiting may be intensified, thirdly, by agonised uncertainty (Mic. 1:12). Therefore the Psalmist admonishes: 'Be still before the Lord, and wait *patiently* for Him' (Ps. 37:7). As a result intense human restlessness is transformed into utter repose in God.

Fourthly, it is the essence of dependence upon God that life be *simple*. Idolatry complicates life, and anxiety obscures the simplicity of relationship a man has with God. Thus the prophet Habakkuk is assured that God's action, 'though it tarry, wait for it; because it will surely come'. In this spirit the early church waited for the appearance of Christ, for whose coming again the believer still waits in a sure and certain hope.

In *Waiting for Godot* there is no community in hope. But in addition to the individual responses to Christian hope we have discussed above, there is the collective response. So the fifth use of the word 'wait' involves the principle of *unity*. Wisdom declares, 'Happy is the man who listens to me, watching [waiting] daily at my gates' (Prov. 8:34). All believers join in the petition, 'Lord, teach us to pray', to learn together that attitude of utter dependence on the Father for everything.

Sixthly, the life of faith requires *tenacity* in covenant and intercession on behalf of others (Gen. 18:22; 1 Kings 17:21).

Seventhly, waiting is a *service* for God (Num. 8:24).

Finally, waiting is in full *expectancy* of what is to be accomplished (Gen. 8:10; Acts 3:5). Thus to 'wait upon God' in all these ways is to have real hope and reliance on Him.

THE NEWNESS OF THE NEW CREATION

Our waiting upon God, our hope in God as Creator-Redeemer, is in anticipation of the new creation. Because its basis is not in man nor in man's world, its structure is totally different from human hope. It is rooted in the covenant God, whose promise is the guarantee of its fulfilment. It has already been evidenced in the life, ministry and resurrection of Christ that has brought a transforming reality into creation. It has been witnessed, too, by the Holy Spirit and His work in the life of believers, personally and corporately. And just as 'waiting upon the Lord' is ultimately defined by our Lord's own prayer life, so too the future, the judgment and the final purpose of God the Creator are all Christ-centred. This calls us to interpret the language of the new creation, to anticipate its community and to be assured of its continuity with the world in which we now live. For the 'newness' of the new creation can be seen in terms of revelation, relationships and redemption.

1. New Creation as Revelation

Behind every level of knowledge there lies a distinctive genre of communication. This is the essence of 'understanding', as we have seen. So we have recognised that the language of creation is not 'scientific', for the latter deals with the secondary processes and relationships of the physical world. Rather, the language of creation is that of *fiat* causation, theological language. We note that in the Bible there are distinctions of genre, such as wisdom literature, history, prophecy, worship. Now we have to examine the language of 'apocalyptic' as we engage in the study of what is commonly called 'eschatology', the end of this old world and the entrance of the new.

The crazy, fearful state of our own world today, challenging us with the environmental crisis, overpopulation and the starvation of millions of people, the threat of atomic war, the dehumanisation of technological society and much else, is helping us all to see the relevance of the Apocalypse.[15] For we call our times 'apocalyptic' in the sense of the sheer magnitude of humanly insoluble issues. Pessimism, terror, the shaking of all foundations—these are the environment of such expressions as the 'end times'. Characteristic of apocalyptic is totality; all is at stake.[16] It has a universal perspective as Noah's flood had, reaching out to total chaos. Its implications are all embracing, as the negative alternative to creation, which is also universal in depth and height as well as in length and breadth. It therefore gives stereoscopic vision to what we might otherwise treat flatly—as a book, a talk or a theological school of thought. Its concern with the whole of human life and the whole of reality requires a new language, a new mode of apprehension. As we well know, bankruptcy, divorce and mental breakdown can give us radically new perspectives. In the Apocalypse, however, we face the ultimate breakdown of a fallen world. Whatever replaces it must therefore be radically, inconceivably, new.

Decisiveness is another trait of its newness. At the Cross two worlds, two creations, met and ultimately diverged: the fallen creation and the new creation. Where time and eternity intersect, that point has immeasurable consequences. In this spirit the apostle proclaimed with all urgency and seriousness: 'Now is the accepted time, today is the day of salvation.' So it involves both present judgment and the anticipation of final judgment. It is therefore both forth-telling and fore-telling, both prophetic in the limited sense and predictive in an absolute sense.[17] The two spheres are mutually exclusive, so that conflict is cosmic in scope and eternal in its consequences. John saw revealed to him an angel, who 'swore by Him who lives for ever and ever, who created heaven and what is in it, the earth and what is in it, and the sea and what is in it, that there should be no more delay' (Rev. 10:6). When such a moment of vision apprehends past, present and future as a single entity, as *now*, then decision is also imperative, *now*.

Rulership is another trait of its newness. In the complacency of life, its disorientation, its emptiness, its nihilism, God will intervene. His silence will end, His absence will be vindicated, and He will display the awesome terror, majesty and might of His power. The world cannot be weightless, a meaningless existence, for He created it all. It is only the loss of the sense of the Creator, the Alpha and Omega, that gives man the delusion that there is no moral governor of the universe. Indeed there is! For He who has primary responsibility for its beginning and its being will also have the ultimate authority for its disposal and the maintenance of His sovereignty. Man cannot wish 'God is dead' and get away with it. So 'knowing the terror of the Lord, we persuade men' with an imagery, symbolism and message that befit the reality of God's sovereignty and of man's rebellion. Everything in the book of Revelation revolves around the throne (which is referred to some forty times). Rule, which is central to creation, is also central to the new creation. The Word of command at the beginning of creation is the Word that will ultimately be obeyed in the eternal rule of God. Meanwhile, conflict is inevitable as long as evil exists: wars in heaven and wars on earth (Rev. 12–14). Hierarchies of conflict are recognised: God and Satan, Christ and the Beast, those who rule over the earth legitimately and the usurping 'kings of the earth'.

Though strange, the language of the new creation is familiar to us. The book of Revelation is saturated with familiar imagery, with such symbols as heaven and earth, kings and rule, churches, the Lamb, the chaotic threat of sea and the grief of tears, the New Jerusalem, the tree of life and the precious stones that once adorned the High Priest's dress in the Holy Place. New creation is new, not by virtue of superseding the old familiar world, but by virtue of making the familiar one clear and meaningful for present life before God. What we have viewed sacramentally in isolated, fragmented parts, we now see wholly, fully and completely realisable. We no longer see things in 'hints and guesses, hints followed by guesses', in the elusiveness of mystery. At last it all becomes significant: the partial ecstasy being fully realised, the partial horror finally resolved. Strange and yet familiar, it is not the mastery of language but of personally being mastered, of being kept more surely by the truth than holding the truth oneself. Detached from this world and its possessiveness, one is not cast into vacuity, but awakened by the familiar Galilean voice that John heard, on the Lord's day, the day of Resurrection (Rev. 1:10). There, one is no longer enchained in the guilt of the past, nor the anxiety of the future, but freed of what T. S. Eliot has called 'the still point of the turning world', the fully lived present. The moment of revelation, it is the experience of the Word of God.

2. New Creation as Relationship

If the creation is expressive of the Word of God—His command, His promise, His revelation—its maintenance is also subordinated to the will of God. Its beginning and its end are both expressive of His will. To us today, living under the atomic cloud, apocalyptic terrors tend to obscure the transcendent possibilities of God, just as the early church might have felt they lived too close to the reality of Caesar's power. Both might obscure the reality of the transcendent rule of God if the alternative is just talk, within the covers of a book, about creation and new creation. But the book of Revelation is not just a book in itself, but the expression of the relationship between God and His people. It is the proclamation of His voice—'Behold, I make all things new'. For Jesus Christ is the Lord of the church, the Lord of history and the Creator of all things.

Just as creation is not merely an objective world, whose phenomena we abstract to study, but the dynamic interaction of relationships, so the new creation is the fullness of relationship. It is not a world into which we are suddenly transposed as in *Alice in Wonderland,* but it is an open relationship into which we have been introduced already by the advent of Christ, who has opened up a new beginning as 'the Way, the Truth and the Life'.

Judgment is the condition and basis of the new creation, for the old has to pass for the new to be brought in. But the initiative of judgment is always seen as the initiative of God. It is the efficacy of the slain Lamb that enables the last seal of the destiny of the world to be broken and revealed. It is the Word of God that dominates the ages in the proclamation of the last trumpet. It is the prayers of the faithful that release the seven vials of plagues. All these symbols express the sovereignty of God, who in His mercy judges—to set bounds, to preserve and to bring in the new creation. God is Himself the absolutely new: 'I make all things new'.

The new relationship that brings in the new creation is then that 'the dwelling of God is with men. He will dwell with them, and they shall be His people' (Rev. 21:3). To identify with Jesus Christ brings about such revolutionary changes in one's personal life, in one's family, in one's job, in one's neighbourhood, in one's world, that now already we can project with the apostle the cosmic reverberations of it all. Paul Minear has summarised the pictures and titles associated with the apostle's understanding of Christ. He is Son of Man, Son of God, the Word, the Lion of Judah, the Lamb, the Root of David, the Offspring of David, the King of kings, the Lord of lords, the Shepherd, the Amen, the faithful Witness, the Bridegroom, the living One, the Alpha and the Omega.[18] Language is exhausted in describing the relationship He has with man, the sovereignty of His will and the reality of His love. For behind all the scenes of what He does, is the love of God in Christ Jesus our Lord; Immanuel, God with us. This new creation community will be the city, 'the New Jerusalem, descending out of heaven from God'.

3. New Creation as Redemption

This prompts us to ask, Why will it be a city? First of all, the garden is the sphere of givenness, where man naturally receives. The city is the sphere much more of choice, where man has the freedom to be, to make, to create.[19] Nature leaves man without choice, the city is the place of choices. When the city becomes the compounding of wrong choices, it is readily seen as the sphere of judgment and of fatefulness, as cities of destruction. But deeper perhaps is the realisation that in the new creation God does not preserve a primitive plan. He placed the Adam in a garden, but He proceeds to place His new community in a city because He has not annulled human freedom. There is no return to a primitive lost age, there is progression into a new relationship of His love.

In the first place, there is forward motion to God's grace because the history of man is not in vain, annulled at one stroke, for ever. How can it be if God in Christ has taken our humanity and entered as Creator into His material creation? New creation is not rupture but continuity, as leaven in the dough; as wine still, though new wine will require new wineskins. The symbols are still the same, though their meaning is changed. We shall have bodies of glory, but transformed bodies. The essential reality, then, of heaven is the transformation of the old into the new, so that in the economy of God's grace not a tear is wasted, nor a groan re-echoing that will not be transmuted into celestial joy. Thus the city, which is the great synthesis of the achievements of man in his exercise of dominion over the world, will all be redeemed. The symbol of the New Jerusalem is the assurance that nothing has been wasted, nothing lost, even though in God's judgment much is destroyed, purified and burned up. It is not dissolution, it is resolution. It is not abolition, it is re-creation.

In the second place, the forward motion of new creation is the tracing out in heaven of what has been done on earth, so it is not mythical but real for man.[20] In the ancient religions, there was always the attempt to do on earth as was done in heaven, for heaven was the prototype of the earthly. Jacob, however, in his dream saw the heavens open and the angels ascending a ladder from earth to heaven (Gen. 28:12). There was a double motion. Jesus fulfilled this when He told Nathanael, 'Truly, truly, I say to you, you will see heaven opened, and the angels of God ascending and descending upon the Son of man' (John 1:51). Now in the Resurrection, says the apostle, 'He who descended is He who also ascended far above all the heavens, that He might fill all things' (Eph. 4:10). This is the purpose of the book of Revelation, to tell us what has happened and will happen now in the heavens as the result of the Resurrection. This is not myth, for it is located within space and time. It has actually taken place. It is history. Creation has been affected by its mighty dynamic power, like a great earthquake. Its epicentre is located on this earth. Now it reverberates throughout all the heavens in its cosmic scope. The redemptive activity of Christ has set in motion the entire series of events that are described in the book. A new song of deliverance can now be sung, 'Worthy is the Lamb'. God has moved more closely to His creatures, for the Lamb has now received power to execute all the purposes of God at the end of time. In all this there is continuity, so that we cannot speak of the new creation as *creatio ex nihilo*. It is the redemption of fallenness, of sinful man, and the consequences of evil in the material realm.[21]

Yet, there is also contrast in the newness of the new creation. With its continuity there is also finality. There has been the Beginning; there will be the End. We live, then, in the 'last days'. When, however, the goal is reached, there will be a 'coming down' of the New Jerusalem, to give complete fellowship between God and His creatures. The 'sea will be no more'; all its chaotic potentials will have ceased. There will be 'no more tears' of creaturely sorrow and pain. There will be the absence of the tree of the knowledge of good and evil, and the presence of the tree of life for the healing of the nations. There shall no more be anything accursed, but there will be healing and happiness. The Temple, with all its priesthood, liturgy, cult, will be no more; there will no longer be religion. The contrast, then,

is that in the new creation God will establish total communion
with His redeemed creation, and everyone will have a new name.

NOTES

1   James Muilenburg, 'The Biblical View of Time,' *Harvard Theo-
    logical Review*, 54, Oct. 1961, pp. 225–252.

2   J. G. Bennett, *The Crisis in Human Affairs*, London, Hodder &
    Stoughton, 1968, pp. 145–166.

3   Stanley L. Jaki, *Science and Creation, from eternal cycles to oscillating
    universe*, New York, Science History Publications, 1974.

4   Quoted by Langdon Gilkey, *Maker of Heaven and Earth*, New
    York, Doubleday, Anchor edition, 1965, pp. 300–301.

5   Roger Hazelton, *God's Way with Man*, Nashville, Abingdon Press,
    1956, p. 123.

6   Langdon Gilkey, op. cit., p. 301.

7   John R. Welch, *Time and Event*, Leiden, E. J. Brill, 1969.

8   See the excellent study by Bertil Gartner, *The Areopagus Speech
    and Natural Revelation*, Lund, C. W. K. Gleerup, 1955.

9   Thomas F. Torrance, *Space, Time and Resurrection*, Grand Rapids,
    Eerdmans, 1976.

10 Quoted by Karl Barth, *Church Dogmatics*, trans. G. W. Bromiley
    and T. F. Torrance, Edinburgh, T. & T. Clark, vol. 3, part 2,
    p. 515.

11 See the helpful interpretation of T. S. Eliot's *Four Quartets* by
    Harry Blamires, *Word Unheard*, London, Methuen, 1969.

12 Quoted by Langdon Gilkey, op. cit.

13 The quotations from T. S. Eliot are taken from Helen Gardner,
    The Composition of Four Quartets, London, Faber and Faber, 1978.

14 James G. S. S. Thomson, *The Praying Christ*, London, Tyndale
    Press, 1959, pp. 129–152.

15 An excellent summary on the nature of apocalyptic literature
    is Leon Morris, *Apocalyptic*, London, Tyndale, 1972.

16 C. F. Evans, *Explorations in Theology 2*, London, S.C.M., 1977,
    p. 170.

17 Richard N. Longenecker, 'The Return of Christ', in *Dreams,
    Visions and Oracles*, edit. Carl E. Armerding and W. Ward
    Gasque, Grand Rapids, Baker Books, 1977, pp. 143–144.

18 Paul S. Minear, *I Saw a New Earth*, Cleveland, Corpus Books,
    1968, p. 33. See also his helpful essay 'The Cosmology of the
    Apocalypse' in *Current Issues in New Testament Interpretation*, edit.
    William Klassen and Graydon F. Snyder, New York, 1962.

19   Charles Williams, *The Image of the City and Other Essays*, London, Oxford University Press, 1958, pp. 92–98, 99–100.
20   Jacques Ellul, *Apocalypse*, New York, Seabury, 1977, pp. 221–225.
21   J. Harrelson, *The Concept of Newness in the New Testament*, Minneapolis, Augsburg Publishing House, 1960.

Postscript

Events in my own life have shown me the reality of the living God, both as Creator-Redeemer and as provident God. Writing this book, I have come to realise that each breath I take, each sentence I write, is only by the grace of God. In these nine chapters, we have seen that there are many reasons why I believe in the Creator. Man is not only the cosmic orphan, but he makes no sense in his humanity without God. Evil and sin are only understood seriously and meaningfully in the light of the Creator. God is meaningful in the reality of a personal Creator. This civilisation we so much take for granted, has been founded on the assumption that we do believe in the Creator. If men do not, then they need to see the radical implications of this in the basic elements of our culture—of being, truth, time, creativity, order and justice, science and the arts, etc. I believe in the Creator as the source of wisdom, in coping with life, as well as in the exercise of the enjoyment of life. It is this faith which enables one to live hopefully in the midst of apocalyptic threats and fears.

What else can one say? Each of us can add his or her own postscript, but mine is simply this. I need the belief in the personal reality of the Creator to help me distinguish idolatry from the real world, to understand the interconnectedness of life far more than even ecologists can recognise and to know how I fit into place, at home in the world.

We have already seen that the apostle Paul and the young church at Corinth made faith in the Creator God a liturgical expression that they sang about, in defiance of pagan idols.

Within a few years of the death and resurrection of Jesus Christ, it was widely recognised in these Christian communities that Christ is the Co-Creator. This was set within the context of their defiance of idols that have 'no real existence', for 'there is no God but one'. For although there may be so-called gods in heaven or on earth—as indeed there are many 'gods' and many 'lords'—yet for us:

> there is one God, the Father, from whom are all things and for whom we exist, and one Lord, Jesus Christ, through whom are all things and through whom we exist.
> (1 Cor. 8:6).

'However,' says the apostle, 'not all possess this knowledge,' which we have seen is still true. *I believe in the Creator* because this reality is the bedrock of existence, by which I can test what are idols and unrealities in life. By it we can test the theological systems of men, to see how clearly they focus on biblical revelation.[1]

We have also seen that, far more profoundly than the ecologists and environmentalists generally realise, the future of the earth is irrevocably linked with the future of mankind. With man the creation stands or falls. Today we see that, environmentally, man has the power and the choice to destroy this planet earth or to preserve it in wise stewardship. Humanly speaking, the odds seem stacked hopelessly against modern man being able to avert eco-catastrophe. We live apocalyptically. Biblically speaking, man has been put at the head of creation by the ordinance of God. His failure involves therefore 'the groaning' of the whole creation in travail, as if waiting for new birth. 'We wait for adoption as sons.' While we wait, however, we have this sure hope, says the apostle, that with our adoption, 'the creation itself will be set free from its bondage to decay and obtain the glorious liberty of the children of God' (Rom. 8:21, 23). *I believe in the Creator,* then, in a responsible attitude to my environment, to take the world seriously, as a steward of its resources. This calls me to a simpler lifestyle, to a surer identity of being 'in Christ', not as *Homo faber*, but taking the responsibility of being a credible witness of new creation with utmost seriousness.[2]

Today modern man has the option either to destroy himself by the loss of hope or to hold on to a sure and certain hope in his Maker and Redeemer. It is a choice between defiance of a meaningless world and existence and confidence in living truly before the Creator of all things. The choice of refusing to trust God is the ultimate basis for the loss of commitment to living fully and authentically. If the world is viewed as unreal and absurd, as so many of our contemporary writers think it is, then things are trivialised, men are depersonalised and life becomes total distrust. Yet trust in the world, sings the King of Siam in the musical *The King and I*, is essential. *I believe in the Creator* because, as the Psalmist says, I can trust Him absolutely. For He created me, and He knows me better than I can ever know myself (Ps. 139).

'Home,' said the poet, 'is where one starts from.' There is no secure resting place in this world. Man, as we have sensed, often feels himself merely a cosmic orphan. As we grow older, the environment we live in gets harsher, more complicated, less like home. The interconnectedness of life becomes more baffling. So, 'as we grow older, the world becomes stranger, the pattern more complicated of dead and living.' The ambiguities of motive and desire intensify the need for reflection and depth in one's soul, so that 'old men ought to be explorers'.[3]

> Old men ought to be explorers—
> Here and there does not matter.
> We must be still and still moving
> Into another intensity
> For a further union, a deeper communion
> Through the dark cold and the empty desolation.
>   T. S. Eliot—*East Coker*

As therefore I explore life with deepening intensity, I cry, 'Lord, to whom can I go, for Thou hast the words of eternal life.' *I believe in the Creator,* for by His Word all things were made, all things hold together and all things have meaning and purpose.

NOTES

1   See Norman Young, *Creator, Creation and Faith,* London, Collins,
    1976, pp. 83–106 for a summary of four theological perspec-
    tives, by Karl Barth, Paul Tillich, Rudolf Bultmann and Jürgen
    Moltmann.
2   See the challenging Christian studies on hope by Jacques Ellul,
    Hope in Time of Abandonment, New York, Seabury, 1972, and
    especially the work of Pedro Lain Entralgo, *La Espera y la Es-
    peranza: historia y teoria del esperar humano,* Madrid, Revista de
    Occidente, 1963, 3rd edition.
3   Helen Gardner, *The Composition of Four Quartets,* op. cit., p. 112.

General References

(Major Works on the Doctrine of Creation)

Bernhard W. Anderson, *Creation versus Chaos*, New York, Association Press, 1967.

Karl Barth, The Doctrine of Creation, *Church Dogmatics*, trans. G. W. Bromiley and T. F. Torrance, vol. III, parts I–IV, Edinburgh, T. & T. Clark, 1958–1961.

G. C. Berkouwer, *Studies in Dogmatics:* vols. on *Providence, Man: the Image of God* and *Creation,* Grand Rapids, Eerdmans, 1952–1962.

Emil Brunner, *The Christian Doctrine of Creation and Redemption,* trans. Olive Wyon, London, Lutterworth Press, 1952.

John G. Gibbs, *Creation and Redemption. A Study in Pauline Theology,* Leiden, E. J. Brill, 1971.

Langdon Gilkey, *Maker of Heaven and Earth,* New York, Doubleday Anchor, 1965.

Richard W. A. McKinney (edit.), *Creation, Christ and Culture,* Edinburgh, T. & T. Clark, 1976.

Hugh Montefiore (edit.), *Man and Nature,* London, Wm. Collins, 1975.

Robert C. Neville, *God the Creator, on the Transcendence and Presence of God,* Chicago, University of Chicago Press, 1968.

John Reumann, *Creation and New Creation, the Past, the Present and Future of God's Creative Activity,* Minneapolis, Augsburg Publishing House, 1973.

Dorothy L. Sayers, *The Mind of the Maker,* London, Methuen, 2nd edit., 1941.

Leo Scheffczyk, *Creation and Providence,* Montreal, Palm Publishers, 1969.

Piet Schoonenberg, S.J., *Covenant and Creation,* Notre Dame, Notre Dame University Press, 1969.

Claus Westermann, *Creation,* trans. John S. Scullion, S.J., London, S.P.C.K., 1974.

Norman Young, *Creator, Creation and Faith,* London, Wm. Collins, 1976.

(Of these, I think Langdon Gilkey, *Maker of Heaven and Earth,* is still the best introduction to the subject, especially for the lay reader.)

The Nature of Evil

The nature of evil is consistent with the overall view of reality. In the history of religion three major systems of thought, apart from biblical faith, have developed distinct attitudes to evil. These are naturalism, dualism and monism. But only dualism has dealt with evil seriously.

1. Naturalism

According to naturalism, creaturely existence is merely the product of natural causes—without purpose or direction, say some; directed purposefully by evolution, say others. Evil is merely what finite creatures can expect to face in the presence of powerful and blind forces which confront and buffet them. Especially in periods of cultural optimism, naturalism has infiltrated great systems of thought as in Carvaka in India, or in Stoicism in the Graeco-Roman world. Stoicism has been of profound influence in Western civilisation, especially through the writings of Lucretius and Cicero, and, in fact, appears very contemporary with much modern secularism.

A modern version of naturalism argues about evil in the following vein. Since man is only a very intelligent animal, the problem of evil should not be exaggerated. It stems perhaps from man's ability to walk upright, to put his head in the clouds, to deny his animal nature, to think himself one of the gods. Man has inherited a reptilian brain, to which have been added two subsequent mammalian brains. It is the collision of his neural pathways that explains man's violent tendencies.[1] Man has a brain inadequate to cope with his false pretensions to god-like powers. The greatest evil and misery in human affairs arises not because men are such rats, but because they make the world reflect back on a false image of themselves. It is man's quest for absolute truth, goodness and justice in the denial of man's non-animality that causes the trouble. None of these absolutes is possible because man is merely animal; in a world of disease, finitude, accident and death these absolutes only mock man's futility. Human nature is in itself not inherently vicious, it just needs the animal requirements of territory, safety and survival. The real evils, such as poverty, disease and pollution, arise not from man but from his environment.

2. Dualism

In dualism evil is rationalised and made intelligible, because evil is conceived to be one of the two constituents of reality: matter. Finite existence is composed of a mixture of matter and form, physical and spiritual, mortal and immortal. So evil is mixed up with good. To be finite is to be subject to evil, and to escape the body is 'the good', just as the immortal soul is eventually to be released from the prison-house of the body. The attraction of such a philosophy is that it appeals to the exercise of the rational, as we find it in Greek thought. The mind can unscramble the two components of reality and treat them separately.

Dualism has had plenty of room for speculation. Some thinkers like Plotinus believed the origin of evil for mankind arose when Adam and Eve 'fell' into the physical state of mortality. Others, like the Manichees, believed the body and soul had always been enemies, as the bad and the good respectively. A hymn of the Manichees declared:

> I have known my soul and the body that lies upon it,
> That they have been enemies since the creation of the
> world.

Augustine, as an intelligent young man, was attracted to Manichaeism. 'For,' he said, 'the Manichees could intelligently ask and answer "where did these sins come from? Where did evil come from at all" '. Since the Manichees were uncompromising rationalists, the religious life could be just a mental game, played out by reason alone. 'And so, from their preaching,' later confessed Augustine, 'I gained an enthusiasm for religious controversy, and, from this, I daily grew to love the Manichees more and more. So it came about that, to a surprising extent, I came to approve of whatever they said, not because I knew any better, but because I wanted it to be true.'

Such a gnostic philosophy syncretised the views of the Greeks with the mystery religions of the Ancient East, just as Christian Science and other gnostic faiths of our day have syncretised views about the nature of evil with contemporary secularism. It leaves the Creator handicapped, doing the best He can with disharmonious materials pre-existing in chaos. So Plato in his *Timaeus* speaks of a limited God who has a compromise with primordial disorder, not an omnipotent god. 'The generation of the universe,' says Plato, 'was a mixed creation by a combination of necessity and reason.' All his god can do is compromise as best he can.

3. Monism

The third perspective is that of pantheism, which teaches that everything is divine. Creatures are not made out of matter only, but out of God. Evil exists only in its isolation and association with finitude, as in the *karma* of Hindu thought. Evil is but the assertion of 'I' and 'mine', of a finite centre that is ignorant of its true identity in the Whole. So evil will disappear as finitude is progressively swallowed up, when the one is absorbed into the many. Contrary to the biblical understanding that all things are real because God created them, pantheism sees all individual things as illusory. Contrary to biblical faith that proclaims deep down that man is a rebel, alienated from God, the pantheist sees that deep down man has the divine within him.

Whereas 'the fall' in biblical thought is the fall of man from his God-intended role and identity, 'the fall' in pantheism is creation itself, as the origin of concrete, particular individuals within space and time. It is 'the fall' from the unity and the changelessness of the One. Thus the shadowy world of 'Maya' is produced by men's inability to see the real unity behind the diversity of the world, in its natural, historical and personal forms. Since the scientific enterprise is involved in the study of individual relationships in a space-time continuum, it is no wonder that neither modern empirical science nor modern technology developed in such a cultural environment as the pantheism of the Ancient East. Nor is it in this milieu that the sanctity of the person and the rights of the individual could ever have developed.

Common to all three interpretations of evil is the acceptance of the primordial basis of evil. It has always existed, for it is rooted in reality. This, therefore, reduces both the awareness of and the sensitivity to it, and lowers the ethical response of man to cope with it. There is a deep sense, especially in Asian cultures, of resignation and even fatalism of spirit, as though evil were better ignored than resisted.

NOTES

1 Larry Ing (edit.), *Alternatives to Violence*, New York, Time-Life Books, 1968, pp. 24–34.

A Critique of Jacques Monod's *Chance and Necessity*[1]

An influential book today on the doctrine of chance as the basis of reality is Jacques Monod's *Chance and Necessity*. He is a brilliant molecular biologist who has explored fully the realm of physical causation in a biological discipline that has made spectacular progress. But it has aptly been said that the trouble with scientists is not that they specialise, but that they generalise, and especially that they apply special techniques to the whole of reality. This is what Monod has done when he reduces all the meaning of life to 'chance'.

Monod seals off his closed system of explanation by describing all attempts to interpret the world as permeated by supra-human purposes, or 'the Good', with a dirty word: *animist*. Ideologies such as Christianity belong to the Stone Age; they are animist. He pre-empts final cause, or purpose, from his schema by introducing the principle of 'teleonomy', that all living things are self-constructing machines, a hangover of the Newtonian mechanistic universe. 'A living being's structure', Monod says, 'owes almost nothing to the action of outside forces, but everything from its overall shape down to its tiniest detail, to "morphogenetic" interactions within the object itself. It is thus a structure giving proof of an autonomous determinism.' He then argues for another principle, that of 'invariant reproduction', so that there is the innate ability of living things to reproduce and to transmit information corresponding to their own structure. Monod believes that the mechanistic theories of molecular biology, genetics and evolution are sufficiently established to further assert that the development of all living matter and its reproductive mechanisms are entirely governed by the operation of chance upon simpler primary materials, without purpose.

Monod's misleading views are so popular today that he has to be challenged, and he can be, in at least three ways. First of all, he does a conjurer's trick with chance. As Professor Donald McKay has shown, 'chance' at the level of micro-matter is another name for ignorance.[2] We do not know the law of causation when we call the outcome of the thrown dice 'chance'. With God there is no chance. As the writer in Proverbs notes, 'The lot is cast into the lap, but the decision is wholly from the Lord' (Prov. 16:33). Monod, however, takes the chance of unknown randomness, converts it into a physical principle and extends it to apply to all meaning of reality. This is really semantic cheating. 'Chance' is thus used in two fundamentally different ways.

The second objection is that Monod does not explain why primeval matter has such qualities that it produces, solely by chance, richly varied life-systems. This is matter with remarkable qualities of variance. No theory that cannot explain the nature of this primary matter, rightfully argues Dr. Mary Hesse, can exclude the possibility of God the Creator.[3]

The third objection is that Monod presupposes 'the principle of objectivity' as the true form of knowledge. But there is no reason grounded in science *per se* for the adoption of this value. Why should this theory of knowledge, for example, be adopted by science over a theistic system of knowledge? Why should it be more 'true' than any other form of knowledge? Truth happens to be a value utilised by scientists, but it is neither their discovery nor solely their monopoly. So it is with this awareness that a humane scientist like Bronowski in *Science and Human Values* and other essays struggles to explain the place of human values in a closed-system universe.[4] In addition to truth, from where do other values of goodness—tenderness, kindness, human intimacy, faithfulness and love—arise?

NOTES

1   Jacques Monod, *Chance and Necessity*, New York, Vintage Books, 1972.

2   Donald M. MacKay, *The Clockwork Image,* London, Inter-Varsity Press, 1974.
3   Mary Hesse, 'On the Alleged Incompatibility Between Christianity and Science', *Man and Nature,* edit. Hugh Montefiore, London, Collins, 1975, pp. 121–131.
4   J. Bronowski, *Science and Human Values,* New York, Harper & Row, 1965.

APPENDIX C

World-Views of Western Civilisation

There is a general complaint today that we lack in the late twentieth century a common world-view or *Weltanschauung*. There have been two major mutations of world-view since the beginnings of Christianity, which we call the Ptolemaic and the Newtonian. They have so profoundly influenced the history of our civilisation that we have to see them as the background to the history of thought and theology right up until modern times.[1] Part of our dilemma in re-emphasising the relevance of creation in the world today is that we do not have a clear framework of understanding that gives coherence and 'makes sense' to legitimise the institutions and values of modern man.

1. The Ptolemaic World-View

The Ptolemaic world-view marked the first change in Western thought. It developed from Greek thought and blended with Christian faith. Based upon the Platonic dualism of unchanging being and changing appearances, against which the early Church Fathers struggled, Ptolemaic cosmology deepened the split in human culture between the celestial and the terrestrial, the ideal and the sensible, the supernatural and the natural, the spiritual and the material. It was a dualism that affected all of culture, religious faith and philosophy of the early and medieval Church, especially in the Latin form of western Christianity which, under the influence of Augustine, was much more dualistic than the orthodox form of Eastern Christianity. Likewise, the ecclesiastical heresies of the period, such as Gnosticism, Manichaeism, Docetism and Arianism, were essentially spin-offs from this world-view.

Superficially at least, the cathedral in the West stood as the single symbol of truth in the socio-economic community of the market town, and sought to embody within its Gothic structure of flying buttresses and soaring nave the unity of a single-minded faith, thrusting heavenward in its aspirations. Springing out of the earth and culture, its gargoyles at the drainage points of the cathedral roof or catching the eye at the end of the pews reminded the worshipper of the incongruities between the will of God in heaven and the will of man on earth. Thus for the medieval Christian, as for Hellenistic man, the unification of all things was salvation. The deepest anxiety lay in this notion of the need to seek on earth what was done in heaven, as the Lord's Prayer was daily chanted. For the unity of the cosmos was fractured; God and man were estranged.

2. The Newtonian World-View

The Newtonian world-view was the second shift of mind-set. It began early in the seventeenth century when the universe began to be seen as mechanical as the clock of Strasbourg. Although its founders were devout Christians—men like Copernicus, Kepler, Galileo and Newton—they inadvertently contributed to cementing the creation into a closed system that operated autonomously and mechanically. Again, it was characterised by a thorough dualism, between absolute space and time as the graticule enclosing contingent events within their embrace. Those theologians who still insist that creation occurred only within space and time reflect this view of reality.

Deism was one of the heresies spun out of the Newtonian world-view in which the autonomous system of 'Nature' and 'Nature's laws' was installed. This was developed to explain all the events of the world, whether it be the fall of the apple by the law of gravity, or the evolution of the ape by Darwin's principle of the survival of the fittest. Consequently, the recognition of God's activity in the creation began to recede when the Creator was only reckoned to be the First Cause, having little or no connection with His world. How God could really 'love the world' the Newtonian world-view could not see. Thus the dualism of a closed creation, self-contained, and a Creator as First Cause, has made the realities of providence, prayer, worship and biblical revelation increasingly remote, if not irrelevant for secular man. For now, as Pope could say with irony:

> God said, 'let Newton be,'
> and there was light.

The concept of the Creator as 'God-of-the-Gaps' is the legacy of this mind-set that is still with us today. Newton invoked it as the device to explain irregularities in the motions of the planets as if God, the cosmic Clock-maker, tinkered with keeping His clock on time. LaPlace later snorted, 'I have no need of that hypothesis.' Unwittingly, this view of creation led to the progressive secularisation of science, which had commenced in the seventeenth century with such strong Christian convictions. A lingering persuasion of the God-of-the-Gaps approach still persists as a substitute for scientific ignorance. It is a dangerous game to play since it leads to the progressive squeezing out of the relevance of God in His world as scientific knowledge advances. If supernatural activity or metaphysical speculation are the only areas designated to belong to God, then we believe in a limited creator, stranded on the island of credulity that ever shrinks before the waves of scientific advances.

3. The Post-Einsteinian World

Today we are too close to the radical shifts taking place to say we have yet formed a radically new world-view or cosmology; it is still being shaped. But modern physics does promise to close the dualism of Western thought, for the first time, with the formula $E = MC^2$ in which the mutual interaction of space-time and all matter/energy in the universe is seen as one. We may anticipate a new way of knowing, in which structure and matter, form and being, are inseparably united.

Yet the cost is great for our human society, because we anticipate the prospects of a material, non-human cosmology that leaves out personal values. This is unique in the history of man, because all previous world-views, whether Egyptian, Babylonian, Ptolemaic or Newtonian, have embraced social values and given sanctions to social institutions within their metaphysical frameworks. Today, however, physical cosmology seems irrelevant to the human condition. We look at the stars, we walk on the moon, we probe the inner secrets of matter or unscramble the genetic code of DNA, but no longer does the whole universe seem capable of answering man's aspirations or interpreting his values.

Thus, whatever shaping of society the post-Einsteinian world will take, it will no longer be possible to enclose reality within Gothic cathedrals. Man seems more like a pilgrim in the dark, seeking to journey from one point of light to the next. Man cries out against the dehumanising institutions he has set up. The language games of Wittgenstein and his followers, who postulate a variety of 'truths', provide no general framework for living, no unified vision of reality. Between the world-view of past and future shaping, man is left without ultimate purpose or enduring significance in secular society, as our modern artists are relating to us in literature and art today.

One example of the pessimism of such faithlessness are the words of the philosopher, Bertrand Russell:

> That Man is the product of causes which had no prevision of the end they were achieving; that his origin, his growth, his hopes and fears, his loves and beliefs are but the outcome of accidental collocations of atoms ... if not quite beyond dispute, are just so nearly certain, that no philosophy which rejects them can hope to stand.[2]

Jacques Monod, the molecular biologist, has similarly argued:

> The ancient covenant [that man has a necessary place in nature] is in pieces; man knows at last that he is alone in the universe's unfeeling immensity, out of which he emerged only by chance. His destiny is nowhere spelled out, nor is his duty. The kingdom above or the darkness below: it is for him to choose.[3]

Thus the unification of all things, within a coherent view of reality that meets human dignity with the unity of the world's complexity, is still the salvation modern man needs. But he has lost his way, since he has lost sight of the biblical recognition of the goodness of the creation, in the scientific celebration of the intelligibility of the universe; and therefore he has lost sight of the moral structure that transcends the physical character of creation.

NOTES

1   T. F. Torrance, 'The Church in the New Era of Scientific and Cosmological Change', in *Theology in Reconciliation,* Grand Rapids, Eerdmans, 1975, pp. 267–293.

2   Bertrand Russell, 'A Free Man's Workshop', in *Mysticism and Logic and Other Essays,* New York, Norton, 1929.

3   Jacques Monod, *Chance and Necessity,* New York, Vintage Books, 1972.

Creatio ex nihilo in the History of the Church

This biblical focus on creation, in Wisdom and by the Word, has often been overlooked in the history of the Church, and it has been replaced instead by a more speculative and uncertain summary of creation out of nothing *(creatio ex nihilo)*. Its intent, to say that God has created all things by His transcendent power and sovereignty, so that He is not determined by any pre-existing matter or principle, is to deny both dualism and pantheism. But unfortunately, it is a form of theological shorthand that can readily be misread. Significantly, it is not a statement made in the Bible, although it has been read into a number of verses. But it is not explicit. It is first explicitly used in 2 Maccabees 7:28. There the martyred mother, urging her youngest son not to fear death, says:

> I beseech thee, my son, look upon the heaven and earth and all there is therein, and consider that God made them out of things that 'were not'; and so was mankind made likewise.

The Vulgate version translates 'were not' as *'ex nihilo'*. Her argument is that because the world itself was created out of nothing and is therefore only a sham world, it will dissolve again into nothing. The Maccabean mother was following a long tradition, for as Pseudo-Plutarch says:

> That things which are non-existent come into being and that many things have come into being of non-existence, has been said not just by nobodies, but by men who have

a reputation of being wise. Already, Hesiod held that 'the Chaos was made first and after this the wide earth (Gaea), the everlasting, safe foundation of the universe, and after that Eros stands out amongst all the immortals, and they say everything arose out of that triad, and that out of nothing'.

According to Arnold Ehrhardt, the concept of *creatio ex nihilo* was first conceived by the Eleatic philosophers and propounded by Theophrastus and by Sophists such as Xeniades of Corinth, who stated boldly: 'The world is created from nothing; it is a sham.' Plutarch says similarly, 'For the creation did not take place out of the non-existent, but out of that which was not beautiful and insufficient.' 'Nothing' therefore tended to mean to the Greeks not something not there, but untruth, something that has no right to be there. Jewish philosophers like Philo wrestled with the compromise between accepting the Greek tradition, which presupposed the infinitude of the world, yet with the sovereignty of the Creator, who made things 'which before were not'. To add to the confusion there was of course the platonic influence that assumed that the world was but an emanation of God, so that it was made out of nothing in the sense of the non-substantial. Such a view could at the same time set forth the eternality of the world, because of the immanence of its divine ruling principle.

Early Christian apologists adopted *creatio ex nihilo* from another perspective. The creed of Hermas thus declares: 'First of all, you have to believe that there is one God, who has founded and organised the universe, and brought the universe out of nothing into existence.' This is repeated by Justin Martyr, Irenaeus and Athanasius. However, the support that it might give to docetic heterodoxy made it suspicious, and so as a creed it vanished from the orthodox faith before the end of the first century A.D. But in the following century, Denys the Areopagite re-affirmed the neo-platonic view of emanationism. Then in the ninth century, Johannes Scotus Erigena affirmed, ' "Nothing" is to identify with God, so that by creating the world out of nothing, God is creating out of Himself.' Avicenna and Averroës continued to propound emanationism in the eleventh century, and finally in 1215 the Fourth Lateran Council adopted *creatio ex nihilo* as the 'scientific' foundation of the doctrine of creation. Thus there was continued the whole scholastic tradition of nominalism that eventually the Reformers had to eliminate.

The debate, however, continues. For in our time, men like Nicholas Berdyaev tell us, 'out of the divine nothing, God the Creator was born,' and Paul Tillich speaks of 'the *nihil* out of which God creates', thus continuing the platonic tradition. Creation to these men is actualisation, the coming-to-be of Aristotle's potentialities and Plato's possibilities. It is in this tradition that A. N. Whitehead and the whole contemporary movement of process-thinking continue to enunciate such views. Another tradition follows Heidegger's *Das Nichts,* which has released the overwhelming contemporary concern by existential thinkers about non-being. Like the hypostatisation of *Sophia* in the Hellenistic world, it is the hypostatisation of a negation. This perhaps is a criticism of Karl Barth, who seems to be far too obsessed with the reality in creation of *Das Nichtige*.

There is, however, here a semantic fallacy that the existence of a word means the existence of a thing. As Ian Ramsey has said, language such as that used by Tillich 'is about as logically naïve and misleading as it possibly could be'. Lewis Carroll illustrates this in his humorous dialogue of the King and the Messenger in *Alice Through the Looking-Glass:*

> 'Who did you pass on the road?' the King went on, holding out his hand to the Messenger for some more hay.
> 'Nobody', said the Messenger.
> 'That's right,' said the King: 'This young lady saw him too. So, of course Nobody walks slower than you.'
> 'I do my best,' said the Messenger in a sullen tone. 'I'm sure nobody walks faster than I do.'
> 'He can't do that,' said the King, 'or he'd have been here first.'

In a similar way, men like Tillich have today brought us back to the dualism which the affirmation of *creatio ex nihilo* was meant to rebut. So we discover that the use of such a theological form of shorthand is in fact largely contradictory of the biblical idea of creation.

More than semantic confusion, it does raise the basic question of whether it is possible for the natural reasoning of man, unaided by the Spirit of God, to know God as the Creator, and then to leap towards a truthful awareness of *creatio ex nihilo*. It is perhaps wiser to recognise that the biblical affirmation of *creatio per verbum* is the only reliable affirmation to make. But it is only by the revealed Word of God, in Christ, through the Holy Spirit, that we can know God as our Creator at all. Thus there was developed in the Apostolic Church the association of Wisdom–Word–Christ, which after the resurrection went on through the illumination of the Holy Spirit to work out all the conclusions that had been reached by the reality of the life, teaching, ministry, death and resurrection of Jesus. Just as the Judaising teachers of Paul's day sought to syncretise Greek philosophy with Moses and the Torah, the writer to the Hebrews clearly sees this as inadequate to express the reality of Jesus Christ. Moses was only a servant in the household of Israel, even though he was the greatest of its servants. But Christ has come, the Son and heir of all things (Heb. 3:1–6). We need to reaffirm the same principle today.

For further study see the following references:

Arnold Ehrhardt, 'Creatio ex nihilo', *Studia Theologica,* IV, 1950, 13f.

Arnold Ehrhardt, *The Beginning,* Manchester, Manchester University Press, 1968, pp. 162–164, 166–168.

Ian Ramsey, *Religious Language,* London, S.C.M., 1957, pp. 71–75.

Leo Scheffczyk, *Creation and Providence,* Montreal, Palm Publishers, 1970, pp. 51, 55–64, 131.

General Index

276

Index of Bible References